MILLER'S

COLLECTING
PORCELAIN

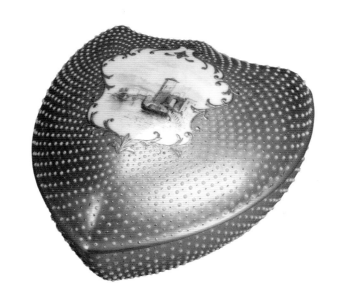

MILLER'S

COLLECTING
PORCELAIN

John Sandon

Miller's Collecting Porcelain
John Sandon

First published in Great Britain in 2002 by Miller's,
an imprint of Octopus Publishing Group Ltd,
2–4 Heron Quays, London, E14 4JP

Miller's is a registered trademark of Octopus Publishing Group Ltd

Commissioning Editor	Anna Sanderson
Executive Art Editor	Rhonda Fisher
Project Editor	Emily Anderson
Page Design	SteersMcGillan Ltd
Jacket Design	Victoria Bevan
Editor	Catherine Blake
Proofreader	Laura Hicks
Indexer	Hilary Bird
Production	Angela Couchman
Special Photography	Chris Halton, Steve Tanner

The publishers will be grateful for any information that will assist them in keeping future editions up to date. While every care has been taken in the preparation of this book, neither the author nor the publisher can accept any liability for any consequence arising from the use thereof, or the information contained therein.

ISBN 1 84000 613 7

A CIP catalogue record for this book is available from the British Library

Set in Granjon and Helvetica
Produced by Toppan Printing Co., (HK) Ltd.
Printed and bound in China

Front of jacket, from left to right: Royal Crown Derby plate from the Duke of York service by Désiré Leroy, 1893, £6,000–8,000/$9,000–12,000; Worcester teapot, Beckoning Chinaman pattern, c.1757, £2,000–3,000/$3,000–4,500; Meissen figure of a Harlequin with a birdcage, modelled by J.F. Eberlein, c.1743, £7,000–10,000/$10,500–15,000; Japanese Arita blue-and-white vase, 17th century, £2,500–3,500/$3,750–5,250; Chinese Export figure of a lady (one of a pair) Qianlong, c.1770, £10,000–12,000/$15,000–18,000 the pair; Meissen dessert basket, c.1890, £700–900/$1,050–1,350; Chamberlains Worcester vase, c.1815, £3,500–4,500/$5,250–6,750

Back of jacket, from left to right: Japanese Imari chrysanthemum-shaped dish, early 18th century, £1,000–1,300/$1,500–1,950; Paris gilded biscuit porcelain centrepiece, c.1810–15, £4,000–6,000/$6,000–9,000; Sèvres plate from the Service des Pêches, 1840, £7,500–10,000/$11,250–15,000; Swansea dessert tureen painted with roses, c.1815–18, £1,500–2,000/$2,250–3,000; Chelsea square-section vase with mazarine-blue ground, c.1765, £4,000–5,000/$6,000–7,500

Half-Title page: Coalport trinket box, c.1910, £800–1,100/$1,200–1,650 (*see* page 127)

Title page: Chelsea-Derby vase, 1772–3, £2,500–3,000/$3,750–4,500 (*see* page 40)

Contents

What is Porcelain?

▲ **A Chinese watercolour, *c*.1800**
Flowing water washes the china clay (kaolin), and also powers hammers to pound the prepared clay.

The Invention of Porcelain

Porcelain is a special and compelling material – it combines cold, hard durability with a delicate fragility and is both practical and beautiful. It has been used and enjoyed for more than 1,000 years and gives untold pleasure to people all over the world. The greatest joy is just to hold a piece of porcelain. Smooth and tactile, there is no substitute for the feel of a perfect glaze, and the realization of its vulnerability. Drop a china bowl and it will shatter, but love and look after it and it will last for all eternity.

Today porcelain is popularly known as "china", for the story begins in that country long, long ago. Since ancient times the manufacture of pottery had been part of a religious ritual, and so each successive culture throughout Asia has taken ceramics very seriously. The finest pottery was always made for the personal use of the emperors, during their reign but especially after death. Whole armies of terracotta warriors and processions of

richly glazed horsemen bear testament to the importance of ceramics in Chinese burial culture. Today we look back with awe at this most advanced civilization, for the Chinese developed pottery-making skills unrivalled in the ancient world.

It is hardly surprising that porcelain was invented in China almost a millennium before the secret was discovered in Europe, for at the time, way back in the 7th century, most of Europe was languishing in the Dark Ages following the fall of the Roman Empire. Nothing is known about the Chinese potters who created the first pure white porcelain. Surprisingly, no mythical story about the discovery of porcelain has been passed down in Asian folklore, so we can only guess how it came about. Most likely it was serendipity. Somewhere in China a naturally occurring source of fine white clay must have contained both kaolin and *petuntse* (felspar) – *see* glossary pp152–3.

▲ A Chinese watercolour
Showing traditional porcelain-making 200 years ago.
The craft of the potter had changed little since ancient times.

▲ Chinese Dingyao porcelain dish, Song dynasty (960–1127)
The thick, ivory-tinted glaze covers subtle carved decoration.
18.5cm (7¼in). **£20,000–25,000/$30,000–37,500**

When fired at sufficient temperature, this unique clay would have fused into a special kind of white pottery that was fully vitrified. Porcelain was born.

No doubt this rather special material would have come to the attention of the emperor. The Tang dynasty (AD 618–906) was relatively peaceful, and scientific investigation of the newly discovered clay would have been encouraged. Tests probably revealed that it was formed from two materials that usually occur separately in nature. Imagine the expeditions sent out by imperial command the length and breadth of China, searching for other sources of the white clay we now know as kaolin. In its natural state, kaolin doesn't occur in thick sediments like other clays. It is formed deep inside a rock by decomposition and is washed out by running water. Milky streams gave indications of kaolin deposits, and eventually led to the discovery of the most important source, near Jingdezhen.

During the first few centuries of porcelain many different sorts of white clay were used, with somewhat different results. Not all of these "proto-porcelains" can technically be classed as porcelain in the modern sense, and not all were translucent. Fine white pottery and other porcellaneous materials were made in northern China during the Song dynasty (960–1127). The best, known as Dingyao, has a translucent white body covered in a creamy or ivory-tinted glaze. Painted decoration was not yet possible, and instead the surfaces of Dingyao bowls were carved with clouds, scrolls, and sometimes fish or animals – decoration that was both exciting and subtle when seen through the deep ivory glaze.

The Tartar invasion of the northern provinces led the Song emperor to establish a new court in the south of China. During the Southern Song dynasty

(1128–1279) there was continued use of simple shapes with carved decoration and plain glazes, which tended to be pale green rather than ivory. A subtle, light-coloured porcelain, known as Qingbai, appears to best effect on a series of conical bowls or round boxes with incised formal patterns. These were more or less mass-produced at Jingdezhen; the early traveller Marco Polo described how he could buy two or three bowls, the colour of azure, for a single Venetian groat. Fine Qingbai vases are now very costly, but it is possible to buy provincially

▶ Provincial porcelain ewer, c.1450–1520
Recovered from a shipwreck off the coast of Vietnam, this ewer from the Hoi An Hoard follows the shape of a precious Chinese prototype.
£3,500–4,000/ $5,250–6,000

▲ A blue-and-white dish from the Yuan Dynasty
Chinese, 1280–1368, 33cm (13in) in diameter. Fourteenth-century porcelain lacks whiteness, but the painting of fabulous beasts is exciting. **£30,000–50,000/$45,000–75,000**

▲ A Korean celadon vase
12th century, in porcellaneous stoneware with inlaid decoration. This masterpiece from the V & A Museum shows that superb early ceramics were not restricted to China.

made bowls of Song Qingbai porcelain for as little as £100–200/$150–300. A darker green glaze is known as "celadon". Celadon wares were made in a number of centres, using both stoneware and porcelain clays. The Chinese initially regarded celadon as inferior, although the dishes later proved very popular with the export trade.

The Mongol conquest of China, under Khublai Khan, led to a short but important era of prosperity during what became known as the Yuan dynasty (1280–1368). The Mongols opened up the export trade, expanding the so-called "Silk Road" to India, the Middle East, and eventually Europe. Porcelain and celadon were traded with the Ottoman sultans, and among the goods received in return was cobalt from Persia. The Persian invention of painting with cobalt in underglaze blue had a profound effect on the development of Chinese porcelain. During the Yuan dynasty the first blue-and-white porcelain dishes were produced, and these are magnificent, full of the Mongol spirit. The porcelain can be dirty-grey rather than pure white, and the blue firing can be uneven, yet Yuan dishes are uniquely exciting. Animals or fish were painted among bold plant patterns on moulded dishes, often of large size. They are, of course, enormously valuable today, and can be admired in most major museums.

Ming Porcelain

In 1368 the first Ming emperor, Hongwu, reclaimed his country. In an attempt to resolve political turmoil he banned foreign travel, so overseas trade was greatly restricted and Persian cobalt was in short supply. Early Ming blue-and-white porcelain designs were consequently less crowded and painted with greater care (they are also increasingly rare). Underglaze red made from copper proved an unsuccessful alternative.

The early 15th century saw the establishment of special kilns to make porcelain exclusively for the imperial court. Throughout the reigns of Yongle (1403–25), Xuande (1426–35), and Chenghua (1465–87), the kilns at Jingdezhen produced what many claim to be the finest porcelain ever. It is certainly the most expensive, for vases, bowls, and even tiny wine cups can be worth as much as one million pounds ($1.5 million). They are superb pieces, technically and artistically. They represent purity of shape and design and are frequently faultless in their potting and execution. By the Zhengde period (1506–21) perfectly controlled green and yellow enamels were used to perfection on dragon bowls, and the joy of being fortunate enough to handle some of these priceless pieces is undescribable.

▲ **A large "Hundred Deer Vase"**
From the Imperial porcelain kilns, with the reign mark of Qianlong (1736–95), and delicate *fencai* decoration painted in *famille rose* enamels. 44cm (17in) tall. **£200,000–300,000/$300,000–450,000**

The imperial pieces can only be seen in top museums and important international auctions, and if a piece does turn up without undisputed provenance it is likely to be a clever fake, made since the 18th century. The best, made recently in China, can fool even some of the greatest experts.

It is possible to buy other 15th-century blue-and-white porcelain for incredibly little. Far away from Jingdezhen, copies were made in "provincial" kilns, situated in parts of what are now Korea and Vietnam. A major kiln site was discovered recently in Vietnam, along with a remarkable, complete ship's cargo of porcelain actually made there. The junk had been fully laden with porcelain destined for trading centres around Southeast Asia. This amazing discovery has led to a total reassessment of Annamese (Vietnamese) porcelain. The best dishes from the "Hoi An Hoard", as it has become known, were painted in blue with fantastic beasts in the same spirit as some Yuan blue-and-white. Other masterpieces were enamelled in red and green with very impressive landscapes. Tens of thousands of small and cheap blue-and-white jars were also recovered from the same shipwreck, and these are today available at less than £50/$75 each.

Korean porcelain developed independently from Chinese traditions during the Ming period.

Back in the 12th century Korean potters had made their own versions of Dingyao, Qingbai, and celadon glazed wares, which are hard to distinguish from Chinese. The most distinctive early Korean porcelain was decorated with inlaid patterns in different coloured clay, a technique perfected by the 12th century and revived much later. Dating Korean porcelain is always difficult, for after defeat by the Japanese in the 16th century no significant Korean ceramics emerged until the Yi dynasty in the 18th and 19th centuries. These look as if they were made centuries earlier, but rare examples can also be far more valuable than they appear.

The 16th century saw a greatly increased output from the Chinese imperial kilns, although the refreshing originality of the early Ming porcelain gave way to more mechanical designs. Jiajing porcelain (1522–66) was confident and impressive in its potting, with bold designs painted in bright primary colours. A series of splendid large jars depicting goldfish among aquatic plants was painted for the emperor. Other wares were decorated with shapes and patterns designed for the Islamic world. The glaze and potting were no longer so perfect, but the decorative effects were dramatic indeed.

Overseas trade was of even greater importance during the reign of Emperor Wanli (1573–1619). Special porcelain was still made for the palace, but the kilns at Jingdezhen were now geared to the mass production of jars and dishes in a limited range of blue-and-white designs. Portuguese mariners established direct trade routes between Europe and China, and vast numbers of late Ming dishes, painted with formal panels of Buddhist emblems, were exported to Europe in Portuguese carracks. The Dutch, who captured some of these trading ships, called the Chinese dishes "Kraak-porzellayne".

▲ **Brush-pot with a "peachbloom" glaze**
Chinese "monochrome" glazes suit very simple shapes, such as this brush-pot from a scholar's table, made in the Kangxi reign (1662-1722). 12.5cm (5in). **£6,000–8,000/$9,000–12,000**

Qing Porcelain

"Chinamania" spread throughout Europe, and the grandest households had "china rooms" to display their collections of Chinese blue-and-white. The factories at Jingdezhen were greatly enlarged to meet this new demand, but special pieces for the emperor and his palace were made in separate kilns. Although the colouring was the same, porcelain for the Asian market was very different from the wares made for export. Blue-and-white continued to dominate production. During the Kangxi reign (1662–1722) a palette of strong colours known as *famille verte* was developed as European trade increased, but in the long reign of Emperor Qianlong (1735–95) a subtler palette of shaded colours was used, which included a prominent rose-pink. Millions of pieces of this *famille rose* porcelain were shipped from Canton to Europe and America. Among the many special designs was a great range of armorial porcelain ordered specially by wealthy families to impress their guests.

The imperial or "Chinese taste" porcelain of the Qing dynasty has enjoyed a significant reappraisal over the past 20 years. Export porcelain has changed little in value, whereas "mark and period" porcelain (bearing the emperor's name as a neatly drawn seal) has escalated in price and reputation. Some Qing imperial porcelain copied the early Ming pieces that were so highly regarded by palace scholars. Other productions were new and original, using *famille rose* enamels of a quality yet to be equalled. Further special pieces in the Chinese taste were decorated with "monochrome" glazes – distinctive colours that have unique textures sealed within. Valuable Qing porcelain in the Chinese taste is well worth careful study. It takes a trained eye to appreciate its subtle qualities, and it also takes experience to avoid the pitfalls. Many copies of Kangxi, Yongzheng, and Qianlong imperial porcelains were made in the 19th and 20th centuries, complete with faithful reproductions of the original reign marks.

Japanese Porcelain

The Japanese were first introduced to porcelain following their invasion of Korea late in the 16th century. Japan forced Korean stoneware potters to go to Japan and establish new kilns near Arita, but porcelain had declined in Korea and the potters themselves had little experience. Early porcelain made in Japan was therefore coarse, and far inferior to the Ming wares of the time. Progress was slow, but by the late 17th century Japan had an established export trade of its own. The Dutch were particularly keen, as porcelain collectors in

▲ **A Chinese dish in so-called *rose verte* enamels**
In Chinese rather than export taste, it dates from the reign of Yongzheng early in the 18th century. 38.5cm (15in) in diameter.
£3000–5000/$4,500–7,500

▲ **A Japanese *Kakiemon* vase, *c*.1690**
This type is called "Hampton Court", as fine examples were displayed in European palaces. 38cm (15in) high.
£35,000–50,000/$52,500–75,000

▲ **Japanese copy of a traditional Chinese design, *c*.1700**
This was made for the Dutch market, as it bears the VOC emblem
of the Dutch East India Company. **£5,000–7,000/$7,500–10,500**

Amsterdam favoured the *Imari* colouring, which
was a Japanese speciality. Named after the port of
Imari, near Arita, the Imari designs combined
underglaze blue with red enamel and gold.
The Japanese made copies of Kraak porcelain
specifically for the Dutch market, with painted
emblems of Dutch trading company the VOC.

Other fine porcelain was made in Japanese
taste. The early Nabeshima wares – plain dishes
with perfect glaze and exceptional painting – were
made for special presentations and had to be perfect
in every way. Dating from the early 18th century,
these are regarded as highly as early imperial Ming.
Although also in Japanese taste, some of the refined
Kakiemon porcelain was exported to Holland and
the rest of Europe. It was refreshingly different,
and caused something of a sensation. Unlike all
other Chinese and Japanese porcelain, Kakiemon
was pure white, with clean lines. It was decorated in
bright enamel colours, but with restrained elegance
that appealed to European connoisseurs at the
end of the 17th century. Only limited numbers of
Kakiemon dishes and vases were available in the
West, and these were treasured as a result.

Japanese porcelain was never able to compete
with Chinese mass-production. Japanese kilns were
unwilling to compromise quality to cut corners, and
eventually production ceased altogether. From
the 1730s Japan entered a period of self-imposed
isolation that was only relaxed after 1850. Unable to
obtain much *Imari* and Kakiemon directly from
Japan, customers in Europe looked for alternatives.
With an eye for profit, the Chinese made *Imari*

patterns to sell to Europeans. At the same time
European royalty financed various attempts at
manufacturing porcelain in the Oriental manner.

The first porcelain actually made in Europe was
very different from anything imported from China
and Japan. For one thing, a source of kaolin had yet
to be discovered, and potters were forced to search
for viable alternatives. Some people believed that
magic played a part, and alchemists became involved
in the search for a kind of philosopher's stone that
would turn humble pottery into pure white porcelain.
The finest European majolica or pottery was made
in Renaissance Italy, and it is understandable that
it was here, in Florence in *c*.1575–87, that Bernardo
Buontalenti, backed by Grand Duke Francesco I de
Medici, produced the so-called Medici porcelain.
Technically this is "frit" porcelain, formed from
white clay and glass fused at a high temperature. It
was nothing like "true" Chinese porcelain, but 100
years before any other European porcelain was
made it was quite an achievement. Some 70 pieces
survive, mostly in museums; two have been sold for
more than one million pounds ($1.5 million) each.
They make a fitting starting point on the quest for
the secret of European porcelain.

▲ **Medici Ewer, *c*.1575–87**
Medici porcelain was the first European attempt to master the
Chinese art. This priceless ewer was made in Florence.

Types of Porcelain

Hard-Paste or "True" Porcelain

Kaolin, popularly known as china clay, is the key to fine porcelain. A form of decomposed granite, china clay is 98 per cent kaolinite. It is a primary or residual clay, found where it is formed. Today it is washed and separated from a rock face using powerful water hoses. Fused at an extremely high temperature with felspar, a crystalline rock known in the porcelain industry as "china stone", it makes the perfect form of porcelain – smooth, durable, and pure white. China stone melts at temperatures of at least 1,350–1,400°C (2,460–2,550°F). As early as the 8th century Chinese potters were able to construct kilns that created this degree of heat.

Early European visitors returned from China with descriptions of the making processes. Their accounts listed kaolin and *petuntse,* the Chinese name for china stone, as the two main ingredients, but they were forbidden to take samples of clay back to Europe. Kaolin was not yet available, and the first European porcelain, made in Italy and France, was the "artificial" or soft-paste type. Accounts of fine white clay contained in rocks mined near Kolditz came to the attention of Johann Böttger, an alchemist working for Augustus the Strong in his castle near Dresden in Saxony. The clay was, of course, kaolin. With this special ingredient, Böttger's experiments finally paid off, and production of true porcelain began at Dresden around 1710. Böttger's porcelain was of a fine hard-paste body, although it was at first beset by firing faults. With a move to Meissen, and a new, purer supply of kaolin from Aue, the recipe was perfected, resulting in some incredibly beautiful porcelain.

The Meissen factory went to enormous lengths to protect its secret formula and processes, for here was the potential to make vast profits. The whole of Europe was obsessed with porcelain, and every kingdom wanted a china factory of its own. King Augustus had good reason to be proud of Meissen porcelain, for the pure white surface was as fine as the celebrated Kakiemon wares of Japan that were prominently displayed in his palaces. Care was taken not to spoil the effect by adding too much decoration, and much early Meissen was sold just in white, or with very limited patterns that did not detract from the powerful shapes. Early figurines were also left white, or sparingly decorated with plenty of white showing. The "Swan Service", modelled by J.J. Kändler for Count Brühl in 1738,

▲ **A Meissen dish from the "Swan Service"**
This dish, 30cm (12in) in diameter, was modelled by J.J. Kändler for Count Brühl in 1738. The extensive use of white glaze was intended to show the beauty of the porcelain.
£20,000–30,000/$30,000–45,000

▲ **Porcelain vase made at the Royal Copenhagen factory**
Early 20th century. It has an exciting underglaze decoration fired at a high temperature. 24cm (9in) tall. **£200–300/$300–450**

is undoubtedly the greatest banqueting service Meissen ever made. The enamelled decoration was very sparse, just sufficient to emphasize the crisp modelling and to show off the pure white porcelain.

In spite of security precautions greed encouraged disgruntled employees to seek fortunes elsewhere. Böttger's assistant, Samuel Stölzel, defected to Vienna to join Claudius du Paquier in making very similar porcelain. His own assistant, Christoph Hunger, took the secret to Venice, while a painter at Vienna, Joseph Ringler, helped to establish factories at Ludwigsburg, Frankenthal, Nymphenburg, and Höchst. Finally, one of Ringler's assistants, Johann Benckgraff, was behind the porcelain made at Berlin and Fürstenberg. Thus the porcelain made all over Germany is quite similar, and we are lucky that each principal maker used a factory mark that uniquely identifies its products.

Once kaolin was discovered in France soft paste was abandoned in its favour, and the hard-paste porcelain body prevailed right across the continent, from Russia to Naples. Paris hard paste is almost indistinguishable from Bohemian and Scandinavian porcelain. Fine hard-paste porcelain is still made all over Europe using a near-perfect recipe. Its firing method differs from almost all soft-paste and bone-china formulae. After an initial low biscuit firing, true porcelain is vitrified together with its glaze in a single high-temperature firing. While underglaze blue was sometimes difficult to control, hard-paste firings enabled skilled ceramicists to produce some exciting glaze effects, particularly during the Art Nouveau period.

Soft-Paste or "Artificial" Porcelain

In France, England, and parts of Italy soft-paste porcelain was the order of the day. In simple terms, this differs from hard paste in that it doesn't contain kaolin. Without access to china clay or the secret of making true porcelain, substitutes had to be found. Many formulae were tried in attempts to reproduce the appearance of Chinese porcelain. The general belief was that porcelain was made by mixing white clay with melted glass. Various mixes of crystalline quartz and sand were added to fine

▼ **Capodimonte drummer, *c.*1755**
Capodimonte porcelain has a unique appearance like melting snow. Examples such as this 25.5cm (10½in) high drummer are rare and expensive. **£10,000–14,000/$15,000–21,000**

▲ **An early French St. Cloud porcelain wine-bottle-cooler**
Early 18th century. The creamy soft paste body is exciting when left in the white. **£5,000–8,000/$7,500–12,000**

▲ **Pickle dish, c.1746**
Made of early English artificial or soft-paste porcelain at the short-lived Limehouse factory. The painting includes a so-called "Long Elija" figure. 13cm (5in) wide. **£5,000–7,000/$7,500–10,500**

▲ **Lenox plate**
Bone China is distinguished by its high translucence. This American plate by the Lenox factory is made from glazed parian – a china body with a noticeable creamy tint.

white clay to create a "frit" that could be finely ground and made into a body for forming and moulding. Some artificial porcelains contained china stone, others animal bone. Methods of production usually included a biscuit firing at about 1,200°–1,300°C (2,190°–2,370°F), then a glaze firing at around 1,000°–1,100°C (1,830°–2,010°F). The glaze, in the form of melted glass, fuses onto the surface but does not become one with the body like hard paste. Soft paste tends to have a thicker, glassy surface, unlike the thin, cold whiteness of hard paste.

A century after Medici porcelain, experiments in France produced a new kind of soft paste, or *pâte tendre*. Louis Proterat probably made some creamy porcelain at Rouen before his death in 1696. The Chicaneau family continued his recipe at St Cloud, where they made the first truly successful European china. Decoration was mostly blue-and-white, but the inspiration was French, not Chinese, and based on contemporary silver. Some was enamelled, but early French soft-paste porcelain is best left white. Very similar creamy bodies were made at Mennecy and Vincennes (the forerunner of Sèvres). At Chantilly attempts were made to produce whiter porcelain by adding tin to the glaze, creating a curious opaque surface not unlike faience. However, Sèvres was by far the most important. Its *pâte tendre* body was whiter than other French porcelains, and

its decoration simply wonderful, with rich colours and intricate tooled goldwork. Owned by the King and free from commercial pressures, Sèvres could concentrate on the best painting and modelling.

In England porcelain was based on private enterprise, with individual factories all struggling to make a profit. Apart from a brief experiment with hard paste at Plymouth and Bristol around 1770, all early English porcelain was soft paste. There were many different kinds: Chelsea made a

▲ **A Minton bone china "Globe Potpourri" vase, c.1835**
Copied from a Meissen hard-paste porcelain original. Popular ornamental styles were copied repeatedly, so the glaze and body are vital identification aids. 20.5cm (8in) high. **£400–600/$600–750**

glassy frit body, while Bow added animal bone. At Worcester the secret ingredient was "soaprock", a steatite mined in Cornwall that gave its artificial porcelain remarkable strength. Early English porcelain copied China and Japan, then Meissen and Sèvres. It was rarely original, but what it lacks in quality it makes up for in charm. Collectors of Continental porcelain can rarely understand the appeal of English blue-and-white, for a primitive Limehouse vase or pickle dish can fetch more than a wonderful piece of early Meissen. In truth, of course, they are as different as chalk and cheese.

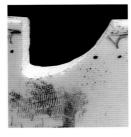 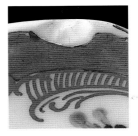

▲ **Rim chips**
These allow an examination of porcelain bodies without the covering of glaze. Soft paste (left) appears granular inside, while hard-paste (right) is shiny with a chip resembling broken flint.

Bone China

Several early English porcelain factories made a "phosphatic" body that contained ash from animal bones. The bone-ash body was rather coarse and not particularly translucent, but it gave the porcelain strength. Towards the end of the 18th century manufactories tried recipes using china clay from Cornwall. A "hybrid hard paste" formula was used at New Hall and copied all over England. Although practical for manufacture and use, the hybrid body was more grey than white, and somewhat granular. English porcelain needed to improve to fight off competition from Wedgwood and other pottery makers. The answer was bone china.

Bone china was roughly 50 per cent burnt animal bone, combined with equal measures of quartz and felspar. The result was strong, white, and above all highly translucent. Josiah Spode is usually credited with its invention in *c*.1800. Other makers soon introduced their own versions, and by the 1820s bone china was made all over England. Although it contains roughly 25 per cent kaolin, bone china is usually described as soft-paste porcelain, as opposed to the hard paste still in use on the Continent. A form of bone china was made much later in the USA, but surprisingly it never caught on in the rest of Europe. Bone china was England's great ceramic invention.

A thin bone-china plate is a beautiful object, particularly when held up to strong light. Its main drawback is vulnerability. China can crack quite easily, and "crazing" can develop when the surface glaze forms a mass of microscopic cracks. Staining can also be a problem, for the body is not as vitrified or glass-like as hard-paste porcelain. With modern china such problems are a thing of the past, and the great English makers still produce superb bone-china tableware that is exported all over the world.

How do you recognize Sèvres or Capodimonte, Chelsea or Bow? Knowing that hard and soft pastes are fired differently and contain different things may be of little help when you are holding a cup in an antique shop. It is useful to examine chips with a magnifying glass. Hard paste chips like glass, while broken soft paste seems granular or rough. Really, though, there is no short cut. Handle as many pieces as you can, and learn how they feel to you.

▶ **Belleek porcelain, *c*.1880–90**
This is made from a malleable parian body that can be squeezed very thinly, making it ideal for delicate modelled flowers. The delicacy of the flowerwork is best appreciated when there is no enamelling. 35.5cm (14in) wide.
£2,200–2,600/$3,300–3,900

How Porcelain is Made

▲ The modeller creates an original sculpture in Plasticine
To allow for shrinkage during firing, this Bronté Porcelain candle snuffer of Nelson must be modelled 50 per cent larger.

Understanding the making process is basic to an appreciation of fine porcelain. If you can picture in your mind all the separate stages, you will view a treasured piece in a new light. Try this exercise. Hold your porcelain and imagine you were the craftsmen making it. Follow each process, and the piece will come alive in your hands. Think of it without glaze – did the potter put the handle on straight? Now glaze it – was the glaze-mix correct, and is it perfectly smooth? Be the painter holding a tiny brush. How skilful was he? How many times did the piece pass through the enamelling kiln? Now look at the gilding. Is it pure gold, smooth and even, and finely tooled? Was it polished properly? Finally, imagine you were the designer, or else the owner of the porcelain factory. Would you have been proud of this pot? I know this sounds childish, but try it. The porcelain will slowly speak to you, and a fine piece will stand out as a result.

It has taken many centuries for an ancient hand-made craft to become an industrial factory process. Many techniques have changed little over a thousand years, whereas other developments have revolutionized the industry. Every type of porcelain, whatever its formula, has to go through a series of stages that turn natural stone and clay into a usable china vessel.

Preparing the Clay

To make any kind of porcelain you must start with clay and stone in the correct proportions, finely ground and suspended in water. The particles must all be exactly the same size if the ingredients are to mix together evenly, so the grinding process is crucial. In olden days a watermill or horses powered a revolving grindstone, but impurities inevitably entered the mix. Today a rotating ball mill is used. A porcelain-lined steel drum, full of flint pebbles or balls of fired alumina – one of the hardest ceramics known, gently grinds the china stone into fine dust. Mixed with water this fine clay is known as "slip". It is then sieved to remove any larger particles, and passed over strong magnets to extract any iron particles, which could ruin everything. Drying the slip used to take months. Today, filtration presses pump the liquid through filter cloths in just a few hours, producing slabs of sticky, malleable clay.

Two hundred years ago strong men spent days cutting, pressing together, and kneading the clay to mix it thoroughly and draw out any air bubbles, as in the heat of the kiln the tiniest bubble of trapped air will explode, wrecking all the potter's efforts. This process, known as wedging, was very hard work. In the 21st century a machine called a "pug mill" chops the clay and squeezes it through a vacuum to suck the air out. Out comes homogenized clay, shaped like a cylinder and ready for forming.

Some processes use clay in a plastic state, taken straight from the pug mill. Another widely used method forms objects in moulds cast from slip. Hand modelling or throwing, on a potter's wheel, is rare in the porcelain industry, as the clay cannot be handled easily when wet and sticky. Moulding processes are far more suitable for porcelain.

Moulds

Creating the moulds is the most important stage in the manufacture of fine porcelain. Making moulds and casting from them involves an alternating succession of positives and negatives. If the original model is a complicated shape it is usually created in modelling clay, such as plasticine. Only basic three-dimensional shapes can be cast from a single mould. A complex figurine, on the other hand, requires separate moulds for the body, the head, each limb, and any additional ornament. At a china factory the senior mould-maker skilfully cuts the plasticine model into separate pieces, and these are individually encased in plaster. The negative casing is itself filled with plaster to cast a positive "case mould", or "master mould", which will be a perfect reproduction of the modeller's work. From this master mould, a considerable number of "working moulds" are made. Master moulds used to be made of toughened plaster or a type of fired clay called "pitcher". A far more durable epoxy resin is now used that considerably extends the life of the model.

Casting and Pressing

Working moulds are made from plaster of Paris. There are two basic methods of casting, using either solid or liquid clay. Press-moulding involves rolling out a slab of plastic clay and squeezing it with the fingertips or a sponge to fill every crevice in both halves of an open mould. The two sides of the mould are then pressed firmly together and allowed to dry. When the mould is opened, the completed hollow shape can be lifted out.

When casting with liquid clay, "slip" is prepared by adding water once more to the prepared plastic clay. An alkaline "deflocculant" is added so that thicker clay mixes flow evenly during the casting process. As prepared slip "ages", its viscosity changes. A skilled caster knows from the feel of the slip when the consistency is just right. Plaster moulds of two or more parts are clamped or tied tightly together, and the slip is poured slowly into a single small opening at the top. As the plaster absorbs a quantity of water from the slip, a layer of dry clay of even thickness forms on the inner walls of the mould. Pouring slip into a mould always looks easy, but it takes experience, not to mention a steady hand – air bubbles trapped within the mould ruin the casting. To make a hollow shape the mould is turned upside down after just a few minutes, and surplus slip poured or shaken out. The clay layer within the mould dries and shrinks a little, so in a short time the mould can be opened and the cast shape removed.

A complete figurine is constructed of many different pieces, each cast from a separate mould. The individual pieces are laid out in order, and an "assembler" joins them together using a thick slip of the same clay, as a kind of adhesive. This process, known as "sticking-up", can be complicated, as each part must be joined at the correct angle. Parts that protrude, such as an outstretched arm, have to be supported using "props" made from the same clay, which will shrink in the kiln at the same rate, otherwise they will move down during the firing process. A fine refractory powder such as highly fired alumina is used to stop these supporting props sticking to the model, or the figurine adhering to the kiln shelf.

Any object that is moulded will usually have seams that need to be "fettled" – scraped away using a knife or rubbed smooth with a sponge or special sandpaper. The care with which a potter removes the seams will have a strong bearing on the quality of the finished product, as will the way in which a manufacturer looks after the moulds. Each time a cast is taken from a plaster mould the inside wears a tiny bit. Repeated use means that the mould becomes worn and the finished products suffer as a result. Replacing working moulds continuously costs time and money. The casters at Bronté Porcelain, pictured below, expect their finely detailed moulds to last for around 25 castings. Other manufacturers may try to produce as many as a hundred casts from one single mould, but so many continuous castings adversely affects the amount of surface detail.

Flatware (plates and saucers) and hollow ware (cups, mugs, and bowls) are usually made from semi-dry or plastic clay. Moulds or dies are used to shape perfectly round objects by means of "jollying" and "jiggering" techniques. To make a cup by jollying, a ball of clay is placed in a revolving plaster mould. A steel tool is pressed inside to force the clay against the wall of the mould and create the internal profile of the cup. Once dry, the cup can be removed from the mould and, after fettling, the handle is applied separately. Jiggering, to make a flat shape,

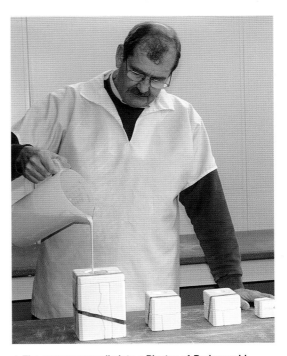

▲ **The caster pours slip into a Plaster-of-Paris mould**
The slip (clay mixed with water) must be of the correct consistency, and a steady hand ensures no trapped air bubbles.

uses a domed plaster mould shaped as the face of a plate. A flat bat of clay is pressed by machine onto the rotating mould. At the same time a steel profiling tool shapes the underside and foot. Full automation today creates perfect tableware with minimal human involvement. A semi-mechanized process did the same job more than 200 years ago, using similar plaster moulds. The potter's fingers did the work of the steel profilers that are used today.

Any irregularities on a round shape are smoothed off by turning the piece on a lathe. Foot-rims can also be turned by hand with skilful use of cutting tools pressed against the vessel or plate as it rotates at speed. As with jollying and jiggering, turning techniques can only be used on a totally round shape. Oval dishes or any other irregularly shaped objects have to be cast or pressed in different moulds. Once the body is dry and smooth, handles or spouts are joined on with a dab of wet clay. Completed objects are now ready for the kiln.

Firing

There are many different sorts of kiln, with separate functions; the largest and most important is the biscuit kiln, where clay is transformed into porcelain.

Man's earliest kilns were simply bonfires, capable of baking basic terracotta but not hot enough to fuse stoneware or porcelain. To achieve concentrated heat the Chinese constructed sophisticated kilns, rising on a hillside in a series of chambers. The fire was stoked in each section, and the heat was drawn through the chambers until it was sufficiently hot to melt the clay, stone, and fluxes together. The basic type of European kiln, developed in medieval times, relied on an outer casing that allowed the heat to circulate and caused a build-up of intense heat within the core or centre of the kiln. Kiln men learnt from experience which parts of the kiln were the hottest, and stacked the unfired porcelain in such a way that the heat at this point was evenly distributed. By the 18th century some bottle-shaped kilns were of massive size, and held a great deal of ware. Months of work forming the delicate porcelain would be ruined if the kiln failed, and so the kiln manager was one of the most important workers in a factory.

Rudimentary boxes, or "saggars", made from high temperature fireclay, protected china from the direct fire, smoke, and dirt inside a kiln. Porcelain was placed inside these saggars and then stacked in tall piles called "bungs". Fully laden saggars were heavy, and it took a long time to load and unload a kiln by hand. In Staffordshire during the 19th century factory owners commonly sent workmen inside the kilns when they were still fairly hot in order to draw out the fired saggars, saving time and heat. The health of these men suffered greatly, and the practice was frowned upon. The development of the tunnel kiln, in which trucks, or "cars", made of refractory fireclay carried unfired ware through the kiln on rails, changed everything for the better.

Tunnel kilns ("continuous" kilns) are used in all larger manufactories today. Inside modern, gas-fuelled tunnel kilns the porcelain no longer needs the protection of saggars. The temperature inside the tunnel is carefully controlled, as is the speed at which the wagons pass through each stage of heating and cooling. After several days the fully fired porcelain emerges at the other end. Smaller factories still use intermittent kilns, mostly powered by electricity. These concentrate the heat in the same way as the old bottle ovens, but modern technology has removed many of the problems. It used to be said that in the old days a good kiln-man knew the temperature was right when his eyebrows began to singe. A kiln manager today simply needs to understand computers.

Bone china "vitrifies" in the biscuit kiln at a temperature of about 1,200–1,250°C (2,190–2,280°F). This porcelain is then glazed and fired again at a lower temperature, between 1,050°C (1,920°F) and 1,150°C (2,100°F). For true, or hard-paste, porcelain the procedure is different. The clay is merely dried thoroughly at the biscuit stage, at about 800–900°C (1,470–1,650°F). It is then covered in glaze, and the body and glaze are vitrified together at 1,300–1,400°C (2,370–2,550°F). The particles forming the porcelain melt and fuse together, and significant shrinkage occurs. The rate of shrinkage depends on the composition of the clay, but all potters need to plan for this and make models that are proportionately larger than the intended finished product.

Glazing

Glaze is a layer of melted glass that coats the surface of porcelain, adding strength and beauty. To assist in the melting of the glaze, and to make sure it flows correctly, chemical fluxes are added to the mix. The most common flux used to be lead – an extremely hazardous material that caused huge health problems for workers. Leadless glazes were developed in the 19th century, and today all glazes used on tableware are totally lead-free. Most glaze mixtures are melted first to form a kind of glass that can be finely crushed. After grinding with clay and water the resulting glaze slip is a liquid with the consistency of thick cream. Glaze used to be applied by hand in a process called "dipping"; a skilled glazer was in effect a juggler, for he had to spin each piece of porcelain in his hands, the sticky glaze swirling across the whole surface, leaving every part covered with an even thickness. The invention of aerographic spraying 100 years ago changed all this. Before firing, any excess glaze must be wiped free from bases and foot-rims to prevent adhesion in the kiln. Some porcelain-makers used spurs and stilts to support their wares in the glaze kiln. These left tiny marks when they were removed – clues to the identity of some early porcelain.

Bone-china glaze is fired at between 1,020°C and 1,100°C (1,870–2,010°F). To create a perfectly

▲ **Three stages in the decoration of a Royal Worcester "Painted Fruit" plate**
The first firing (left) and second firing (centre) show how the depth of colour develops. A final firing (right) adds a real gold rim.

▲ A fireclay "car" loaded with painted porcelain emerges from the tunnel kiln
In the clean atmosphere of a modern, gas-fired kiln there is no need for protective saggars, as long as no pieces touch one another.

smooth surface, glaze needs to be fired at just the right temperature, preventing bubbles or blisters, known as pinholes, forming on the surface. It must also "fit" the body perfectly – fusing and shrinking with it. If the glaze's expansion coefficient is too high, crazing will occur as the glazed vessel cools after firing. Crazing, a network of tiny cracks in the glaze, can also slowly develop after many years, especially if an object is stored in damp, hot, or cold conditions.

Decoration

The artistry of the porcelain-decorator knows few limits. From simple coloured glazes to intricate hand-painting, all ornamentation is permanently sealed by fire. Take care of porcelain and the decoration will endure. China-painting will never fade, but metallic decoration may tarnish. In most cases we can enjoy today the same colours and exciting sheen that were first seen when the precious object was taken from its kiln, possibly centuries ago.

Glaze is widely used to preserve decoration underneath its transparent layer. Underglaze decoration basically means blue-and-white, as a blue pigment, created using cobalt oxide, has been applied to Chinese porcelain since the Yuan dynasty. Cobalt oxide, prepared as a fine black powder, is mixed with water and painted directly onto the biscuit porcelain. During the glaze-firing a chemical reaction with the boro-silicate-based glaze creates a rich blue colour that is sealed forever within the glaze. Iron and copper oxides can make other underglaze colours, but with nothing like the reliability of underglaze blue. Differently coloured clay can be used to create some stunning underglaze decoration. *Pâte-sur-pâte* involves building up decoration in low relief on a coloured background. When skilfully applied the result is visually stunning, sealed beneath a clear transparent glaze.

Most porcelain decoration is applied on top of the glaze. Ceramic colours are mostly oxides of different metals mixed with powdered glass that acts as a flux. During firing in an enamelling kiln the china colours themselves become a translucent coloured glass that fuses with the glazed surface of the porcelain. Enamel firings are generally between 750°C and 800°C (1,380–1,470°F). Not all colours mature at the same temperature, so a succession of enamel firings is usually necessary to create rich, painted decoration in a full range of colours. Enamels change significantly in the kiln, too. Some powdered metallic oxides look completely different from the final colours that will appear after firing, and china-painters have to learn how to predict the end result. It also takes years of practice to apply the powdered colours with the correct mixture of fat oil so that they adhere to the glazed surface and do not run when the porcelain is fired.

Printing has largely replaced underglaze hand-painting in the porcelain industry. The technique was invented at Worcester in the 1750s. Thin copper plates with finely engraved decoration were filled with underglaze colour that was transferred to the surface of the porcelain using either thin sheets of paper or slabs of jelly-like glue. Although still time-consuming and exacting, transfer printing was inevitably much cheaper than freehand painting. The printing process became more mechanized in the 19th century, and revolutionized the industry.

With transfer printing only one colour can be printed at a time. Multi-coloured printing, which painstakingly places one colour on top of another, was developed in the 1850s. Colour printing by lithography, or "decalcomania" as it is known in the USA, provides fully coloured decoration with little expenditure. It produces transfers in ceramic colour onto thin paper or plastic sheets that are then placed onto the glazed surface to be decorated. Modern "decals" are made by photographic processes or silk-screen printing. They can be exceptionally detailed, and easily mistaken for hand-painting. The one disadvantage of these transfers is the difficulty of laying flat paper on the curved surface of a vase or teapot. A flat decal may crease as it is rubbed down, leaving unsightly streaks across the print.

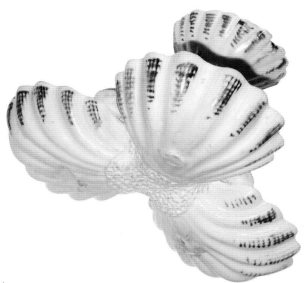

▲ **Bow pickle stand, 1750s**
The individual feet that should have supported this stand broke off in the biscuit firing. The broken stumps were glazed over and fired anyway, so that the pickle stand could be sold.

Gilding is the last decorating process, as gold fires at the lowest temperature – around 740°C (1,365°F). Real gold is mixed with an amalgam that burns away during firing, leaving a thin layer of gold fused to the surface. In the 18th century, gold was mixed with a variety of substances – honey at Worcester, and garlic oil, it is said, at Sèvres. In the 1770s chemists at Sèvres discovered that gold mixed with mercury gave a very bright finish, and mercury gilding has been used ever since. It appears dull when the porcelain is drawn from the kiln, and has to be burnished. This involves polishing the surface with a smooth hardstone such as agate or hematite, or rubbing it with very fine zircon sand. Real gold, properly burnished, looks stunning and gives fine porcelain the finish it deserves.

There are cheaper substitutes. Meissen invented a "gloss gold" in the 1840s that emerged shining from the kiln. "Bright gold", in liquid form, is widely used today for the same reason, although it fires as a very thin layer that wears off easily. These and other artificial golds don't begin to compare with the beautiful finish of the real thing, especially when it is tooled by a master. You could apply gold as a solid mass to porcelain, although this would be very wasteful. Instead "raised-paste" gilding builds up the pattern as a thick enamel paste. After tooling, and maybe several kiln firings, fine burnished gold is applied. This is one of the most time-consuming and costly methods of decoration, but pieces finished in this way can be incredibly beautiful.

▲ **Chelsea red anchor period teabowl**
To prevent adhesion in the kiln this was fired on three tiny clay pegs, which have left tell-tale "stilt marks" on the base.

Forming a Collection

▲ **John Sandon conducting a sale of porcelain in London's New Bond Street**
An important auction generates much excitement, but the auctioneer makes sure the atmosphere is not intimidating.

What is Available & Where

In our modern high-tech world there are more opportunities to buy antiques than ever before. Only the depth of one's pocket limits the choice available to collectors. It is vital, therefore, to be focused from the start, and resist the temptation to just buy anything that takes your fancy. Indiscriminate buying can result in a disappointing muddle; each piece may be admirable in its own way, but you could end up with a meaningless assemblage.

Specialization is the key. You can specialize in more than one thing, of course, and indeed I have several different collections myself, each built around a specific theme. In this book I suggest all manner of themes for collecting, and there are plenty more besides. Deciding what to collect is very personal, but once you have chosen you must set yourself boundaries. If you collect within firm parameters, you will end up with an interesting and worthwhile display. When I sit at my table at the BBC's *Antiques Roadshow* I see in front of me the full contents of many china cabinets. It is the themed collections

that are memorable, be they teapots or candlesticks, blue-and-white, or the product of one great factory. Stick with a particular theme, and you will derive enormous pleasure from your porcelain collection.

Buying From a Dealer
The relationship between dealer and collector is very important. Few people have the time to traipse around auction rooms or spend hours surfing the Internet, or indeed have the expertise needed to be sure of getting value for money. A professional dealer, specializing in one particular area, has inside knowledge that is worth paying for. This is the crux of the dealer/collector relationship. An experienced dealer buys the best pieces from salerooms all over the world and gathers them together in his gallery. He will also buy pieces privately from old collections that will not be offered on the market. Above all, a reputable dealer will provide a guarantee that his stock is authentic and correctly described.

Unless you are very knowledgeable yourself, you have to trust the integrity of a dealer. The great majority are steadfastly honest, with a real interest in the objects that they sell. However, to stay in business they have to make a profit. Their often considerable overheads have to be built into the prices they ask for their stock, and the price guides given in this book are optimistic auction values, not dealer prices. You may be lucky enough to find the same piece on sale cheaper elsewhere, but with a top dealer you are paying for convenience and experience. Walk into the shop of a specialist china dealer and you will find a wide selection of pieces likely to be of interest – all identified and clearly priced. Without the pressure of an auctioneer's hammer about to fall, you have time to consider how badly you want a particular piece. Most dealers love to talk about their stock, and from such conversations it is usually possible to gauge how much the seller really knows about his subject.

If a collector becomes a regular customer, a friendship will probably develop. This can be very important, for dealers will usually offer special prices to customers they know well. Also, if a dealer knows your particular interests he will keep an eye out for similar items in the future, and offer them to you ahead of anyone else. A good friendship means you can ask a dealer for advice before a major auction, and may even commission the dealer to bid for you, paying an agreed commission for this advice. Auctioneers are perfectly happy with such an arrangement – many dealers bidding in the salerooms are buying for specific collectors rather than for their own stock.

You need to be sensible when buying from dealers. You have to consider how much they really know about their subject, remembering, of course, that a general dealer will not have the same level of knowledge as a porcelain specialist. Is the asking price fair? Shopping around is a perfectly natural way to check prices. Don't be afraid to ask questions – you need to know as much as you can about the piece, where it was made, and especially when. Ask the dealer to write this down so that you have a record of what you were told. Above all, ask about its condition – is there any damage, visible or hidden? If a piece has been restored it is very important to know exactly what has been done. Buying damaged porcelain is fine as long as you are quite aware of what you are getting. Any reputable dealer will be delighted to give you reassurance. On the other hand, someone who appears unwilling to give you this information on a written receipt should not be trusted. Honest dealers who have made a genuine mistake will be happy to refund you, as their reputation is at stake; others may not.

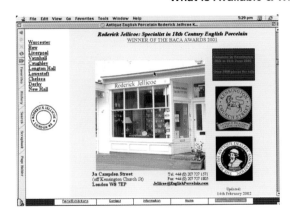

▲ **Dealer's Internet website**
Fine porcelain from specialist shops in Kensington Church Street can be viewed in the comfort of your home, by logging online.

Buying at Auction

No longer the sole domain of the dealer, auction houses have become user-friendly, welcoming places where private collectors can enjoy refreshments as they browse the antiques on offer. Many sales today are displayed in room settings, and it is possible to take the whole family along to viewings. Private collectors have become the auctioneer's lifeblood, and in many areas they have almost completely replaced the traditional antiques dealer. In a recent porcelain sale that I catalogued, private buyers outnumbered dealers by three to one, taking home the majority of the lots on offer. Twenty years ago such a situation would have been unimaginable.

Auctioneers have changed their attitude to the needs of private collectors. This is most evident in the catalogues, which now resemble glossy magazines, with beautiful colour photographs and descriptions that read more like photo-captions from lifestyle magazines than academic listings. These catalogues are expensive to produce and quite costly for collectors to buy, although sale categories have become more specialized and it is possible to subscribe only to catalogues that interest you. More catalogues can also now be viewed on the Internet.

Auctioneers charge consigners a percentage for selling, and also a premium to the buyer. This ranges from 10% to 20%, and there is usually VAT or sales tax on top. Buyers' premiums are a fact of life, for without them most auctioneers could not operate. The income enables salerooms to host specialized sales where collectors can find large numbers of items of particular interest. In major porcelain sales in London or New York it is easy to justify the buyers' premiums, as the finest porcelain is available backed up by catalogues compiled by some of the world's leading experts. In provincial

▲ A stand at the International Ceramics Fair held in London each June
The finest stock of the world's top dealers is gathered together in a single location, presenting collectors with a unique opportunity.

salerooms it is rare to find such knowledge, and one often pays heavily for the privilege of bidding on objects that are, in fact, described incorrectly.

If you are paying for the expertise of the auction house you should make the most of it and ask to speak to the specialists who catalogued the pieces. Don't be afraid to ask the same questions you would of a dealer. Enquire about the provenance, the likelihood of finding a better example, and in particular about the condition. Auctioneers are not obliged to list damage in the catalogue, although many do so. Detailed reports on condition are usually available on request, but don't leave it until the last minute, as they take time to prepare. A written report is useful even if you have viewed a sale, for you have a stronger case if an expensive buy turns out to have been misrepresented.

Anyone is welcome to come along and bid at a public auction, although in some cases a credit check may be necessary. Estimates of the likely selling prices are available, but don't assume this price is the most a lot will make. With competition on the day, auctioneers' estimates are frequently exceeded. Telephone bidding is possible on more expensive lots if you cannot attend a sale, or you can leave an absentee bid to be executed by the auction house on your behalf. It's all a matter of trust. Most auctioneers

handle absentee bids with impeccable integrity, and if you set yourself a price limit it is the same as being there. Owing to the fragile nature of porcelain it is usually best to collect any purchases as soon as possible after a sale, and it is often worth taking suitable soft packing material with you just in case.

Buying on the Internet

The Internet has transformed collecting. With practice you can search the catalogues of future porcelain auctions all over the world, and visit the stocks of dealers from Southampton to Seattle. The pros and cons of buying porcelain over the Internet are debated whenever collectors get together. What is clear is that more and more people are now using their computers to buy and sell delicate porcelain.

Most specialist dealers now have their own website (*see* picture on p.23). Auctioneers' catalogues are also available on-line. The same common-sense advice applies: ask for as much information as possible before you buy. E-mail or telephone for a full condition report and extra information on colouring or markings – indeed anything you cannot see for yourself. Remember to enquire about shipping costs and take this into account, for many auctioneers contract-out packaging and postage to specialist shippers and their charges can be expensive.

Internet auctions are a very different phenomenon. eBay is by far the biggest, but there are many other on-line auctions, and a staggering quantity of porcelain is available. You have to decide your maximum bid from the information given – at best inadequate, at worst totally misleading. Descriptions often show astonishing ignorance on the part of the sellers. As a result there is inevitably an element of risk involved. When your Internet purchase arrives in the mail a few weeks later, will it be as described? Indeed, will it be in one piece? It seems that many Internet sellers are as careless with their packing as with their listing and photography. There are bargains to be had, but there are also many pitfalls, and it will be a long time before the Internet replaces live auctions and shows.

Buying at Antiques Fairs & Flea Markets

Major fine-art fairs have always been held annually as showpieces for top London dealers, but in the 1960s and 1970s a very different kind of antiques show became fashionable. A new breed of part-time antiques dealers, without shops of their own, started to travel around Britain exhibiting in town halls and hotel ballrooms. Without the overheads of a high-street gallery, exhibitors at these new antiques fairs could undercut their professional colleagues. Regular fairs introduced the world of antiques to a new generation of collectors. At the same time, dabbling in antiques became a popular hobby, with more and more dealers exhibiting at even bigger fairs. Giant flea markets and car-boot (garage) sales have given antiques fairs a cheaper and down-market image. There is always the chance of discovering rare porcelain unrecognized amongst bric-a-brac, but this happens very rarely. Most of today's exciting "finds" in boot fairs are fakes, shipped over in bulk from the Far East. Covered in "dirt", these fakes are slipped into boxes of apparent junk and fool a surprising number of novice collectors.

Over the past 20 years a new phenomenon, the ceramics fair, has transformed the retailing of antique porcelain. Dealers united in their interests take a wide selection of pottery and porcelain to a single venue, where in one weekend more collectors will pass through than would visit an antiques shop in a year. Ceramic fairs have brought a real tonic to the porcelain trade. Some of the biggest dealers in early porcelain don't bother with shops any more and just trade from these fairs. Meanwhile, at the top of the market, international ceramics fairs in London, and more recently in New York, present to dealers and enthusiasts the world's finest porcelain. Whatever you collect, and wherever you choose to buy your porcelain, remember above all else to buy the very best that you can afford.

▲ **Car-boot (garage) sales**
Rare and valuable finds do turn up at these sales, but you have to get there early and need a great deal of luck.

▲ **A selection of odd lids**
These make an unusual, informative collection, and there's always the chance that one day you'll find a matching base. **£4–40/$6–60 each**

Themes for Collecting

Many collectors buy porcelain without having a real theme in mind; they simply buy anything that takes their fancy. This is all very well, but collecting with a purpose is far more satisfying. One of the principal aims of this book is to suggest different subjects for collections – the variety is endless, and the choice totally personal.

That said, there are certain guidelines that are definitely worth bearing in mind. It is no use trying to collect something that is too specialized, or too obscure. If you cannot find new items on a regular basis, you will most likely lose interest. If you own a rare or curious object and see another that is similar, it is natural to want to buy it and begin a collection, but if you can't easily find any more then admit defeat and collect something else. Also, avoid collecting things that are always the same. I once saw a collection of 12 almost identical examples of Meissen's "The Lady Racegoer" with her hands in a feather muff. By itself this is a charming figurine, but 12 all the same standing in a row

added nothing to each other. The purpose of a collection is for the whole to be worth more than the sum of its parts.

You should collect within your range of expertise and budget. If you are going to collect very rare porcelain, make sure you have a thorough knowledge of your subject, or are guided by an acknowledged expert. Try not to collect something you can't really afford, and avoid any field where the best pieces are simply out of reach. You should always buy the best you can, for there is nothing more disappointing than a collection of mediocre porcelain. Never buy bad examples, or excessively damaged pieces, just because these are all you can stretch to. It is much better to choose an area of collecting within your budget, and then you know you can acquire really good examples. Always aim for quality – you may end up with just ten good objects but it is far preferable to have those than 100 poor ones for the same money. Your collection won't be as big, but it will be far superior in the long run.

The space you have available is an important consideration. Collections can take over an entire house, and you have to have the room to display your porcelain attractively as well as safely. Teapots are popular with porcelain collectors, but they are surprisingly large. Forty teapots will fill an entire wall of a room. Twenty plates hung in rows will do the same. If you have the space, such collections can look wonderful, but if it is a problem then stick to smaller things. It is no coincidence that tiny objects, such as scent bottles or pickle dishes, cost far more proportionately than large pieces of porcelain.

There are three principal themes for collecting – style, shape, and origin – and each of these is considered separately in this book. Most collectors choose a single maker, such as Sèvres, or Derby. They usually limit their scope further through focusing on a period, such as 18th-century Chinese porcelain, or early 20th-century Royal Worcester. You can specialize in one type of factory decoration, such as Derby *Imari* patterns, or a particular shape, such as Meissen figures. If you have shape as your theme you may acquire pieces by many different makers. For example, collectors like to buy teapots from as many separate factories as possible. Blue-and-white is the most collected type of decoration in England (where so much was made), and it is also

▲ **A selection of Kakiemon porcelain**
This group includes Japanese originals and 18th-century copies made at Meissen, Bow, Chelsea, and in China.

popular in The Netherlands, but it is unfashionable in the rest of Continental Europe. But try not to let fashion dictate what you collect– whether buying on a shoestring, or as a serious investment, follow your own instincts and stick to what gives you pleasure.

▲ **Staffordshire porcelain cats, 1830s–'50s**
These form part of the Sheila Davis collection of several hundred cats in pottery and porcelain. £200–450/$300–675

Collecting By Style

Trace the influence from one continent to the next or concentrate on a particular period

▲ **A Ming *guan*-shaped jar, 15th century**
From the "Windswept Scholars" group. Finely painted decoration from this period is as exciting as it is rare. 38cm (15in) tall.
£25,000–35,000/$37,500–52,500

Asian Porcelain & Its Influence on Europe

Porcelain from China and Japan was prized by wealthy Europeans three centuries ago and had an enormous influence on every early European manufactory. Asian porcelain is still as popular as ever, and is widely collected around the world.

Ming & Later Imperial Porcelain

The quality attained by the Chinese porcelain-makers in the early Ming period is truly incredible. Many of the vessels produced in the imperial kilns in the 15th century simply cannot be faulted, and it is amazing to think that certain pieces really are more than 500 years old. *Doucai* ware – porcelain decorated with colours outlined delicately in blue – includes the celebrated "chicken cups" from the reign of Chenghua (1465–87). These tiny painted bowls have commanded prices above £1 million ($1.5 million). The finest Ming porcelain was reserved for the emperor, and the insistence on perfection was bound up with religion: porcelain

that survived the kiln firings without a single blemish was treasured and preserved in the imperial palaces as religious art, valued above any jewels or riches.

With rebellion in the 19th century came looting of the palaces, and for the first time Imperial porcelain became available in the West. The Imperial porcelain was in the Chinese taste, using symbolism and symmetry generally unknown outside Asia, and was totally different from the export porcelain sent in quantity from China and known throughout the world. Many of the finest pieces were not from the Ming period but of later Qing date. These were produced in the Imperial kilns in the 18th and 19th centuries with a similar religious attention to quality. The results are truly remarkable.

Maybe it is because they were so perfect, and consequently did not look ancient, that these Chinese-taste porcelains were not understood in Europe and the USA. Export porcelain remained far more valuable to Western collectors for many

▼ A Chinese porcelain *Kendi*
This was a type of hookah popular for export to the Middle Eastern market in the mid-17th century. The animal form is ususual, and novelty shapes always sell for a premium. 19cm (7½in).
£3,000–4,000/$4,500–6,000

◄ A fine saucer-dish in Chinese taste
From the Qianlong period with a six-character mark. The underglaze blue dragon and cloud pattern are enamelled in green.
£15,000–25,000/$22,500–37,5000

▲ A "mark and period" porcelain tray
Inscribed with poetry written by Emperor Jiaqing (1796–1820); the poem describes the brewing of tea, indicating that this dish would have been used in a tea ceremony. 16cm (6in) wide.
£2,500–4,000/$3,750–6,000

decades, until the market underwent a reassessment in the 1980s. Qing "mark and period" porcelain (which has a reign mark corresponding to the date of manufacture) suddenly became as valuable as early Ming. Collectors in Asia competed to reclaim their wonderful ceramic heritage, and the true meanings of the designs, especially the markings, were reviewed. What matters most is the authenticity of the reign mark. A great deal of copying went on. Qing emperors instructed their potters to copy famous pieces of early Ming in the palace collections to show that standards remained just as high, and often Qing copies were given spurious Ming markings. Other pieces made in the late 19th and 20th centuries were given the designs and marks of Kangxi and other 18th-century emperors. Many of these copies are superb pieces in their own right, but are naturally worth only a fraction of the value of the real thing. Unfortunately it takes a very experienced eye to tell the two apart (*see* pages 138–41).

The Imperial kilns at Jingdezhen were not the only source of porcelain production during the Ming dynasty. The term "provincial porcelain" is used to describe a great range of wares made in other parts of Asia. Excavations in Korea and Vietnam, as well as other regions of China, have identified many manufacturing centres. Patterns identical to highly prized imperial wares were made for everyday use. The "Hoi An Hoard", the recently recovered contents of a shipwreck, included several hundred thousand pieces of porcelain datable to the late 15th century, made in part of what is now Vietnam. Sold via the Internet, shipwreck cargoes such as this have made it possible to acquire Ming period vases, dishes, and ornaments for remarkably little money. Provincial porcelain made in the 18th and 19th centuries for the Asian rather than the Western market is generally coarse, but not without charm. Some can be bought today incredibly cheaply, for less than the cost of most modern tableware.

▲ **Chinese porcelain armorial plate, Kangxi period**
Early 18th century, showing the arms of Meade. Export porcelain plates made to special order are always superbly potted.
£650–900/$975–1,350

▼ **"Gentleman's Mandarin", c.1775**
Qianlong period. European collectors called this rich decoration "Gentleman's Mandarin", and although they didn't understand the Chinese stories depicted, they loved the comical figures. 13cm (5in) high. £250–350/$375–525

Famille Rose & Canton Enamelling

Enamelled porcelain made in China for the Western market is classified according to palette. Pieces made during the Kangxi reign (1662–1722) are known as *famille verte*. The most distinctive colour is indeed a bright emerald green, used with black, red, blue, yellow, and purple. (A rare version using black as a solid background colour is called *famille noire*.) However, shading was limited until a new range of enamel colours was introduced from Europe during the reign of Yongzheng (1723–35). These could be shaded to produce subtle effects, and this new palette is known as *famille rose*. A bright opaque pink, softly toned with white, predominates, although it doesn't occur on every piece.

Famille rose characterizes Chinese export porcelain from the 1740s until the early 1800s, during the Qianlong and Jiaqing reigns. It continued though the 19th century, although it was then known by different names. In Europe the term "Canton" is generally used, while in America "Rose Medallion" is a popular name, for designs in *famille rose* were often placed in reserved panels or medallions.

Chinese export porcelain falls into two main categories: porcelain produced in bulk to standard patterns and designs, and porcelain made to special order for private trade. On 18th-century trading ships, representatives of the Dutch and British East India Companies, known as "super-cargoes", were responsible for purchasing vast quantities of porcelain dinner and tea services to be auctioned in London and Amsterdam. The captains and senior crew were allowed to buy a limited quantity of goods themselves, to sell for profit when they returned home safely. This private trade involved taking special orders to China, where patterns and shapes could be made that were not generally available in the shops at home. Expensive fancy goods such as snuff boxes or perfume bottles of Meissen porcelain, or fashionable silver candlesticks, were taken to Canton and left behind to be copied at Jingdezhen. Anything up to a year later, the completed order would be taken back to eager customers in Europe. The most important private trade involved armorial and crested porcelain

▼ **"Tobacco Leaf" pattern tureen, *c.*1775–80**
Qianlong period. The "Tobacco Leaf" pattern is incredibly decorative, and it is hardly surprising that it is as popular today as it was in the 18th century. 20cm (8in) wide.
£10,000–14,000/$15,000–21,000

◄ **Canton *famille-rose* jardinière, early 19th century** These decorative wares were initially aimed at the Middle Eastern market, but enjoyed popularity in the USA where they became known as "Rose Medallion". 42cm (16⅓in). **£3,000–4,000/ $4,500–6,000 (a pair)**

▲ **Garden seat, mid-19th century**
Intended for the conservatory in a grand Victorian home, this seat is based on the shape of an ancient Chinese drum. With its rich Canton enamelling, it is a highly decorative ornament. 49.5cm (19in) tall. **£3,000–4,000/$4,500–6,000**

(*see* pages 62–63). Elaborate drawings of coats-of-arms were given to china painters in Canton, to be faithfully copied onto plates and teacups. The family history behind these coats of arms is one of the most fascinating areas in the study of Oriental porcelain.

During the reign of Qianlong (1735–95) a huge amount of *famille rose* porcelain was exported to Europe. Set patterns, mostly Chinese in origin, depicted flowers or formal landscapes with birds and animals, and a wide range of figure subjects. Scenes were often taken from Chinese literature, so the stories meant nothing to customers in Europe – rather, the little Chinamen and family groups were amusing to Western eyes. Sets of mugs were used for drinking hot beer or cider, plates were for dining, while tea and coffee sets allowed wealthy homes to entertain in style. Imported Chinese porcelain was expensive, and owners were frightened to use their precious tea sets. Consequently, a large amount of *famille rose* has been preserved in display cabinets, and can therefore be relatively cheap

today. Pieces with special decoration in the European style – copies of Meissen, or scenes taken from Dutch and English prints – are, of course, much more expensive.

Trade with Europe was reduced around 1800 and a new market was found in the United States. American trade porcelain includes many distinctive patterns, such as "Fitzhugh", made in a variety of bright colours, and all are very collectable today. Nineteenth-century Canton export porcelain, including Rose Medallion, was largely aimed at the Turkish and Middle-Eastern market, although many examples found their way to Europe and the USA. While they were highly decorative, the quality of the enamelling generally declined and collectors need to seek out pieces that are finely painted. Twentieth-century Chinese enamelled porcelain mostly follows traditional Chinese taste and Imperial patterns rather than the old export designs. The best examples, often of eggshell-thinness, are well worth collecting, but don't be misled by spurious reign marks (*see* pages 138–41).

▼ Chinese wine pot, Kangxi period
Late 17th century. This will have been used as a teapot in Europe, or else put on display as a precious curio from the Orient. £1,400–1,700/$2,100–2,550

◄ Chinese teabowl and saucer, c.1770
Qianlong period. Of very small size – the saucer is 9cm (3½in) in diameter – this was made for the Dutch market, where "toys" were very popular. £100–150/$150–225

▲ Chinese "Nankin"-type dinner plate, c.1780–90
Part of a set, painted entirely by hand and beautifully potted. Sets like this were imported to Europe in enormous quantities, and examples are remarkably inexpensive today. 20cm (8in) in diameter. £50–80/$75–120

Blue-&-White Export

The Chinese used mass-production methods to make blue-and-white porcelain in incredible quantities. A fair quantity was available in Europe as early as the 1690s, and proved popular as a form of interior decoration. Queen Mary II lined entire rooms of her palaces with blue-and-white porcelain and started the fashion for "chinamania" that soon spread across the Continent. Plates, cups, and saucers were mounted in rows on walls above mantelpieces designed to display sets of vases known as "garnitures". Porcelain was keenly collected, and the wealthiest princes and nobility engaged in intense rivalry to form bigger and better "china rooms".

In the 18th century, imported Chinese blue-and-white porcelain was known in England and America as "Nankin", even though most was shipped from Canton, Macao, and Batavia. Blue-and-white was much cheaper than enamelled porcelain and was used on a daily basis in many well-to-do homes. Early in the century Chinese blue-and-white appealed to collectors, and copies

were made in Delft and other pottery centres across Europe. By the middle of the 18th century, Nankin was no longer scarce and was used every day as the fashion for tea-drinking spread. Tea sets were designed with teapots, jugs, and sugar bowls to match the cups and saucers. In Europe, tea was drunk in the Chinese way – using "tea bowls" without handles. Filled with hot tea, these bowls were not easy to use, and many countries adopted the habit of drinking tea from the saucer instead – hence a "dish of tea". Teacups with handles were rare until the 19th century.

Porcelain-makers across Europe copied Chinese blue-and-white porcelain, especially in England, although it was only as a result of transfer-printing in blue-and-white that British porcelain could match the Chinese imports in price. Cheap labour-costs at Jingdezhen meant that large quantities of delicate tea bowls and saucers, as well as thin dinner plates, were painted with highly intricate designs. Some copied the appearance of English transfer-printing, with tiny shaded lines all painted by hand.

▼ **Chinese butter tub,** *c.***1760–70**
Qianlong period. The rare shape of this dish was specially ordered as a copy of a European silver original.
£3,000–4,000/$4,500–6,000

Eventually these Chinese wares could no longer compete with cheap British printed pottery, and as a result Chinese blue-and-white porcelain suffered a decline at the beginning of the 19th century.

Its great revival came in the 1880s when influential collectors such as Oscar Wilde encouraged a new wave of chinamania. The department store Liberty, in London's Regent Street, imported huge quantities of cheap Chinese blue-and-white vases to sell to new customers who wanted their homes to have Oriental-style interiors. These vases were mostly copies of old Kangxi originals that had by then become quite valuable.

A great many Chinese blue-and-white vases copying antique examples were imported, especially to Britain, and these were almost always given fake Kangxi and Qianlong reign marks. The vases were intended as cheap decoration, and can still make impressive displays in modern homes, but once again be careful not to be taken in by the false markings. These later Chinese vases lack the precision and delicacy of the Kangxi originals.

Collecting
Cargo Porcelain

▲ **Chinese export dinner plates**
Recovered in 1985 from the wreck of the *Geldermelsen*, sunk in 1746 and known as the "Nankin Cargo". Fascinating history at an affordable price. **£200–300/$300–450**

In 1985 Captain Michael Hatcher headed a salvage operation to recover Chinese porcelain from the wreck of the *Geldermelsen*, a Dutch East-Indiaman that sank on its way to Europe in 1746. One hundred thousand pieces of Chinese blue-and-white porcelain were brought to the surface and sold in Amsterdam as the "Nankin Cargo". The sale recreated a scene from 18th-century auctions, at which whole dinner sets and thousands of cups and saucers were sold to dealers and collectors. Millions of pounds were raised, and the sale started a new "chinamania", as pieces were re-sold worldwide for enormous sums of money.

A few years later the "Diana Cargo" of Chinese blue-and-white porcelain was auctioned. This was followed by the Vung-Tau, the Hoi An, and the Tek-Sing cargoes – three more enormous shipwrecks that each yielded several hundred thousand pieces of Oriental blue-and-white. The result of these salvage operations and subsequent auctions, some conducted via the Internet, is that Chinese porcelain is now as plentiful as it was in the 18th century.

The best finds are expensive, but many simple dishes and bowls that may be some 300 years old can now be bought for as little as £5/$8. Even 15th-century pots from the Hoi An wreck can cost as little as £20–40/$30–60. What a wonderful opportunity for enthusiasts to form a fascinating, inexpensive collection.

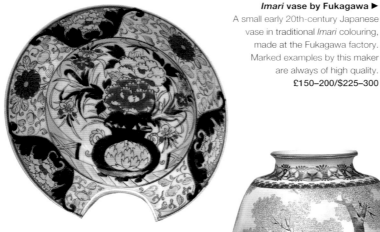

▲ Barber's bowl, late 17th century
Made in Japan during the Edo period
to a traditional *Imari* design. However,
the shape was clearly made for export
to Europe. 26.5cm (10in) in diameter.
£1,000–1,300/$1,500–2,000

Imari vase by Fukagawa ▶
A small early 20th-century Japanese
vase in traditional *Imari* colouring,
made at the Fukagawa factory.
Marked examples by this maker
are always of high quality.
£150–200/$225–300

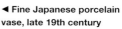

**◀ Fine Japanese porcelain
vase, late 19th century**
Made for the home market rather
than for export, and painted with
remarkable care. The best Japanese
porcelain from this period is rarely
appreciated in the West.
£2,500–3,500/$3,750–5,250

Japanese Porcelain

The continuation of traditional designs means that it is often quite difficult to date Japanese porcelain. Patterns and shapes from the late 1600s were revived two centuries later and were exported in large quantities to Europe and the USA. Dishes and vases in the well-known *Imari* colouring are highly decorative and particularly popular with collectors today.

Arita was the main centre of manufacture, and from there porcelain was exported via the nearby port of Imari, which is how the porcelain got its name. Early blue-and-white porcelain made at Arita largely follows Chinese prototypes, but it is rare and therefore quite expensive. The Japanese porcelain-makers favoured a distinctive palette, combining underglaze blue with red and orange enamels, and gold. This found great favour in Europe, especially in Holland where *Imari* porcelain was keenly collected early in the 18th century. Fearing cultural contamination, Japan chose isolation from world trade and from the 1740s onwards hardly any Japanese porcelain found its way to the West. Instead *Imari* patterns were copied by Chinese porcelain factories to sell in Europe. The term "Chinese *Imari*" is used for these wares made in China as copies of the patterns no longer available from Japan.

Once Japan reopened its doors in the mid-19th century the majority of porcelain that was produced revived the old *Imari* patterns. Pairs of vases, some of massive size, and splendid dishes for hanging on the wall were shipped in quantity to Europe. A lot of Japanese *Imari* was relatively inexpensive, and it is important for collectors to consider the quality of the painted decoration and, if possible, compare examples. Two dishes of similar size can be of very different value, depending on the care taken over the enamelling.

Many very individual types of porcelain were made in Japan in the late 19th century, and the work of top artists such as Makuzu Kozan can fetch incredible sums. One prolific factory, Fukagawa (meaning "fragrant orchid"), produced porcelain of high quality in a great range of different styles.

▲ Kutani-style vase
One of a pair of early 20th-century Japanese export porcelain
vases, decorated with good quality figure subjects, 30.5cm (12in)
in height. Matching pairs are always worth proportionally more
than single vases. **£800–1,100/$1,200–1,650 per pair**

Collecting
Kakiemon

▲ Kakiemon dish and Meissen copy
(Top) A Japanese lobed dish in the "Flaming Tortoise"
design, late 17th century. **£8,000–12,000/$12,000–18,000**
(Below) A Meissen octagonal dish, *c.*1730, copying a
Kakiemon original; the design is known as "Hob in the Well",
28cm (11in) diameter. **£15,000–20,000/$22,500–30,000**

At Hirado very beautiful blue-and-white porcelain
was produced. It was incredibly precise and quite
different from contemporary Chinese exports.
At Arita many colourful pieces that copied
traditional Chinese and Japanese patterns continued
to be made, while at Kutani *Imari* designs were
adapted by replacing the underglaze blue with
painted black enamel.

During the 20th century Noritake became the
principal centre of porcelain manufacture. A lot
of Noritake was copied directly from popular
European porcelain, especially Limoges, Vienna,
and Royal Worcester, to sell cheaply in china shops
around the world. Noritake is best known for its
inexpensive tea sets made for the export trade
(*see* page 111), decorated with traditional Japanese
subjects such as Samurai or views of Mount Fuji.
Eggshell-thin cups frequently have a geisha girl
moulded in the bottom – several million were made
in the 1920s and 1930s. While cheap sets are no
more than novelties, the few Noritake tea sets that
were finely enamelled are well worth collecting.

The most valuable of all Japanese porcelain,
Kakiemon is also widely regarded as some
of the most beautiful ever made. Traditionally
this wonderful white porcelain is associated with
a single family of Japanese potters, descendants of
Sakaida Kakiemon, although it is now known to
have been produced in a major kiln at Arita from
around 1670 until 1710. The porcelain is beautifully
white (known in Japan as *nigoshide*), and forms
the perfect background to a distinctive palette of
enamels. Patterns are never crowded, and the
subtlety is incredibly pleasing. In Europe kings
and rich aristocrats treasured the few pieces of
Kakiemon porcelain available (at enormous cost).

Once porcelain was reinvented in Europe, and
Japanese export had ceased, factories at St Cloud,
Chantilly, Meissen, Chelsea, Bow, and Worcester
all made direct copies of precious Kakiemon
originals. It is extremely difficult to distinguish the
best of these, especially those made at Meissen,
from the originals. Collecting Kakiemon
porcelain is not a cheap pastime, but it can be very
rewarding for the pieces do have a unique beauty.

▲ French porcelain inkwell, c.1830–40
Enamelled in Paris, this inkwell combines *Chinoiserie* decoration
with a classical Empire shape. 15cm (6in) long. **£400–600/$600–900**

◄ Meissen *Chinoiserie* tea canister, c.1725–30
This features *Chinoiserie* figures in the manner of J.G.
Höroldt. Meissen's incredible range of Chinese style
figures were always superbly painted. (Lacking cover).
9cm (3½in) high. **£2,500–3,500/$3,750–5,250**

Chinoiserie & Japanesque

Since medieval times, trade along the Silk Road
had brought exotic produce from China to
Europe, and with it mystical legend. Inspired by
the porcelain and fancy silks, Europeans conjured
up in their imaginations their own ideas of what
life must be like in China. Few people had seen a
real Chinaman, and instead they invented a fantasy
world populated by Europeans dressed up in
Chinese clothes. Failing to understand the
perspective shown in Oriental art, European artists
assumed differences in scale were characteristic
features of the Chinese style of painting. As a result
Chinoiserie was invented.

Early European porcelain was expensive to
make and cost more than most imports from China.
Rather than attempt to copy Chinese porcelain
directly, many European makers chose *Chinoiserie*,
as it appealed more to Western taste. In effect it was
more Chinese than the real thing, emphasizing the
comical figures, crazy pagodas, and fantastic
beasts. The greatest exponent of *Chinoiserie* was

J.G. Höroldt at Meissen. In his vivid imagination he
devised the most fantastic world of pretend Chinese
families, where tall, elegant ladies serve tea to portly
mandarins, acrobats and conjurors perform their
tricks, and elephants march in procession – but
always too small for the fine gentlemen who ride
on their backs. Höroldt drew sheets of *Chinoiserie*
designs for other painters at Meissen to copy, and
consequently it is difficult to distinguish the work
of the master from his many pupils.

Chinoiserie suited the mid-18th century spirit
of rococo, and was practised right across Europe.
Books of Chinese designs were published, the most
influential by Jean Pillement, a French artist,
whose work was copied by porcelain-makers in
Paris as well as in England, at Chelsea and
Worcester. Pillement's Chinamen were always
Europeans dressed up in rich costumes and playing
harmless games. Following the neo-classical period,
Chinoiserie enjoyed a great revival in Regency
England with the building of the Brighton

▶ **Minton vase in *Cloisonné* style, c.1871**
Inspired by the Orient, but not a direct copy. Instead the design is probably the work of Dr Christopher Dresser. 28cm (11in) in height. £4,000–5,000/$6,000–7,500

▼ **A Royal Worcester copy of a Japanese bronze drum**
Decorated in the manner of James Callowhill in raised gold and platinum, with a date code for 1883. Worcester made a vast range of *Japanesque* designs. 15cm (6in) wide.
£300–400/$450–600

▲ **A Davenport jug, *c.*1812–15**
Painted with Chinese figures in a cartoon-like style that was a specialty of this factory. 15.5cm (6in) high.
£500–700/$750–1,050

Pavilion. Porcelain-makers including Davenport, Spode, and Wedgwood copied Pillement's drawing books once again, while Höroldt's Meissen work was also copied afresh.

In the 1860s, after more than a century of self-imposed isolation, Japan reopened its doors, and Victorians discovered the wonders of Japanese art. Japanese wares of every kind were seen for the first time at international exhibitions, and caused a sensation. Porcelain-makers in Paris and England rushed to make copies of Japanese artefacts. Minton and Royal Worcester led the world in a new style of porcelain that became known as *Japanesque*. Japanese bronzes, ivory, lacquer, and cloisonné were either copied exactly or else adapted to suit European and American customers. Elements from Chinese, Indian, and Middle-Eastern art were combined with Japanese designs to create a new, eclectic style. Gilbert and Sullivan lampooned Japanesque in their comic operettas *The Mikado* and *Patience*, the latter poking fun at the Aesthetic

Movement that grew out of the cult for all things Japanese. Collectors filled their houses with Oriental art, antique and new, and Minton copies fitted in perfectly. One of the greatest collectors was R.W. Binns, owner of the Royal Worcester factory, whose private museum of Japanese art contained thousands of artefacts intended to inspire his workmen. Dr Christopher Dresser, who produced some designs for Minton, is regarded as the foremost British designer working in the Japanesque taste.

The fashion for Oriental art has become timeless. Japanese design, of course, had a great impact on the Art Deco period in the 1920s and 1930s. Interior decorators in Europe and the USA favoured *Chinoiserie* schemes throughout the 20th century, especially in the 1920s and 1960s. This can make dating relatively modern porcelain made in the style of the 18th century confusing. The Royal Pavilion in Brighton continues to inspire lavish decorations, while firms such as Meissen still produce *Chinoiserie* patterns first made in the 1730s.

▼ **A Nymphenburg group, c.1760–70**
"Troubled Repose" by F.A.Bustelli, the greatest of the rococo modellers, featuring an impressed shield mark. 23.5cm (9in) in height. £6,000–10,000/$9,000–15,000

▲ **Vienna rococo clock case, c.1755**
Marked with a shield in blue. The form is asymmetrical without a single straight line, and yet the design is perfectly balanced. 31cm (12in) in height.
£4,000–6,000/$6,000–9,000

Rococo & Rococo Revivals

Great fashions in art have a habit of repeating themselves. Rococo was the epitome of good taste during three very different periods, while at other times it was ridiculed and reviled. Derived from the French word *rocaille* (meaning decorative rock), the name "rococo" was itself a parody, used to poke fun at rockwork grottos and an obsession with seashells. Each period of rococo was a reaction against the formal art style that preceded it. It was a protest against classical symmetry, for the basis of rococo is the total absence of any straight lines.

Both France and Germany claim to have invented the rococo style in architecture and music, for the spirit of rococo encompasses every branch of the arts. However, in porcelain there is no contest – the first great rococo designs were made at Meissen. Rococo was a sculptural style, best reflected in the fluid figure subjects of J.J. Kändler that captured so perfectly the new spirit of the age. Asymmetric scrollwork began to appear everywhere during the late 1730s and the 1740s. The masterly "Swan

Service", modelled by Kändler for Count Bruhl in 1737, led a revolution in ceramic design that culminated in the great rococo figures and wares made at Meissen in the period 1745–50. Every other German china factory adopted rococo, especially Nymphenburg, where F.A. Bustelli modelled a series of figures to rival even those of Kändler himself.

In France, rococo was somewhat gentler than in Germany. Porcelain made at Vincennes, the forerunner of Sèvres, used lightly modelled leaf and plant scrolls as ornament and borders. Watteau, the great French rococo artist, provided figure subjects and paintings for the Vincennes craftsmen to copy. In Italy, rococo was captured perfectly in the porcelain of Capodimonte, particularly in the figure models by G. Gricci (*see* page 15). English porcelain was just starting to develop when rococo was at its zenith in Europe. Chelsea, Bow, and Derby figures epitomize English rococo, while Chelsea vases from the Gold Anchor period (1758–69) are as eccentric as they are exciting.

◄ Minton vase, *c.*1835
Made during the first major rococo revival. The inspiration is Meissen porcelain of the time, for this Minton vase is marked underneath with a copy of Meissen's crossed swords in blue. 25.5cm (10in) in height.
£500–700/$750–1,050

▼ Royal Doulton plate, 1890s
Finely gilded with a border of rococo ornament. The whole plate is smothered with decoration. 23cm (9in) in diameter.
£250–350/$375–525

◄ Chelsea vase from the "Gold Anchor" period, *c.*1765
One of a pair, or from a matching garniture, with fantastic tooled gilding that suits the eccentric shape. 27cm (10½in).
£4,000–6,000/$6,000–9,000

Discoveries in the classical world took art and design in a different direction after 1770, and rococo suddenly became old-fashioned. For 50 years formal, classical symmetry dominated porcelain design, and it was not until the 1820s that irregular scrollwork and delicate flowers came back into fashion. Paris and Dresden once more led the way. Old Meissen figures by Kändler became popular again, and modelled porcelain flowers were a most desirable ornament. In the 1830s porcelain-makers in Paris and Limoges copied old Dresden too, taking the more eccentric 18th-century models and adding extra scrollwork and flowers in brighter colours. New Meissen porcelain was sold in every china shop in England in the 1830s, and copied extensively. "English Dresden", as it was called, was made by all the great factories, including Worcester and Derby, and especially Minton, Rockingham, and Coalport, where some old Chelsea shapes from the Gold Anchor period were reintroduced. Coalport porcelain with modelled rococo scrollwork and

applied china flowers was known as "Coalbrookdale", and enjoyed great popularity between 1835 and 1845.

High-Victorian taste was torn in many different directions – English Gothic, German medieval, Italian Renaissance, and finally Chinese and Japanese. Rococo was forgotten until the 1890s when the craze for eccentric ornament saw a new, and this time short-lived, revival. Dresden led the way again, with figures of cupids supporting flower-encrusted lamps and centrepieces, and mirror frames awash with irregular rococo scrolls and further applied cupids. Limoges in France reintroduced many old rococo designs, albeit in new colours with lots of shaded gold. Eventually world taste had had enough, and Art Nouveau was born.

It is important to learn to differentiate between the three rococo periods, roughly spanning 1740–65, 1825–45, and 1885–1900. Each one is more extreme than the last; early rococo is wonderful, late rococo is very decorative. They are totally different, and appeal to widely different markets today.

◄ **A single vase from a Chelsea-Derby garniture**
Marked with a gold anchor. In 1772–3 this was the latest London fashion and the height of elegance. 34cm (13in) in height. **£2,500–3,000/$3,750–4,500**

▲ **A Naples porcelain milk jug**
Dated c.1780–90, copied from an ancient Etruscan ewer; the scene shows Naples as it would have appeared on the Grand Tour. **£1,200–1,600/$1,800–2,400**

◄ **Meissen figure of Cupid, c.1775–80**
From the Marcolini period, with crossed swords and a star mark. The altar of love is formed from a classical pillar, and the base is ornamented with a Greek key design. **£600–800/$900–1,200**

The Classical Taste

A detailed knowledge of the classical world was an essential part of every aristocratic education. The "Grand Tour" was not a new idea, for travellers had visited Italy to study architecture and art long before most of the "sites" were discovered. However, the discovery of the ruins of Pompeii and Herculaneum changed everything. Beneath the volcanic ash the entire life of ancient Rome was laid out in full and glorious colour. Visitors to the diggings in the 1770s saw the Pompeian wall paintings in their true colours, and realized that ancient Rome had not been monochromatic. Among the travellers who took the Grand Tour was a young Scottish architect, Robert Adam. Adam became Britain's most influential interior designer, and households the length and breadth of the land commissioned his "neo-classical" rooms, with specially designed furniture and fireplaces. Tableware and ornaments for the mantelpieces were needed next, and these were provided in pottery by the Wedgwood factory, and in porcelain by Derby and Worcester.

London was the hub of the new neo-classical taste. The finest classical porcelain was made at the former Chelsea factory, owned by William Duesbury of Derby and trading as Chelsea-Derby. Between 1770 and 1775 almost the entire output of the factory was classically inspired and refreshingly different. Across London, in Soho, the china painter James Giles used a new formal style of painting to decorate blank Worcester porcelain with classical urns and landscapes with ancient ruins. However, this English porcelain was not original but copied new porcelain from Germany and Paris, where neo-classicism had completely replaced rococo.

Classical design dominated the final quarter of the 18th century. Travellers who visited the ruins of Pompeii brought home Doccia and Naples porcelain painted with local views. At Meissen, under the new direction of Count Marcolini, Kändler's rococo figures were replaced by the work of a new classical modeller, Michel Victor

▶ **Worcester vase by Flight, Barr and Barr**
This vase, dated c.1825, was painted by George Davis and has magnificent gilding. While classically inspired, the decorative effect is straight out of Regency England. 30.5cm (12in) in height.
£5,000–7,000/$7,500–10,500

▲ **Coalport porcelain bough pot**
Painted by Thomas Baxter in his decorating studio in London, this pot is signed and dated 1801. The shape is very formal to suit a classical-inspired interior. 19cm (7½in) high.
£5,000–7,000/$7,500–10,500

Acier. German tableware was now classical in design, much of it painted with Grecian urns or portrait medallions of Roman emperors. In France, in the years leading up to the Revolution, even the Sèvres factory substituted classical design for some of its rococo ornament.

After the French Revolution a new style of classical decoration became fashionable in Paris that rendered the formal ornament of ancient Rome in new, brighter colours with intricate gilding. The style was adopted throughout Europe, especially in London where Paris porcelain sold alongside Coalport and Worcester copies, many of them painted in London. With the 19th century came an even greater interest in the ancient world. Napoleon's campaigns in Egypt and Nelson's Nile victory brought Egyptian designs into the public eye. Simple classical-style porcelain was now too plain for a Europe-wide market that wanted more colour, more exciting shapes, and much more gold. In France the style was known as "Empire",

inspired by the personal taste of Napoleon who cast himself as a new Roman emperor. Splendid vases with painted classical scenes and handles in the shape of eagles, sphinxes, and caryatids were made in Paris and then copied in England, Germany, Austria, and Russia. Britain's version of the French Empire style is referred to as "Regency" – a somewhat loose term given to the more extravagant decoration of the early 19th century. The Worcester factories of Chamberlain & Co., and Flight, Barr and Barr made some of the finest Regency porcelain, much of it in classical taste, at least in shape. However, the decoration relied now on brightly coloured grounds, and splendid gilding to frame beautifully painted panels. In Germany and Austria the equivalent of Empire taste is called "Biedermeier", and here again the magnificent porcelain made at Berlin and Vienna between 1805 and 1830 left its classical roots far behind in favour of gorgeous coloured grounds and fine goldwork.

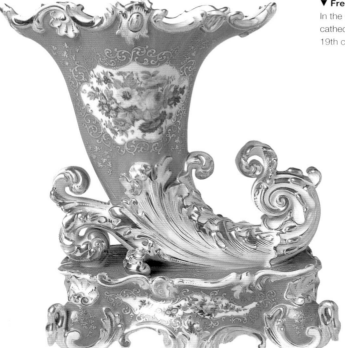

▲ **Cornucopia vase by Jacob Petit,** *c.***1840**
Petit was a French porcelain-maker, famed for his lavish ornamentation. A pair of these would have looked splendid on a massive mantelpiece. 30.5cm (12in) high. **£500–700/$750–10,500**

▼ **French porcelain mantel clock,** *c.***1840–50**
In the Gothic taste, this eccentric style is based on a medieval cathedral, although the colouring belongs in the middle of the 19th century. 51cm (20in) high. **£3,000–4,000/$4,500–6,000**

High-Victorian Taste

The Victorian era spans seven decades, and during this period many different tastes and fashions came and went. The generic term "Victorian" can be very misleading, as it is used for just about anything made in the 19th century. This was a period of great prosperity for Britain, with the expansion of the British Empire and the growth of global trade. The markets that were developing in the USA provided great opportunities for Britain's factories. To be successful, porcelain-makers had to understand different markets around the world, and keep up-to-date with changing fashion. This meant participating in the many international exhibitions that were then being staged in major cities. For the Victorians, these events involved far more than just a great day out.

The catalogue of the Great Exhibition, held in London in 1851, is a wonderful summary of taste at the time. The Exhibition displayed the finest porcelain from all over Europe alongside the very best English examples. Manufacturers learnt from each

other and copied whatever was successful. At these massive trade shows were "Exhibition Pieces" made for display, as well as fancy goods of all descriptions. Illustrations of porcelain on show in the 1851 and 1862 exhibitions reveal that when it came to High-Victorian taste there were no half measures. Everything is smothered with ornament, with no room to spare.

Paris and Dresden remained the principal influences on English porcelain, while the Meissen and Berlin factories led the way in establishing new fashions. German porcelain embraced a new style known as *Historismus*, which was basically a revival of medieval, Gothic, and Renaissance art presented in a very Victorian way. In France the Sèvres factory, and especially the Paris firm of Jacob Petit, took rococo ornament to new heights, while the firms of J. Gille and Porcelaine de Paris made large porcelain figures in new interpretations of historical costumes. The most successful English porcelain factories, Minton and Copeland, copied these latest

▼ **A Derby Crown Porcelain Co. vase**
In the Islamic taste, and *c.*1885, this vase is absolutely crammed with arabesque ornament. The quality of the raised goldwork is as impressive as the design. 33.5cm (13in) in height.
£1,300–1,600/$2,000–2,400

▲ *Pâte-sur-pâte* **Minton vase, 1869**
One of a pair, with panels by Lawrence Birks depicting the twelve months of the year. The gilding is equally lavish. 43cm (17in) in height.
£15,000–20,000/$22,500–30,000 (the pair)

▼ **French porcelain mirror frame**
In the Dresden taste, *c.*1880. While it lacks the quality of Meissen, every inch is smothered with china flowers, Cupids, and other ornament. 76cm (30in) high.
£2,000–3,000/$3,000–4,500

Continental styles. They also engaged craftsmen from France to bring a different, refreshing look to many of their productions. Obsessed with all things French, Minton also made reproductions of the best Sèvres porcelain from the 18th century.

Alongside these Continental styles, Minton and Copeland exhibited a new kind of porcelain, one that was totally English. "Parian" allowed the life-sized marble statues on display at the exhibitions to be copied in small versions to bring home as souvenirs. Plain white and sculptural, parian wasn't fancy, but it reflected the best art of the time and allowed collectors to bring "masterpieces" into their front parlours. These figures were combined with glazed, painted, and gilded dishes and baskets to form the most elaborate table centrepieces.

A preoccupation with Oriental art dominated the 1870s and 1880s. Copies of Eastern designs could be simple or heavily ornamented, depending on your taste. Royal Worcester specialized in copying the appearance of old ivory and produced many truly magnificent vases, as well as simple jugs and pitchers for everyday use. Several porcelain makers in Limoges produced Japanese- and Indian-style porcelain, much of it for the American market.

By the 1890s popular taste had become totally mixed, but it hardly mattered for most Victorian interiors were a mass of different kinds of clutter. Vases and figurines from all parts of Europe copied old Dresden, Vienna, Capodimonte, and Sèvres, but you can not mistake the Victorian versions for the real thing. Early 18th-century porcelain had a subtle elegance that was lost on the Victorians; 19th-century makers wanted to go one better, exaggerating every feature, squeezing in extra ornament, and generally going over-the-top. These pieces were not made for connoisseurs; their purpose was to impress, and to show off the new wealth of the middle classes who wanted new ornaments, not antiques. The true collectors, who had previously bought simple, classical styles and had moved on to Japanese designs, now cried out for something different.

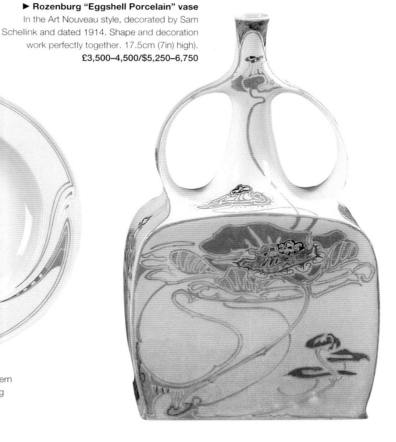

► **Rozenburg "Eggshell Porcelain" vase**
In the Art Nouveau style, decorated by Sam Schellink and dated 1914. Shape and decoration work perfectly together. 17.5cm (7in) high.
£3,500–4,500/$5,250–6,750

▲ **Meissen plate, *c*.1903**
Meissen appreciated the importance of modern design, and commissioned work from leading artists and architects, in this case Henri Van de Velde. £1,000–1,500/$1,500–2,250

Modern Taste – Art Nouveau & Art Deco

When the spirit of Art Nouveau arrived a hundred years ago, one of the most exciting periods in art was born. Yet, surprisingly, most porcelain makers ignored this revolutionary style, which was transforming the glass and pottery industries. Porcelain factories remained staunchly traditional, and although firms such as Minton produced great Art Nouveau designs using their pottery bodies, their attempts at porcelain were half-hearted and unmemorable. Fine Art Nouveau porcelain is rare; it was generally limited to a few special pieces that were far more expensive than pottery. However, these are worth seeking out.

Art Nouveau porcelain was largely made on the Continent. The three most important factories produced some stunning designs, although again only as a sideline, to be sold alongside traditional copies of 18th-century pieces. The French national porcelain manufactory at Sèvres used the *pâte-sur-pâte* technique to make spectacular vases in a totally new Art Nouveau style. The German state

factories at Meissen and Berlin also opened new art departments to experiment with running and dribbling coloured glazes and *pâte-sur-pâte* decoration. Their Art Nouveau porcelain is exceptional in beauty and originality, but is not well known. In 1900 Meissen continued to sell copies of 18th-century figures by Kändler, and these generated huge profits that subsidized the experimental new productions. Meissen's figures of children by Konrad Hentschel are much rarer than its 18th-century figures, a fact that is now appreciated by a new generation of collectors. The value of Art Nouveau Meissen has escalated in recent years, especially tableware by avant-garde designers such as Henri Van de Velde.

New techniques in underglaze painting developed at Meissen were copied with great success by the Royal Copenhagen porcelain manufactory in Denmark. The subtle painting was sometimes combined with innovative modelled shapes based on plant designs. Yet Royal

◄ **Royal Copenhagen Vase**
Dated *c*.1905 and decorated
by Christian Thomsen, whose
exciting Art Nouveau designs
were inspired by nature.
20cm (8in) tall.
£600–900/$900–1,350

▶ **Sèvres figure
of a dancing girl**
Dated 1900, this
is part of a series
made for a table
decoration,
designed by
Agathon Léonard.
Unglazed biscuit
porcelain
emphasises the
sculptural quality
of the piece.
52cm (20in) high.
**£8,000–12,000/
$12,000–18,000**

▶ **Minton vase, *c*.1912**
Designed and decorated by
John Wadsworth, combining
classical form with *secessionist*
ornament, a style unusual on
English porcelain. 18.5cm (7in)
high. **£500–700/$750–1,050**

Copenhagen came into its own during the Art Nouveau period as a maker of figures – children, dancers, and satyrs, all delicately coloured to enhance the sculptural quality of the modelling.

The subtle underglaze colouring used at Sèvres, Meissen, and Copenhagen was copied even in Russia, where wonderful Art Nouveau vases were made by the Imperial Porcelain Factory. Royal Doulton made intriguing Art Nouveau porcelain with its "Titanium Ware", painted in underglaze colours. Royal Worcester's "Sabrina Ware" aimed at similar subtle glaze effects, but with poor glaze control the results were somewhat hit and miss. Among the most beautiful Art Nouveau pieces are those made by the Rozenburg factory in The Hague. Although technically a high-fired pottery, Rozenburg eggshell is usually thought of as a kind of frit porcelain. Vases, cups, and saucers of "eggshell" thinness, painted by Sam Schellink and others, have original and uniquely delineated plant designs.

Sèvres made a collection of stunning figures of the exotic French dancer Loïe Fuller, issued in white biscuit porcelain as a series of flowing sculptures. The Royal Dux factory in Austria and Ernst Wahliss in Vienna also made well-modelled figures of Art Nouveau maidens, although they were sold with traditional colouring. Elsewhere in Vienna the Wiener Werkstätte was devising a new school of artistic design which would later be known as "Secessionist". Its most direct influence was on pottery and glassware, but some modern porcelain was made along Secessionist principles. In due course the Secessionist style developed into Art Deco.

The Bock coffee set (*see* page 46) is a dazzling example of modernism in Continental porcelain. Even more dramatic was some of the post-Revolutionary Russian porcelain made in the early 1920s to designs by major avant-garde artists such as the Suprematists, Vasilii Kandinsky and Nikolai Suetin. The best of these Russian pieces

▼ **Limoges parrot jug,** *c.*1930
A covered jug ingeniously designed as
a parrot, by Swiss sculptor Edouard-Marcel
Sandoz. 18.5cm (7½in). **£300–400/$450–600**

▲ **A striking Modernist Joseph Bock coffee set,** *c.*1920
Designed by Jutta Sitka for Bock, a totally original and very
exciting design at the time.
£3,800–4,500/$5,700–6,750 (the set)

are so valuable today as modern art that they fall
outside the scope of this book, but do watch out
for clever fakes made recently in Russia. At
Noritake in Japan, tea sets with modernist patterns
of interlaced coloured circles were made to designs
by the architect Frank Lloyd Wright. Excitingly
different, they are also pretty rare. The new
abstract styles took time to catch on, but European
commercial designers gradually noticed what had
happened. Art Deco had left Art Nouveau behind.

Pottery-makers dominated the world of Art
Deco. In England, Clarice Cliff was the most
innovative designer, and her work was heavily
copied. However, porcelain was somehow felt to
be too delicate, and bold Art Deco hardly fitted.
Some of the best modern-designed tableware was
made in England, by Doulton and particularly by
the Shelley factory, which specialized in tea sets.
Angular shapes, triangular handles, and square
plates were original, but the traditional porcelain-
buying public was rarely brave enough. Customers
chose sets of modern shapes with watered-down
Deco patterns, or even old-fashioned roses that

seem incongruous on such angular pieces. Their
value today very much depends on how
dramatically Art Deco the patterns appear.

The discovery of Tutankhamun's tomb in 1922
revived the Western fascination with Egyptian art,
and this ran hand-in-hand with Art Deco. France,
in particular, took great interest in the angular
shapes and bright colours, and many original
pieces came from factories at Limoges. The best
were by outside designers such as the eminent
sculptor Edouard-Marcel Sandoz, who created
comical animal and bird tea sets, and the fashion
house Robj, which devised perfume and liqueur
flasks in the form of curious figures. Colourful
copies of Limoges and other bold Art Deco pieces
were made cheaply in Japan, and this Noritake
ware is a growing field for collectors.

Between the two world wars, Scandinavia and
Germany created wonderful figure and animal
models in porcelain. China factories mostly
commissioned models from freelance artists who
were often used to working in marble or bronze.
As a result their creations frequently have a

▶ **Cleopatra and Henry V figures**
Vivien Leigh as Cleopatra and Lawrence
Olivier as Henry V, designed by Susan
Parkinson as part of a series of early
1950s theatrical figures for Briglin.
29.5cm (11in) high. **£200–300/$300–450**

▼ **"Variations on a Geometric Theme"**
One of a set of six Wedgwood bone-china
plates designed by Eduardo Paolozzi,
issued in 1970 as a Limited Edition of 200
sets, each plate 25.5cm (10in) in diameter.
£1,500–1,800/$2,250–2,700 (set of six)

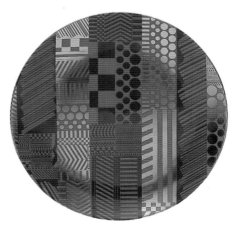

◀ **"The Dancers" by Doris Lindner, 1933**
For Royal Worcester. This Art Deco figure
group was available in simulated stone-
effect, or fully coloured as here.
£700–900/$1,000–1,350

sculptural feel, and are very different from the traditional porcelain figurines for which Dresden was famous. Original Art Deco porcelain models were made by firms such as Rosenthal, Ens, and, of course, Meissen. Their sculptural qualities are best seen when unspoilt by painted decoration. Collectors today tend to regard these as unfinished and unexciting, and as a result some wonderful pieces can be surprisingly inexpensive.

In England, traditional china factories failed to understand modern sculpture. Royal Worcester noticed what was happening in Germany and bought some designs from two Rosenthal artists, but issued them in totally inappropriate colouring. Doris Lindner, a freelance sculptor working in London, had designed a series of Art Deco figures for the home furnishings store Heal's. Worcester bought her models, but instead of colouring them with delicate stone textures it painted them in bright colours, just like most of the Doulton figures from the 1930s. Customers were not interested, and as a result most of the Worcester and Doulton Art Deco-style figures are incredibly rare today.

The onset of World War II brought closure to most porcelain factories, and when production restarted in the late 1940s markets were severely restricted. The relaxation of these restrictions in the early 1950s gave designers a chance to rethink. The Festival of Britain epitomized the era, with innovations in technology headed by television, and a desire by artists to be different. Rounded, amoebic forms replaced the hard, angular shapes of 1930s Deco. Stripes and polka dots were the dominant patterns, with black and white or red the principal colours favoured by designers. Pottery was still more important as a ceramic medium, but some exciting porcelain was made in Germany, Poland, and Scandinavia, as well as the USSR. Brighter colours came in during the 1960s, but by this time most porcelain factories had lost direction. A surprising number of makers relied on traditional designs for tableware. During the 1960s a new collectors' market grew up for limited editions – fine porcelain sculptures and commemorative and pictorial plates that brought salvation to a struggling industry.

Collecting by Decoration

Surface design or colours can inspire an endless variety of possible themes

Blue-&-White Porcelain

This most familiar form of decoration is almost as old as porcelain itself, for it was perfected during the Yuan dynasty around 700 years ago. Chinese potters discovered that patterns painted onto unfired porcelain using fine powder ground from ingots of Persian cobalt could survive the intense heat of the kilns, leaving a design in brilliant blue sealed within the glaze. During the early Ming dynasty superb blue-and-white porcelain was made for the Chinese emperor and his palace, and these pieces can command hundreds of thousands of pounds/dollars today. However, it is possible to collect Ming blue-and-white on a modest budget – not the Imperial quality, but so-called "provincial" wares such as the coarse porcelain made in Vietnam. Large amounts recovered from shipwrecks are available (*see* page 33).

Chinese blue-and-white porcelain was exported to Europe in considerable quantities during the 17th century. Beautifully decorated and thinly potted, Chinese porcelain was collected for display rather than for use. "Chinamania" was the term given to the obsession of princes who constructed china rooms in palaces to show off their collections of blue-and-white. By the 18th century a vast amount of blue-and-white was being imported from China for everyday use in well-to-do households. In spite of this, demand continued to exceed supply, and there were fortunes to be made producing copies in Europe. Curiously, while it was a treasured commodity two centuries ago, Chinese blue-and-white survives today in large quantities and is now surprisingly inexpensive. Many finely painted plates or cups and saucers from the 18th century can be bought for less than £50/$75, which presents endless scope for collectors.

The many European copies of Chinese blue-and-white porcelain constitute a fascinating area for study. The earliest successful production, from the end of the 17th century, took place in France at Rouen and St Cloud, where a creamy soft-paste porcelain was used, decorated with European-style

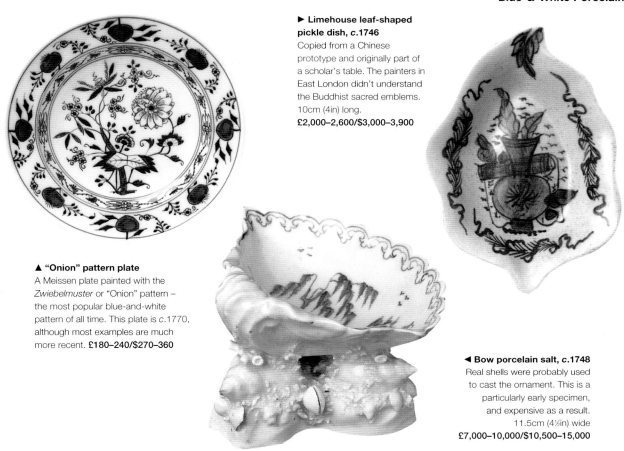

▶ **Limehouse leaf-shaped pickle dish, c.1746**
Copied from a Chinese prototype and originally part of a scholar's table. The painters in East London didn't understand the Buddhist sacred emblems. 10cm (4in) long.
£2,000–2,600/$3,000–3,900

▲ **"Onion" pattern plate**
A Meissen plate painted with the *Zwiebelmuster* or "Onion" pattern – the most popular blue-and-white pattern of all time. This plate is c.1770, although most examples are much more recent. **£180–240/$270–360**

◀ **Bow porcelain salt, c.1748**
Real shells were probably used to cast the ornament. This is a particularly early specimen, and expensive as a result. 11.5cm (4½in) wide
£7,000–10,000/$10,500–15,000

baroque ornamentation painted in bright blue. At Meissen during the 1720s copies of Chinese vases and teacups were made in "true" porcelain, and these can be easily mistaken for real Oriental porcelain. Meissen, Berlin, and Vienna all made tea wares copying popular Chinese designs. Two patterns, "Onion" and "Immortelle", enjoyed great popularity and are still made today by Meissen and other Dresden factories, and by Royal Copenhagen. However, as a general rule German blue-and-white porcelain of the 18th century proved difficult to control during firing, and early examples are uncommon. It seems somewhat strange, therefore, that Continental blue-and-white is not particularly expensive today. This is because there are far more collectors for early English blue-and-white than there are for the productions of any other country.

In England, various early porcelain factories made blue-and-white to compete with Chinese imports. Many productions were intentionally passed off as real Chinese, and as a result of this few makers used factory marks of their own. Initially, exact copies of Chinese plates and tea wares were made using artificial or soft-paste porcelain. The largest factory was at Bow in East London, where most of the output was modelled on Chinese and Japanese prototypes. Bow succeeded by exporting much of its porcelain to America – a fact proved by large numbers of Bow porcelain fragments recovered during archeological investigations at American historical sites. Indeed, the blue-and-white porcelain made by the only early American factory, Bonnin and Morris in Philadelphia, closely resembles that of Bow.

In order to make blue-and-white porcelain commercially viable, English factories had to produce it cheaply so that it could sell for less money than the imported Chinese wares. Sadly this proved impossible for most British makers. Instead they had to devise a product that would sell in china shops in England even though it cost more than real Chinese blue-and-white. Worcester found the

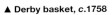

▲ Derby basket, *c.*1758
Taken from a dessert set. 18th-century baskets make wonderful decoration, especially when carefully painted, as in this example. 18.5cm (7in) wide. **£1,400–1,800/$2,100–2,700**

► Worcester cylindrical mug, *c.*1762–5
Painted with a mock Chinese pattern known as "Walk in the Garden". This would have been used for hot beer or cider. 8.5cm (3in) in height. **£900–1,200/$1,350–1,800**

▲ Chinese Export teapot and cover
Dated *c.*1785–90. The shape is based on a Leeds creamware prototype that was sent to China for copying. The gilding was added back in England. **£350–500/$500–750**

perfect formula for success by producing objects that could not be bought from importers of Chinese porcelain. It placed blue-and-white Chinese-style decoration on shapes that were copied from the latest and most fashionable English silver. Sauceboats and cream jugs, pickle dishes and shells for serving sweetmeats, handles for cutlery, holders for salt, inkwells, and candlesticks – all manner of objects modelled in the rococo taste were sold in London and other major cities. By 1760 English porcelain was no longer treated with suspicion, and blue-and-white production spread to all corners of Britain.

Early English porcelain-makers didn't have access to kaolin, and each factory developed its own formula, which was kept a closely guarded secret. Some firms followed Worcester's lead and used "soaprock" from Cornwall as a principal ingredient to give porcelain strength. Others used burnt animal bones instead. These two types of porcelain, known as "steatitic" and "phosphatic", each have a different effect on the look of the glaze and colour of the blue-and-white decoration. It is important

to study these subtle differences carefully, as the various English makers copied each others' shapes and designs. Liverpool, for instance, was home to several rival manufacturers in close proximity, and it is clear that some workmen moved from one factory to another. The factories of Philip Christian and Seth Pennington in Liverpool were maybe a quarter of the size of Worcester. By comparison, the short-lived Liverpudlian factories of Samuel Gilbody and William Reid were tiny – perhaps one-twentieth of Worcester's size. All made very similar shapes and patterns. Examples from the little factories are very hard to find, and can often only be distinguished by subtle differences in the colour and texture of the glaze. But it can be rewarding to recognize blue-and-white made by some of these less well-known, short-lived factories, and such rare pieces of early English blue-and-white are incredibly valuable.

Many blue-and-white collectors are interested in concentrating on one factory, the most popular being Worcester, Caughley, or Lowestoft. The

▼ **Liverpool cream jug, *c*.1780s**
From the factory of John and Jane Pennington. This shape was copied exactly from an English silver cream jug of a similar date. 12cm (5in) high. £750–1,000/$1,100–1,500

Collecting
Printed Blue-&-White

▲ **Caughley "Dutch Jug", *c*.1780s**
With a mask spout and "S" mark, printed with the "Fisherman" pattern. Caughley specialized in transfer-printing in blue and white, and managed to avoid blurring, even on moulded shapes such as this. 31cm (12in) in height. £700–1,000/$1,000–1,500

most profitable time for the English factories was the 1770s, following the invention of transfer-printing. Large amounts of blue-and-white were exported to The Netherlands and America, but success was brief. Chinese imports became cheaper, and the English pottery industry grew under the influence of Josiah Wedgwood and Josiah Spode. Blue-and-white pottery was cheaper still, and by 1800 porcelain decorated in blue was in decline. Blue-and-white tea sets by Miles Mason and others continued into the 19th century (*see* page 82), but by this time pottery had really taken over.

There was a great blue-and-white revival in the 1880s when cheap Chinese copies of early Kangxi porcelain flooded into Europe. As inexpensive decoration, the vases and jardinières from the late 19th century offer good value to collectors today, but this market is limited, as so much modern Oriental blue-and-white porcelain continues to be mass-produced in the Far East. With the exception of the Christmas plates from Copenhagen (*see* page 102), very little original blue-and-white was made in the 20th century.

A British invention revolutionized the porcelain industry in the 18th century. English blue-and-white had always been decorated by hand, in the Chinese manner – a delicate and costly technique. At Worcester, around 1756, Josiah Holdship perfected a method whereby a pattern engraved into a metal printing plate was transferred onto unglazed porcelain. Instead of relying on the skills of individual painters, finely detailed patterns could be printed in underglaze blue in quantity, with each piece identical. Worcester used blue printing extensively in the 1760s and 1770s, but Holdship's secret was never patented and other factories soon copied Worcester's lead. Several makers in Liverpool and in Shropshire – the Caughley factory in particular – used transfer printing to produce great quantities of cheap blue-and-white porcelain. Even the Chinese attempted to compete, using highly skilled painters to recreate by hand the shaded effects seen on printed porcelain. It is not difficult to tell printing from hand-painting. Using a strong magnifying glass, look among shaded areas for close parallel lines rather than solid washes of blue. Later in the 1790s the fashion for the "willow" pattern on printed pottery spread to Staffordshire porcelain.

◄ Chelsea plate, c.1755–85
Of so-called "Hans Sloane" type, with botanical decoration. This specimen of *Acacia Spinosa* is copied from a contemporary print by Philip Miller. 21.5cm (8½in) in diameter
£4,000–6,000/ $6,000–9,000

▼ Meissen flower pot, c.1740
Painted in the style known as *holzschnitt blumen*, with flowers based on engravings. It has a crossed swords mark and is 11cm (4in) in height.
£2,000–3,000/$3,000–4,500

► Derby plate, c.1805–10
With botanical decoration painted with a high level of realism, possibly the work of William "Quaker" Pegg.
£1,200–1,500/ $1,800–2,250

Floral Decoration

Nothing suits the fine white surface of porcelain more than flower painting. Chinese flower decoration tends to be somewhat stylized, but the best painting in *famille rose* can be breathtaking, with price tags to match. Following the invention of porcelain at Meissen the factory's aim was to create decoration that was different from Chinese styles. European flower painting was a most inspired invention. During the 1720s Meissen introduced *Deutsche Blumen* – recognizable German flowers painted as if they had fallen at random onto the surface. The painter J.G. Klinger is associated with *Ombrierte Deutsche Blumen* – a style wherein the flowers cast shadows onto the porcelain. Meissen flower painting had an enormous influence on all porcelain decoration, and pretty flowers are today synonymous with Dresden.

The Chelsea factory took Meissen's flower painting into a new dimension, thanks to the availability of a new book, by Philip Miller, of botanical illustrations. Naming its pattern after the

scientific collector Sir Hans Sloane, Chelsea copied prints of flowers onto its porcelain with botanical accuracy, using suitable books of illustrations as sources. The Derby factory bought books of English flower prints and around 1790 produced services of plates and dishes, each painted with a single plant that was named on the reverse. William Pegg, Derby's finest flower painter, copied botanical illustrations, and created even more splendid compositions of his own. In 1789 the King of Denmark commissioned the Copenhagen porcelain factory to make a special royal presentation service using plant specimens taken from a book of Danish flowers. The resulting legendary *Flora Danica* set has been much reproduced in the 20th century.

Most decorators in porcelain factories created their own compositions from their imaginations and didn't need real flowers to copy. At Sèvres, in the 18th century, a large team of gifted flower painters worked in a very gentle style, ideally suited to soft-paste porcelain and quite different from the

▶ **Pair of Royal Worcester plates, 1912**
Made for the Australian market, depicting Australian flowers copied from the botanical paintings of Marion Ellis Rowan. £250–400/$375–600

▲ **Royal Copenhagen plate, *c*.1980**
Reproducing the famous *Flora Danica* service. The original 18th-century set is displayed in the Rosenburg palace, but many versions have been made since. 28cm (11in) in diameter.
£250–400/$375–600

◀ **Nantgarw dessert plate, *c*.1820**
With distinctive flower painting, probably the work of a London decorator. It bears the impressed factory mark "Nant Garw CW". Flowers always look wonderful on the pure white Welsh porcelain. 25cm (10in) in diameter.
£1,500–2,000/
$2,250–3,000

Meissen painting. In Vienna around 1815–20 Joseph Nigg, arguably the finest flower artist ever to paint on porcelain, produced some unbelievable work, most notably a series of magnificent plaques. At this time painters at Sèvres, Paris, and Berlin came close to the excellence of Vienna, while in Britain the best flower painting was executed in London by independent china painters. Some used Swansea and Nantgarw porcelain blanks, while other superb floral artists, including David Evans and the flower-painting genius William Billingsley, worked at the Welsh factories themselves. Billingsley trained at Derby, and his original method of painting flowers quickly in thick, wet enamels influenced many.

The Victorian era was the heyday of the dessert service. A great many homes owned a set of china fruit plates and dishes that were as much for show as for use. Many were botanical, with a different flower in the centre of each piece. The best, by Royal Worcester and Minton, are cleverly painted with lavish borders, while many other cheaper sets

served their purpose as decorative reminders of summer flowers all year round. A lot of dessert sets, painted with English wild flowers and heathers, sold in Australia. China dealers in Sydney asked for something more appropriate, and in 1912 they commissioned Royal Worcester to make special pieces painted with Australian flowers, copied from original paintings by the Australian artist Marion Ellis Rowan. Similar sets were made for South Africa, painted with exotic local flora. Worcester's tradition of fine flower painting continued into the '60s when Daisy Rea created delightful floral tea sets.

In Australia and, especially, in the USA china-painting guilds were established in many towns and cities early in the 20th century, encouraging amateur china-painters. American artists practised on white chinaware imported from Limoges. Some were semi-professional and sold their porcelain, but most of it was made as gifts for friends and family. While not particularly valuable, amateur-painted Limoges can be very individual.

▲ **Meissen platter, c.1745–50**
From an ornithological dinner service. Meissen
specialized in bird decoration, always painted
with remarkable accuracy. 39cm (15in) wide.
£3,000–4,000/$4,500–6,000

▼ **Sèvres cup and saucer with extra cup**
Painted by François Alonçle, one of the most
influential bird artists working in the 18th
century. **£3,000–4,000/$4,500–6,000**

Bird Painting

The magnificent ornithological table services
made by Meissen around 1740 broke new
ground in porcelain decoration. Previously the
Chinese had placed birds among plants as part of
complicated compositions, and the Japanese had
used birds in their dramatic Kakiemon decoration.
What made the Meissen porcelain different was
scale. These birds were the primary subjects, not
just supporting ornament, and were realistic, painted
with ornithological accuracy. There is rarely any
doubt as to which species is depicted, exotic or tame,
fancy or farmyard. The quality is exceptional.

Meissen naturally influenced other German
factories, including Ludwigsburg, Frankenthal, and
Höchst. It also had a very direct effect on English
porcelain. Chelsea borrowed a collection of Meissen
bird-painted vases and tea wares and made exact
copies during the Red Anchor period (1752–56).
Worcester then copied these Chelsea vases but in a
more comical style, most notably with a series of vases
bearing a design known as the "Mobbing Birds".

The only early English bird-painter known by name
is I. Rogers, who signed one Worcester mug in 1757.

Far more is known about the bird painters at
Sèvres, for the factory encouraged its artists to use
unique workmen's marks. Bird painting was an
important part of production at the French royal
factory. Their senior bird painter was Nicholas
Alonçle, a versatile artist who devised two very
different kinds of birds, real and "Fancy". The
Fancy birds are part peacock, part pheasant, with
some parrot thrown in, inspired by the ho ho birds
of China and touched by the spirit of rococo. The
misty, atmospheric Sèvres landscapes provided the
perfect background for these rather curious feathered
beasts. Once the fabulous fowl were seen in England
nobody wanted the Meissen style of bird any more.
Chelsea and London enameller James Giles changed
to Fancy birds in the 1760s, and all factories,
including Derby, Bow, and Bristol, followed suit.

Worcester took the style to its extreme around
1770, with its imaginary bird painting in panels on a

◀ **"Mobbing Birds" pattern Worcester vase, c.1757**
This design is associated with the painter I. Rogers, although many different hands worked in this style. 21cm (8in) in height.
£4,000–6,000/$6,000–9,000

▶ **Royal Worcester vase**
The shape is known as "Mrs Hadley's Hand", after the modeller James Hadley. The bird painting is associated with the painter John Hopewell. 12.5cm (5in) in height. **£450–550/$700–800**

▲ **Derby centre-dish, c.1825**
From a dessert service painted by Richard Dodson, with carefully-observed real birds in imaginary landscapes. It has a red factory mark.
£700–1,000/$1,000–1,500

◀ **Hard-paste porcelain mug**
Plymouth or Bristol, with "tin" mark, c.1770. The Sèvres style of bird painting is believed to be the work of a Frenchman, M. Soqui. 13cm (5in) high.
£1,500–2,000/$2,250–3,000

dark blue ground. Known by different descriptive names – "Fabulous", "Aggressive", "Agitated", "Dishevelled" – Worcester's varied kinds of Fancy birds are stylized and all somewhat crazy-looking, in bright primary colours, with none of the subtlety of Sèvres. Pieces were enormously expensive 30 or even 70 years ago, but values have fallen, and now they present an amazing opportunity for collectors. During the 1780s the Worcester painter George Davis ("Doctor Davis") developed particularly splendid Fancy birds. His subsequent work, for both Flight's and Chamberlain's factories, is quite extraordinary and influenced a new generation of porcelain decorators (*see* picture on page 41).

Richard Dodson, a painter at Derby in the 1820s, also placed colourful birds in imaginary settings. In many ways his work is as crazy as Davis', but his birds are real and, like illustrations from books of colourful prints, he shows different species crowded together in a single tree. With the Victorians came an interest in scientific study and collecting stuffed birds to display at home under glass domes. Dessert services from England, France, and Germany were painted with a different bird on each piece. Minton birds are remarkably accurate. Royal Worcester birds were more formal, especially those rendered in a style of painting associated with the artist John Hopewell, which was very popular around 1870. The finest bird painters of the last 100 years all worked at Royal Worcester. Charley Baldwyn painted flying swans, James Stinton loved game birds, especially pheasants, and Walter Powell, my favourite bird artist, brought flamingos, storks, and parrots to life in atmospheric settings heavy in mood and mist. William Powell (no relation) was the most prolific, responsible for a phenomenal number of jugs and cups and saucers painted with the little birds he loved to watch in his garden. Royal Worcester porcelain painted by the senior bird artists has risen dramatically in value, and deservedly so. However, early Meissen seems to remain cheap in comparison.

▼ **Meissen bowl with *Fäbeltiere* decoration, *c*.1730**
Decorated with colourful and imaginary beasts
associated with the painter A.F. von Lowenfink.
£1,000–1,400/$1,500–2,100

▲ **Vienna plate from the
Liechtenstein Service, dated 1829**
Each piece was painted with different
animals elaborately named on the reverse.
This plate depicts llamas. 20.5cm (8in) in
diameter. £400–600/$600–900

◄ **Chelsea dish of so-called "silver" shape**
Dated *c*.1750, painted by Jefferyes Hammett
O'Neale, with a raised anchor mark. O'Neale is the
best-known English porcelain animal painter. 24.5cm
(9½in) wide. £15,000–20,000/$22,500–30,000

Animal Decoration

Detailed animal paintings are surprisingly uncommon on early porcelain. Painters clearly had difficulty making animals appear real, and many of them look cartoon-like. Oriental art is dominated by fanciful animals, especially dragons and *kylin* (lion-dogs). Real animals are rare, although rabbits, mice, and rats do feature in some designs. Tigers are found on Japanese Kakiemon porcelain – friendly rather than ferocious – and direct copies of these pieces were made in Europe.

It was the curious, imaginary beasts from the Orient that inspired the earliest animal painting at Meissen in the 1720s and 1730s. Known as *Fäbeltiere,* these items are highly individual. This style of animal painting is associated most with A.F. von Lowenfink, whose strange imagination created very exotic creatures. Elephants appear in the *Chinoiserie* painting of J.G. Höroldt and his followers in a confused scale, showing that European china-painters had no idea of the true size of an elephant. Accurate depictions of animals relied on detailed

source prints for the decorators to copy. Some of the best Meissen animals, on tableware from *c*.1750, were copied from very much older engravings.

In Vienna, at Du Paquier's factory around 1740, some remarkable animal painting was executed in *schwarzelot* (black monochrome) enamel. The subjects mostly relate to hunting, and it is the chase after stags and boars that accounts for most of the animal decoration in 18th-century Germany. On Meissen tea sets, huntsmen in colourful jackets ride out in pursuit of quarry panicked by ferocious hounds. Far more gentle sport is depicted on German porcelain after 1750, and also on delicate Sèvres pieces of the time. When the hunting was over, noblemen and ladies of the Saxon and French courts would enjoy role-playing games and dress as shepherds and shepherdesses. Sheep and cattle were depicted in rustic settings, inspired by Dutch painting as well as designs by Watteau.

The advent of fine painting on Empire and Biedermeier porcelain saw animals depicted

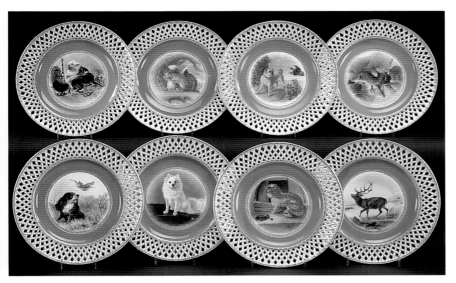

▲ Minton dessert service
Painted by Henry Mitchell with dogs and other
animal subjects. Mitchell specialised in copies
of Landseer's paintings.
£500–700/$750–1,000 per plate

► Royal Worcester vase, dated 1938
Painted by Harry Davis, who could paint many
different subjects but is famous for his Highland
sheep in atmospheric settings. 15.5cm (6in) tall.
£1,600–2,000/$2,400–3,000

beautifully on cabinet cups from France, Austria, and Germany. Hunting scenes remained the most popular, along with horses and hounds. Exotic animals are rare, although a few special services were made illustrating the inhabitants of zoos.

In England the painter J.H. O'Neale introduced a unique style of animal painting at Chelsea around 1750, bringing the fables of Aesop to life as charming cartoons. He painted similar fables at Worcester c.1768–70. These pieces were exceptions as other animal subjects are rarely found on English porcelain, which is strange as Derby produced many modelled animals, establishing a tradition for sheep and dog figures that was followed in Staffordshire. Painted dogs can be found on fine Regency porcelain from Derby, Worcester, and Rockingham. In Victorian times English china factories engaged fine artists to decorate expensive vases and dessert services. Some of the top painters could at last do justice to animals: Royal Worcester's Robert Perling painted farm animals, and at Minton Henry Mitchell

specialized in dogs, some copied directly from the paintings of Landseer. Porcelain painting relied on an ability to copy. The celebrated Berlin plaques, by the best independent artists in Dresden and Vienna, often depict animals as fine art to be framed on a wall.

Popular painting styles influenced fine Edwardian porcelain. Sheep in winter scenes by the Scottish artist Farquharson influenced painting at Royal Doulton in flambé, titanium, and other glaze effects, as well as the work of Harry Davis at Royal Worcester. The fashion for Highland landscapes created a ready market for Highland cattle on porcelain by John and Harry Stinton. These sold in Australia and New Zealand, where expatriate Scottish farmers ranched herds in the outback and looked at their Worcester vases with nostalgia. Worcester and Doulton still sell well in Australia today. Meanwhile "cute" animals on sets of decorative wall plates are more popular than ever, but they are produced by photographic litho-printing on collectors' plates, rather than by hand-painting.

▶ **Berlin presentation vase, *c.*1855**
Decorated with a finely observed view of the palace at Potsdam. 69.5cm (27½in) tall.
£40,000–50,000/$60,000–75,000

▼ **Meissen cabinet cup and saucer, *c.*1850**
Painted with three different views of Venice, with bright gold borders and crossed swords mark.
£1,200–1,500/$1,800–2,250

▲ **Derby bough pot, *c.*1830**
From a garniture of three, painted with different "picturesque" landscape views. 19cm (7in) wide.
£1,200–1,600/$1,800–2,400

Landscape Decoration

There is a considerable distinction between simple, imaginary landscape painting and "topographical" decoration, where a detailed painting of a real building or city view is copied carefully onto fine porcelain. Some landscapes are little more than crude sketches, while the best are the most fabulous works of art. At first the Oriental presentation of perspective in landscape painting was hard for Europeans to understand; the Chinese scale of buildings and mountains confused them, and they created "willow" pattern-style *Chinoiserie* scenes instead. Rococo ornament in 18th-century Europe was suited to rustic landscape "vignettes" – simple scenes painted within scroll-moulded panels or border reserves. Serious attempts to depict actual buildings were rare until neo-classicism took over.

The most interesting and effective painting comes from Italy, where travellers on the Grand Tour took back as souvenirs Doccia and Naples porcelain depicting local scenes, including the smoking volcano Vesuvius. Englishmen returned home with Naples and Parisian porcelain painted with views, and these inspired a new style of china painting. The fashion for travel and sketching led to a new movement in art, where artists attempted to create the perfect "Picturesque" landscape, improving nature itself. Idealized compositions were filled with imaginary obelisks and ruined columns, like the follies built on country estates by landscape gardeners such as Capability Brown. Derby factory painters created wonderful Picturesque views on expensive cabinet cups and tea sets. On the base of Derby porcelain was written the title of its subject, notably local landmarks such as Dovedale and the High Tor near Matlock. Most of the views, some titled simply "In Italy", were totally fictitious, created in the minds of Derby painters such as Zachariah Boreman and "Jockey" Hill. At Worcester, Thomas Rogers, Enoch Doe, and Thomas Baxter painted superb scenic views. Porcelain souvenirs featuring views of Bath, Cheltenham, and Malvern were sold at these

◄ **Copeland and Garrett plate,** *c.***1840**
From a "named view" dessert service, painted with the bridge at Eltham in Kent, copied from a series of travel books. 22.5cm (9in) in diameter. **£200–300/$300–450**

► **Cheap German souvenir mug,** *c.***1890s**
The ground is in pink lustre, the printed scene copied from a picture postcard. 8cm (3in) in height. **£25–30/$40–45**

◄ **Worcester vase,** *c.***1825**
An elaborate vase by Flight, Barr and Barr with full factory marks; the view of Downe Castle, Perthshire, is painted with characteristic care. 24cm (9½in) tall. **£3,000–4,000/$4,500–6,000**

popular spa towns, while numerous scenes of Worcester and Derby were also sold to earn profits for their factories, which understood this market.

Similar markets were explored on the Continent. Artists at Meissen painted endless views of Dresden and German spa towns, while in France Sèvres and other, independent, china decorators painted Parisian views on plates and cabinet cups. In Prussia profit was of secondary consideration as the state factory in Berlin was commissioned to make special diplomatic gifts. A team of highly trained topographical painters faithfully copied views of state and municipal buildings. Berlin porcelain with landscape decoration was highly prized by its recipients – the most favoured statesmen were presented with sets of massive vases, or tea sets with a different view of Berlin on every piece. The quality is usually breathtaking, and they are understandably expensive to buy today.

Victorian scenic dessert services provided an opportunity for escapism. Owners could stare longingly at romantic scenes of Switzerland, India, Scottish lochs, and majestic castles, and dream of touring the world as they moved round their dining tables. The snow-capped Alpine peaks and the atmospheric Highland views were painted not from life but from illustrated books, for china painters didn't travel. The exotic views were painted in factories in Stoke-on-Trent or Limoges.

By Edwardian times, cheaply printed souvenirs had replaced hand-painted views. Visitors to seaside resorts brought back giftware showing the beach, pier, and winter gardens on cruet sets and cups and saucers. If you bought a souvenir at Coney Island or Blackpool Tower, the chances are it would say "Made in Germany" underneath. The pictures were copied from picture postcards, sent to massive factories in Bohemia and reproduced using simple engravings, or later by photography, for an original cost of a few pence. Antique landscape souvenirs are still generally inexpensive, and are well worth consideration for collecting on a budget.

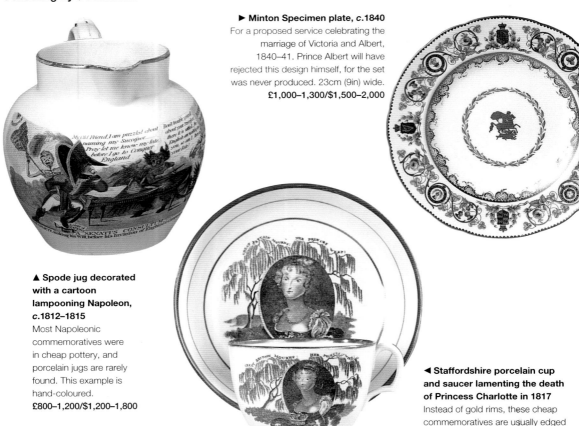

▶ **Minton Specimen plate, c.1840**
For a proposed service celebrating the marriage of Victoria and Albert, 1840–41. Prince Albert will have rejected this design himself, for the set was never produced. 23cm (9in) wide.
£1,000–1,300/$1,500–2,000

▲ **Spode jug decorated with a cartoon lampooning Napoleon, c.1812–1815**
Most Napoleonic commemoratives were in cheap pottery, and porcelain jugs are rarely found. This example is hand-coloured.
£800–1,200/$1,200–1,800

◀ **Staffordshire porcelain cup and saucer lamenting the death of Princess Charlotte in 1817**
Instead of gold rims, these cheap commemoratives are usually edged in pink lustre. £100–140/$150–200

Commemorative Porcelain

By its very nature commemorative decoration is topical, and sells while an event is still fresh in people's minds. Pottery tends to be cheaper than porcelain, so it is hardly surprising that most commemoratives are made from earthenware. However, the quality of porcelain souvenirs can be very high, and there is huge scope for collectors.

Painted portraits of Queen Anne and George I on delftware were unflattering cartoons. This was all to change in 1757, at the Worcester factory. While England's ally, Frederick the Great of Prussia, was winning memorable victories in Europe, the British public wanted souvenirs. Worcester printed his image as a detailed black transfer onto thousands of porcelain mugs, and sold them all over the country. By comparison, mugs of Britain's own King George II sold in far fewer numbers. Popularity of the subject dictated the number of souvenirs sold, and consequently the rarity: two centuries later, a Worcester mug of George II is worth four times as much as the King of Prussia.

Worcester's invention of transfer-printing was supposed to be secret, but through espionage Liverpool printers Sadler and Green were soon applying their own version of the King of Prussia's portrait to Liverpool and Longton Hall porcelain, as well as to Wedgwood creamware. As pottery was cheaper, within two decades the market in printed commemoratives moved completely from porcelain to earthenware. Street stalls sold cheap pottery mugs to mark naval and military victories.

Leading porcelain-makers looked to more select markets. Jewellers and specialist china shops sold finely painted vases and cabinet cups celebrating Nelson, Wellington, and other popular heroes. Britain's wars with France led to a huge range of memorabilia. Derby and Worcester, supplying the top end of the market, painted detailed naval encounters and portraits of admirals and commanders on mantelpiece vases and lavish cabinet cups and saucers. Some Coalport and other cheaper mugs and jugs poked fun at Napoleon

► Souvenir of the coronation in 1902
Made, not in Staffordshire, but in Germany. When held up to the light, the bottom reveals a *lithophane* portrait of Edward VII (*see* right). **£50–70/$75–100**

▼ Staffordshire commemorative mug for the American Bicentenary in 1976
Many millions of souvenirs were made for this popular celebration, and so the value remains small. **£4–6/$6–9**

► Mug celebrating the 100th birthday of Queen Elizabeth, the Queen Mother, 4th August 2000
Her death in 2002 spawned an even greater quantity of commemoratives, and few are likely to increase in value.
£3–5/$5–7

with satirical cartoons. Across the Channel, Napoleon himself encouraged the Sèvres factory to produce special pieces for his own use. Many European porcelain factories were state-financed, and made special productions for diplomatic gifts. Portraits of generals and other prominent figures were painted on Sèvres, Berlin, Meissen, Naples, and Russian porcelain. Identifying the subjects can be difficult, but fascinating history lessons can be built around a study of commemorative porcelain.

By the time of Queen Victoria's jubilees, in 1887 and 1897, printed porcelain had become inexpensive and suitable for mass production. The coronation of Edward VII followed in 1902, and all of the great porcelain factories produced commemoratives of some sort. Doulton made fine beakers with colour-printed portraits as well as cheaper versions in a single colour. Worcester, Derby, Coalport, and Minton all made cheap plates, as well as more costly vases, to mark every royal event. Very expensive porcelain was made

for use by the Royal Family, and pieces from royal services can make fine, if expensive, collections.

Political souvenirs are popular, especially pieces made for US presidential campaigns. Wartime commemoratives cover every historical conflict up to modern times. The souvenirs made for international exhibitions and world fairs constitute a very popular field for collectors, as does travel memorabilia.

The American Bicentenial in 1976, the Silver Jubilee of Elizabeth II in 1977, and the marriage of the Prince and Princess of Wales in 1981 each yielded many millions of commemoratives, so very few pieces are worth more than when they were made. Any unsold Golden Jubilee plates and mugs from 2002 will take years to sell out. As a general rule, less expensive commemoratives hold their value better than the more costly pieces, and an item issued as a "Limited Edition" is not always destined to increase in value. It is best to collect for historical, not financial, reasons in this area.

▶ Russian porcelain custard cup, *c*.1785
From the Gardner factory in Moscow, painted
with the Order of St. Vladimir, with a "G" mark.
The set was commissioned by Catherine the
Great. 11:5cm (4½in) high.
£3,000–4,000/$4,500–6,000

**▼ Soup tureen in "Dragons
in Compartments" pattern**
Dated *c*.1796, part of a
magnificent service painted
with the arms of Parker
impaling Palmer, from the
Chamberlain factory,
Worcester. 29cm (11in) high.
**£7,000–9,000/
$10,500–13,500**

▲ Teapot enamelled in *famille rose*, *c*.1750
This shows the arms of Creston impaling Playford,
from a Chinese export armorial service of
the Qianlong period. 12cm (5in) high.
£2,000–3,000/$3,000–4,500

Armorial Decoration

The medieval traditions of European heraldry
were incomprehensible to the Chinese, but
their painters were master-copyists. Decorators in
Canton reproduced complicated armorial designs,
which they faithfully copied onto tea sets or dinner
services. In the mid-18th century this became a
valuable international trade. When a trading vessel
arrived in China, the ship's captain and the
"super-cargo" – the representative of the trading
company – carried with them detailed drawings of
armorial shields and devices. Most were part of
the "private trade" conducted by the ship's crew,
placing orders for porcelain to be painted to special
designs. Many months, or even up to two years
later, the sets would be ready and would be
returned to Europe in a subsequent shipment.

Every notable European family wanted to
impress its guests by using its own Chinese armorial
porcelain. A wedding would require the ordering
of a new Chinese set with updated heraldry, to be
delivered two years later. There would have been a

ready market for European-made armorial
porcelain if it could have been produced at a price
that matched the Chinese. Mostly this proved
difficult, and the earliest Meissen and other
European armorial porcelain was a luxury, made
for royalty and the very wealthiest households.
Particularly fine porcelain with coats of arms was
made in Germany and Italy, but in the mid-18th
century surprisingly little was produced in France
and England. It is not clear why Chelsea chose to
avoid this particular form of decoration. Worcester
and some other factories made a certain amount,
but all early English armorial porcelain is rare.
It seems customers preferred Chinese.

The end of mass importation of Chinese
porcelain, around 1800, gave English porcelain-
makers an opportunity to take over this important
market. It was very much a luxury trade, involving
only a few factories. Even Derby played a relatively
small part, while Coalport, Spode, and certain other
Staffordshire makers produced some special orders.

► **Crested china model of a field gun, 1914–20**
Souvenirs relating to World War I are popular with collectors. This example is made by Carlton China. 13cm (5in) long.
£50–70/$75–100

▲ **Rockingham plate from the coronation service of William IV**
Ordered in 1830, the set was more than six years in the making. 24cm (9½in) wide.
£5,000–7,000/$7,500–10,500

◄ **Berlin presentation cup and saucer, c.1840**
With elaborate armorial decoration and characteristically rich gilding, the cup is 13.5cm (5in) high.
£700–1,000/$1,000–1,500

The bulk of armorial production was made by the two rival factories of Chamberlain's and Flight's in Worcester. Royal patronage was everything. Flight's won a commission from the Duke of Clarence in 1788, followed by several orders for King George III himself. In 1802 Chamberlain's was patronized by Lord Nelson. Both these factories made services for the Prince of Wales (later the Prince Regent, and then George IV), who adored armorial porcelain. This royal patronage encouraged aristocratic and well-to-do families to order lavish armorial sets of their own.

Many rich armorial presentation cups and saucers were made in Germany, especially at the Berlin factory, but it was in England during the 1830s and 1840s that the market in armorial decoration truly flourished. The new king, William IV, ordered sets from Rockingham and Flight's, and further lavish sets were made for Queen Victoria. Occasionally single pieces from royal services come onto the market and can fetch several thousand pounds/

dollars. Armorial plates with no royal connections are far less expensive. Rich heraldic decoration was very dear when it was made. Allowing for inflation, many examples can be bought today for far less than it cost to make them 150 years ago.

The most affordable category of armorial porcelain is "crested china". Its popularity stems from the remarkable output of W.H. Goss, a Staffordshire firm that became a household name. Goss china miniatures – tiny pieces with coloured heraldic badges – were sold in souvenir shops all over Britain. Many other makers followed, and some pieces with English crests were made in Germany and Japan. Goss and crested china enjoyed a keen following among collectors 20 years ago. The market has been static since, and well-made pieces can be bought today for relatively little. Look out for items made during World War I, such as tanks, aeroplanes, and ambulances. Although more expensive, these are historically interesting as well as decorative.

▼ An early Meissen teapot of *Böttger Porcelain*, c.1720
Enamelled in Holland in the Japanese taste. 10cm (4in) high.
£8,000–12,000/$12,000–18,000

Collecting by Maker or Country

Specializing in a single manufacturer creates a focused collection

▶ **Meissen group of Harlequin and Columbine**
These Commedia Dell'arte figures are among the most spectacular Meissen pieces. Dated c.1743–8 and modelled by J. J.Kändler, 15.5cm (6in) tall.
£20,000–30,000/ $30,000–45,000

The Great Factories – Meissen

Meissen has been Europe's most important porcelain factory for three centuries. It was the first to make "true" or "hard-paste" porcelain in the Chinese manner. The story of the first Meissen porcelain is the stuff of legends. An alchemist, Johann Böttger, claimed to know the secret of the philosopher's stone, fabled to turn base metal to gold. Imprisoned in a castle in Dresden by Augustus, King of Saxony, Böttger failed to produce gold, so he was put to work instead to discover the ingredients of porcelain. This was Augustus's great obsession, and he had a vast collection from China and Japan. Böttger developed the recipe for a fine white porcelain, known today as "Böttger Porcelain". Production began c.1710, although it took many years to perfect. By 1719, the year of Böttger's death, superb, smooth white porcelain was made, as fine as the Kakiemon of Japan. Much early Meissen porcelain was sent to Augsburg for decorating by court goldsmiths and enamellers known as *Hausmalerei*, and is highly prized today.

Böttger's former assistant, Samuel Stölzel, who had defected to set up a rival factory at Vienna, returned in 1720 bringing with him a brilliant young painter, J.G. Höroldt, a genius at *Chinoiserie* decoration. Höroldt taught other painters to work in his style, and as chief decorator he attracted to Meissen enamellers who excelled at landscape, flower, and figure painting. During the next 40 years every piece of Meissen was decorated to the highest possible standards, enriched with the finest gilding. The sheer quality of Meissen painting prior to 1760 means that many pieces, while not exactly cheap, are extraordinarily good value.

During this period Meissen invented the porcelain figurine, thanks to the arrival of J.J. Kändler, a new modeller who revolutionized figure-making and was the greatest sculptor in miniature. He could adapt his style to any subject required, and was incredibly prolific. In the 1730s and 1740s he made the field his own; his finest achievement was the Commedia Dell'arte series of harlequins.

◄ Meissen sucrier, *c.*1745
Painted with Watteau figures, this sucrier has a crossed swords mark. A magnifying glass is necessary to appreciate the quality of the best Meissen painting. 9cm (3½in) high.
£1,200–1,500/ $1,800–2,250

▲ Meissen powder box, *c.*1870
With a finely painted view of Dresden. Notice the superior gilding that sets Meissen apart from all of its competitors. 8.5cm (3in) in diameter.
£450–600/$700–900

Older books on Meissen porcelain imply that worthwhile production ended with The Seven Years War (1756–63), but fine porcelain continued to be made at the factory. Its fortunes during the so-called "Academic" and "Marcolini" periods (1763–1814) were mixed, but the 19th century saw Meissen regain its position as Europe's premier porcelain factory. It succeeded by concentrating on quality and tradition. The great models and designs of the 18th century proved enormously popular in Britain and the United States. Kändler's figures were reissued in new colouring, with pretty painted faces and dainty costumes, and always the most careful attention to detail. Meissen encompassed new Victorian ideals and produced exciting Art Nouveau porcelain around 1900. However, during the 20th century its output relied too heavily on the past. The market has reassessed later Meissen porcelain, and 19th-century pieces have rocketed in value, acquiring a strong collectors' following. Some are rightly almost as valuable as 18th-century examples.

Recognizing
The Crossed Swords

▲ Meissen's crossed swords mark
The shape of this mark is an important guide to dating.
Top left: straight swords, *c.*1740. **Top right:** a dot between the hilts, Academic period, 1763–74. **Bottom left:** a star above the swords, Marcolini period, 1774–1814. **Bottom right:** curved swords with pommels, *c.*1850–1900.

The arms of Saxony include two crossed swords, and this emblem has been painted on every piece of Meissen since the 1720s. The shape and form of the crossed swords are an invaluable guide to dating. In the 18th century each sword was painted as a straight line. Some of the earliest examples use swords placed almost at right-angles (although an angle of roughly 30°–40° became standard). The swords were always painted in the centre of the base, but figures with rough bases and no glaze were given a mark at the back of the model, near the base.

During the "Academic" period (1763–74), a dot was placed between the hilts or handles of the swords, giving rise to the alternative name of "Dot Period". When Count Marcolini was director of the factory (1774–1813), a star or an asterisk was used instead, usually painted above the hilts. The Academic and Marcolini marks are the most commonly faked Meissen ones.

Post-Marcolini marks were often somewhat scruffy, but from the 1840s until the early 20th century the swords were most carefully painted. Each was gently curved, and a dot or "pommel" was placed at the tip of each hilt. Between 1926 and 1939 a dot was placed between the blades of the swords. Post-war productions have thin, curved swords, with no dots or pommels.

▼ **Frankenthal group of a
shepherdess and her lover,** *c.*1758–64
Modelled by J.F. Luck, with a CT and
crown mark. The delicate scrollwork
around the base is characteristic of
Frankenthal rococo modelling
£2,000–2,700/$3,000–4,000

▲ **Fürstenberg teapot,** *c.*1765
Painted with birds. The sparse decoration is
intentional, for it emphasises the smooth, white
porcelain. The teapot has an "F" mark in blue,
and is 12cm (5in) high. **£600–800/$900–1,200**

Germany & the "Dresden" style

The first, and the best, European porcelain
was made in Germany. The close proximity
between Meissen and Dresden led to much
confusion, for both names were broadly used.
Many Dresden factories copied Meissen and, as a
result, "Dresden China" became a household
name around the world.

Germany in the 18th century

Following the success of Meissen, every kingdom
and principality wanted its own porcelain factory.
Throughout Germany generous offers were made
to entice workmen away from Meissen and impart
the secrets of china-making. This worked, and
beautiful porcelain was made as a result. It is hardly
surprising that these varied productions borrowed
heavily from the artistry and traditions established
at Meissen. The porcelain body used at each factory
is remarkably similar, as the recipe was passed, or
stolen, from one maker to another. Initially Samuel
Stölzel, Böttger's assistant at Meissen, took it to

Vienna, where he worked with Claudius du
Paquier. Christoph Hunger assisted Stölzel before
he ran off to Italy with the formula, working with
Vezzi in Venice. Joseph Ringler worked as a painter
at Vienna and learnt as much as he could about the
porcelain-making processes before setting off to sell
the secrets to all and sundry. Ringler was involved
in the establishment of factories at Nymphenburg,
Ludwigsburg, Frankenthal, and Höchst, while his
assistant, Johann Benckgraff, left to set up porcelain
factories at Berlin and Fürstenberg.

The quality of the porcelain made at each of
these factories is very high and it is most unusual
to encounter serious firing imperfections, with
the exception of Ludwigsburg where there were
problems with a dirty, smoky glaze. Painting
styles were noticeably similar too, for enamellers
also moved from factory to factory, and all copied
Meissen to varying degrees. We are most fortunate,
therefore, that the different 18th-century makers
marked the majority of their productions.

▶ **A Limbach figure of a fruit seller,** *c.*1780. Thuringian figures are far removed from Meissen and other major German factories, but they have a naive charm of their own. £250–350/$375–525

▼ **A Berlin cabinet cup in the Biedermeyer taste,** *c.*1815-20, with sceptre marks in blue. Berlin always maintained the highest standards – the fine flower-painting here is accentuated by brilliant burnished gold. £800–1,200/$1,200–1,800

▲ **Ludwigsburg plate,** *c.*1770 With a distinctive basket-moulded border and characteristic landscape painting. It bears a crowned "Cs" mark. £500–700/$750–1000

Meissen remained the biggest and the most influential factory. The others made dinner and tea sets in rococo style, mostly painted with somewhat similar landscapes, flowers, or birds. Figure subjects are rare but can be full of charm, especially pieces by Jakob Osterspey at Frankenthal. Tableware by the smaller makers is scarce compared with Meissen's vast output, yet is usually less expensive, thus providing enthusiasts with a good opportunity to build up a fascinating collection. Figure-modelling by the different factories is far more distinctive, owing to the individual skills of the sculptors responsible, and some wonderful series of figures emerged. Franz Anton Bustelli at Nymphenburg modelled a relatively small number of subjects, but his Commedia Dell'arte series is regarded as the greatest ever interpretation of rococo in porcelain. Meissen's *cris de Paris* set of street vendors inspired the *cris de Wien*, a series of Viennese street sellers with huge charm. At Ludwigsburg, in Württemberg, G.F. Riedel designed an extensive set of miniature figures recreating the local carnival – the "Venetian Fair" – staged there annually. Also worthy of the closest attention is the work of Konrad Linck and Karl Gottlieb Luck at Frankenthal, Simon Feilner at Fürstenberg, and Johann Peter Melchior at Höchst.

Because of Meissen's position in the history of European porcelain it attracts the most serious collectors, with the result that Ludwigsburg and Höchst figures always fetch less. Vienna figures seem ridiculously inexpensive, but Berlin is dearer – especially its finely decorated 19th-century productions. At the bottom of the price scale are the products of the many small factories in Thuringia, where a number of minor china factories operated towards the end of the 18th century. Makers including Limbach, Wallendorf, and Kloster Veilsdorf produced painted tea wares inspired by Meissen, and all manner of figures, principally in the classical taste. Much of this porcelain is crude compared with that of the rest of Germany, but even so it remains remarkably cheap considering its age.

▶ **Vienna-style vase, c.1870s**
Following the closure of the Vienna
manufactory, some fine decoration was
carried out by former State factory
decorators. This example is painted with
the Judgement of Paris and has a "shield
mark". 68cm (27in) in height.
£3,500–5,000/$5,250–7,500

▲ **Vienna cabinet cup and saucer, 1811**
Painted and signed by Jakob Schufried
with views of Vienna and the Gardens
of the Belvedere, with shield marks.
£6,000–10,000/$9,000–15,000

"Dresden" & "Vienna"

Meissen is situated 12 miles from Dresden. In the
18th century the porcelain made there was known
around the world as either "Saxon" or "Dresden"
china. As a result, Dresden became a household
word while the name of Meissen was virtually
unknown. In the 19th century Meissen lost its state
monopoly, and many other china makers were
established in the Dresden area. At the same time
Dresden became home to many independent china
painters who enamelled porcelain with copies of
old Meissen patterns. To avoid confusion, the
original great factory resorted to the name of
Meissen, which allowed the others to mark their
products "Dresden" without fear of prosecution.

It is most important, therefore, to distinguish
between actual Meissen porcelain, and "Dresden"
made in the Meissen style. Dresden is not a single
maker, it is a style of porcelain, copied from
Meissen. Dresden-style porcelain is made all over
the world, and the term is used very loosely,
especially as many makers used copies of old
Meissen marks.

Some important makers of Dresden porcelain
were based in other parts of Germany. The firm of
Voigt in Sitzendorf made porcelain table
centrepieces, and lamp bases with encrusted
modelled flowers and cupids. Instead of the
Meissen crossed swords, Sitzendorf porcelain is
marked with two straight lines with one further
line across. Carl Thieme's factory in Potschappel
near Dresden made decent-quality porcelain,
including large vases encrusted with china flowers.
Its mark was the letter "T" above a cross. At
Plaue-am-Havel in Thuringia a third major
factory also produced flower-encrusted centrepieces and candelabra, marked with two double
lines crossed like a noughts and crosses grid.
Dresden centrepieces from Sitzendorf, Potschappel,
and Plaue can be enormously decorative, and
although they are not as well finished as Meissen,
they represent good value for money. For this
author to admit to liking Dresden figures is rather
like a great classical musician confessing to enjoying
lift (elevator) music. Yet hundreds of thousands of

▼ **Dresden vase with Watteau figures, c.1875**
A copy of a classic Meissen 18th-century original, dated and decorated in the Wolfsohn workshop with Watteau figures. "AR" mark, 17cm (6½in) tall. **£160–200/$240–300**

◄ **Dresden-style vase made at Plaue-am-Havel**
Early 20th century. While the quality is intentionally cheap, as a fancy ornament this is an effective piece of decoration. 36cm (14in) tall. **£250–350/$400–500**

▲ **Conductor from a Dresden monkey band, early 20th century**
Far removed from the quality of the Meissen original, this costs one tenth of a 19th-century Meissen. Scissors mark, 17cm (6½in), **£100–150/$150–200**

people have grown up with fond memories of figurines looking down from the mantelpiece. This is what Dresden porcelain is all about.

In Dresden itself, independent decorators enamelled porcelain with copies of old Meissen patterns. The best known of these was Helena Wolfsohn, who began in the 1840s decorating substandard white Meissen. By the 1860s her firm's production was extensive, each piece bearing a copy of Meissen's early mark, the "AR" cipher for Augustus the Strong. Wolfsohn is best known for cups and saucers with coloured grounds and panels after Watteau, which are usually referred to today as "Augustus Rex". Her factory was prosecuted on several occasions for imitating Meissen, and in 1882 Meissen procured an injunction banning the use of the "AR" mark. Instead Wolfsohn used the letter "D" below a crown, the first of the so-called "Crown Dresden" stamps, which added to the confusion. Wolfsohn's porcelain is not in the same league as Meissen, but at a quarter of the price it should not be ignored.

There was no such injunction concerning the shield mark of Vienna, for the state factory closed down in 1864, after which anyone was free to make copies. Vienna had been responsible for superb enamelled porcelain during the 19th century, especially plates and cups and saucers painted with views and figure subjects. When the works were closed, some former factory painters set up on their own as independent china decorators. Other Vienna-style porcelain was painted in Dresden, marked with copies of the old Vienna shield. The mark became known as the "beehive" mark, because of the shape of the shield when viewed upside down. The great majority of decorative porcelain bearing the Vienna beehive mark has nothing to do with the original Vienna factory, and, like "Dresden", the name "Vienna" became little more than a popular style reproduced all over Germany. What matters most is not where the Vienna porcelain was made, but how well it is painted and gilded. Much "fake" Vienna porcelain is superbly decorated in its own right.

▶ **Single Sèvres plate from the *Service de Departements*, painted by A. Poupart, 1823**
An important commission with topographical decoration of the Château de Pau. Elaborate factory markings, 23.5cm (9in) in diameter.
£7,000–10,000/$10,500–15,000

▼ **Rare Sèvres hyacinth vase, *c.*1763–5**
Painted with panels of Cupids and amatory trophies on a deep cobalt blue ground, with a crossed LL mark.
£6,000–10,000/$9,000–15,000

▼ **Double cream pot**
From a simple Sèvres table service, *c.*1770. Sets with basic flower painting were made in great quantities in the 18th century and are not hugely expensive.
£300–400/$450–600

The Great Factories – Sèvres

To the great French porcelain manufactory, royal backing meant far more than finance from the King. Louis XV created a state monopoly, with injunctions that prevented any rival chinamakers from using the same rich decoration or any gilding. It was also illegal to import any porcelain other than Chinese. If you wanted fine porcelain, you had no choice but to patronize the new factory at Vincennes. Customers didn't mind, for its beauty was unlike anything they had seen before.

After roughly twelve years of experimentation at Vincennes, the growing factory moved to Sèvres in 1753. Here it continued to develop new colours in a style that differed totally from Meissen. The porcelain was made of a creamy soft paste (*pâte tendre*) that set off the delicate rococo decoration to perfection. The painting sinks completely into the soft glaze, giving the enamels a very subtle, somewhat melted appearance. This is ideal for colourful depictions of fruit and flowers, and gives atmospheric backgrounds to landscape, bird, and figure paintings. Delightful shepherdesses and sweet children were copied from paintings by François Boucher. Similar figures were modelled by leading French sculptors to create the most charming groups cast in unglazed or *bisque* porcelain. Without glaze, Sèvres porcelain has a smooth silky surface like the finest marble.

Sèvres is famous for its special backgrounds. The colours are bright and remarkably even. A stunning turquoise (*bleu celeste*), bright green (*pomme verte*), glowing rose pink, brilliant yellow, and several tones of blue were used as grounds to frame painted panels, finished off with exceptional gilding. Gold on Meissen and Chinese porcelain had been smooth and flat. At Sèvres it was applied thickly, and then tooled to add delicate patterning and texture. Sets of vases and magnificent dinner sets were presented by the King as diplomatic gifts. Favour at court meant you dined in style.

The French Revolution severely curtailed production, but the prestige of a state porcelain

► **Sèvres vase with *pâte-sur-pâte* decoration, c.1900**
By Taxile Doat, an influential decorator whose work is rarely seen.
In the 19th century Sèvres was an innovative manufacturer and
developed many new decorating techniques. Size unknown.
£2,000–3,000/$3,000–4,500

Understanding
Sèvres Factory Marks

▲ **Sèvres factory marks**
These contain complicated codes that reveal vital information.
(Left) Year code A for 1753, the first year this system was
used. The painter's mark at the top is for the landscape
painter André-Vincent Vielliard.
(Right) Year mark X for 1775 and painter's mark K for the
figure painter Charles-Nicolas Dodin. The gilder's mark at
the top is for Guillaume Noel.

factory was recognized by the new regime, and
some of the most stunning presentation porcelain
was commissioned by Napoleon. Although
turbulent French history resulted in sporadic
production during the 19th century, many
magnificent sets were made for special government
and royal commissions. Splendid vases were
created to show off in Victorian exhibitions, and
some of the finest Sèvres porcelain of all was made
during the Art Nouveau period.

   Sèvres porcelain is collected widely, and not
just in France. It has enjoyed a keen following in
Britain and the United States ever since rival 19th-
century collectors paid incredible sums for early
coloured-ground vases. This led to the creation of
vast numbers of fakes, and now copies of Sèvres
outnumber the real thing to an unbelievable
extent. It is impossible to collect Sèvres without an
extensive understanding of the markings, colours,
and painting styles. The real thing is beautiful, so
it is worth learning how to avoid the pitfalls.

No other porcelain factory left us so much
information about its artists and decorators.
The factory mark was a special royal symbol –
the letter "L" mirrored, which was the cipher of
Louis XV. This should have been sufficient
identification, but instead Sèvres added a code
system that uniquely identified the painters and
gilders who had worked on each item, as well as
the year of production.

   A very simple letter code was used to
indicate the year a piece was made. In the
centre of each "LL" cipher a single letter was
placed, beginning with A in 1753, B in 1754,
and so on, until Z in 1777. The factory then
started again with double letters (AA, BB, etc.),
until after the Revolution. Other code systems
were used during the 19th century, such as
incised dates: a simple date system was incised
with a needle underneath cups and plates – just
the month of manufacture and the last two
digits of the year. On some pieces a date mark
was printed in green, such as "S.47" for Sèvres
1847, and so on.

   The painter of each piece added the factory
mark as well as a personal device – a letter or a
symbol – to show who was responsible. Lists
survive at the Sèvres factory identifying most
of the painters' marks, and there are even
sketched portraits of some senior painters. The
gilders subsequently added marks of their own
so that they too would be credited. Checking
the marks on a piece of Sèvres is very satisfying.
As long as the subject matter and date match
other recorded pieces by the same artist, the
chances are that the piece is genuine.

◄ Mennecy custard cup, c.1760
A delightful shape made in creamy, soft-paste porcelain. Incised "DV" mark for the Duc de Villeroy. 8cm (3in) high.
£1,500–2,500/$2,250–4,000

▼ Chantilly Mustard Pot, c.1735
Hunting horn mark in red. The shape derives from a French silver original, and the decoration is copied from earlier Japanese Kakiemon. **£700–1,000/$1,000–1,500**

► Bonbonniere, c.1755–60
French, probably made at Mennecy, in the shape of a dromedary. The Chantilly and St Cloud factories also specialised in novelty boxes that were aimed at collectors rather than for actual use.
£2,000–2,500/$3,000–4,000

France, Paris, & the Empire Style

Long before the discovery of true porcelain at Meissen in Germany, French potters were experimenting with different ingredients in an attempt to find the right mix. What they were missing was kaolin, the raw material already used for centuries by the Chinese. However, chemists in France believed that porcelain could be made from glass mixed with white clay. Europe's first success-ful porcelain was made using a mixture of alchemy and luck. Discovered by Louis Proterat at Rouen before 1690, it was a curious creamy material with a surface like melted snow, known as "artificial" or "soft paste", or "*pâte tendre*" in French. The first commercial production was by the Chicaneau family at St Cloud, around 1695.

Blue-and-white made at St Cloud was very different from Chinese imports. Designs were baroque in style, with blue scroll-pattern borders known as "lambrequins". The shapes were also totally different. Knife and fork handles were a speciality, and cups with trembleuse saucers (*see* page 113) were made for infirm aristocrats with shaky hands. Novelty snuff boxes began a French tradition continued at Mennecy, a factory making soft-paste porcelain owned by the Duc de Villeroy. Little boxes in the shape of animals, figures, and flower baskets were mounted in silver, and delicately coloured. The third major French factory, at Chantilly, produced porcelain with a very different appearance – it had a unique, silky surface created by an opaque tin oxide-based glaze. Under the direction of the Prince de Condé, Chantilly specialized in reproductions of Japanese Kakiemon porcelain.

As a plaything for his mistress, Madame de Pompadour, Louis XV bought a new china factory that had been established on the outskirts of Paris prior to 1740. To ensure the success of this Vincennes porcelain, the King banned all other French manufacturers from using gilding and certain specified colours. His edict effectively forced Mennecy and Chantilly into decline while

▶ **Hard-paste porcelain coffee can and saucer, c.1795**
In the Classical taste, finished off with high quality gilding. This example is marked by Nast, a major firm of decorators in Paris, c.1790–95. Many similar cups and saucers are unmarked and therefore difficult to identify.
£700–1,100/$1,000–1,500

◀ **Pair of French vases, c.1810**
Intended for flowers or fruit, these formed part of a lavish Empire-style dessert service by the Paris factory of Pierre Neppel in the Rue de Crussol. The biscuit porcelain is finely modelled and the gilding is outstanding. 30.5cm (12in) high.
£15,000–20,000/$22,500–30,000

the royal factory flourished, moving to Sèvres in 1756. Sèvres made a delicate soft paste that was whiter than other early French porcelain, and every piece was finished to the very highest standards. Shapes and decoration represent unrivalled artistry, and, in turn, Sèvres influenced every other European china-maker.

When a source of kaolin was found in France Sèvres felt that it should exploit the discovery by introducing its own hard-paste porcelain in 1769. The factory was clearly convinced of the beauty of soft paste, for it continued to make the soft *pâte tendre* body alongside the hard white *pâte duré*. Sèvres adapted to changes in fashion as rococo gave way to the classical taste. Brilliant gilding became of great importance and was used to frame painted panels of wondrous quality. The Sèvres factory produced a vast range of "ordinary" chinaware painted with simple flowers and used as everyday porcelain in the aristocratic households. When entertaining, the same homes

used prestige Sèvres dinner sets, while magnificent vases graced their mantelpieces.

The royal edict that stifled opposition was relaxed in 1766, and a few new manufactories were established that made hard-paste porcelain until the Revolution. Louis XV's brother, "Le Monsieur", owned a china factory of his own at Clignancourt in Paris where elegant porcelain was made with delicate enamelling and richly gilded borders. As Queen a few years later, Marie Antoinette gave her patronage to another firm in the rue Thiroux, Paris, where porcelain was marked with her crowned "A" cipher. Tableware with pretty border patterns became the staple products of a number of Paris firms, particularly the Locre factory, known as "La Courtille". During the 1780s and 1790s much Paris porcelain was exported to England and greatly influenced British porcelain decoration. Paris porcelain was also very popular in the United States, and the Chinese too copied the latest French patterns.

◄ **Porcelain temple,** *c.***1815**
One of a pair, by the Paris
makers Darté Freres. The
Empire taste took classical
inspiration and smothered it in
brilliant gold. 39cm (15in) high.
**£10,000–15,000/
$15,000–22,500 per pair**

▲ **Fake Sèvres plate,** *c.***1880–90**
Purporting to be a Sèvres plate from
Louis Philippe's "Hunting" service, this
copy was made at Limoges. Many
Limoges china factories specialized
in fakes of Sèvres – copies which are
decorative in their own right. 23.5cm
(9in) in diameter. **£60–100/$90–150**

► **French porcelain mantelpiece
clock,** *c.***1835–40**
By Jacob Petit of Paris, in the
frivolous style of the rococo revival.
£400–600/$600–900

Paris enjoyed brief prosperity under Napoleon, and truly lavish porcelain was made in the "Empire" style. Shapes were influenced by the classical world, and by Napoleon's campaigns in Egypt. Vases were given caryatids or sphinxes as handles, in richly gilded biscuit porcelain. Gold emblazoned every piece of Paris porcelain, enriching brightly coloured backgrounds and framing superb painted panels. Much of it was made in Limoges, where fine porcelain clay was readily available. Blank Limoges wares were enamelled and gilded by many independent china decorators in Paris. Meanwhile the Sèvres factory continued to make important services for the imperial court, followed by rich commissions for the restored monarchy.

Much French porcelain is unmarked and difficult to identify, as each maker used an identical pure white body. Most is known today simply as "Paris", or in the United States as "Veaux Paris", even though Limoges became the largest centre of manufacture. Large quantities survive and are generally inexpensive, mostly because so much is just plain white with gilding. Fancy shapes can be

used as effective decoration, but avoid examples where the gold is rubbed. A weakness of French gilding means pieces are prone to severe wear. Restorers cannot match the pure gold, and rubbed Paris porcelain looks somewhat scruffy. Richly painted and gilded pieces are, of course, expensive.

Mid-19th-century French porcelain is typified by the fancy shapes of the rococo and Gothic revivals. Jacob Petit, a Paris maker, is best known for clock cases and horn-shaped vases awash with modelled leaf scrolls and applied china flowers, highly decorative and undervalued today. Also admired are the *bisque* porcelain figures made by Gille (later Vion and Baury), which specialized in costume figures with very detailed painting. The products of one of the largest French porcelain-makers are virtually unknown today, for Porcelaine de Paris made copies of old Dresden figures, candelabra, and mirror frames which were given fake Meissen marks and thus caused much confusion. Samson, another legendary Paris factory, chose to copy other makers' products and marks, and its name is now synonymous with fake porcelain (*see* page 139).

Probably made by J. Gille & Cie., these fanciful coloured depictions of Native Americans represent the excesses of high-Victorian taste. 70cm (27in) high. **£1,200–1,600/$1,800–2,400**

Understanding *Sèvres style*

▲ **Highly decorative vase, *c*.1860s**
With spurious 18th-century Sèvres factory mark. Possibly by Bettignie, a French maker famed for intricate jewelled decoration. 26cm (10in) high. **£1,200–1,500/$1,800–2,250**

Tableware-makers in Limoges have dominated French porcelain since the late 19th century. Opportunities were exploited by David Haviland – an American china dealer who set up a factory in France making china for the US market. Other members of the Haviland family opened their own porcelain factories in Limoges, where many further makers were established. Limoges is not a single maker, therefore, but a succession of rival firms making popular porcelain for everyday use, much of it exported.

A great deal of white Limoges porcelain was shipped to the United States and Australia, where it was enamelled by members of amateur china-painting guilds. Examples by the more accomplished painters can be extremely decorative but rarely cost much money (*see* page 89). More recently, Limoges has become famous for miniature or "toy" porcelain, and souvenirs with cheaply printed decoration, as well as for a huge range of snuff boxes and other novelty boxes reviving the 18th-century French tradition. However, very few Limoges boxes on sale in antique shops are in fact antiques.

The old Sèvres *pâte tendre* was treasured even in the days of King George IV who, as Prince of Wales, was obsessed with Sèvres. His acquisitions established the basis of the present Royal Collection. By the mid-19th century old Sèvres with coloured grounds was worth phenomenal sums, and this led to faking on a huge scale. Copies fall into two main types. After the Revolution thousands of genuine pieces, in white or with simple patterns, were sold to decorators who created clever fakes by adding coloured grounds. The other type of forgery was unintentional. People admired great Sèvres vases in grand homes, so factories in England and France produced affordable versions. The best had jewelled decoration and elaborate ormolu mounts and handles, and were often marked with the old Sèvres cipher of Louis XV. For over a hundred years they were referred to as "Sèvres vases". For every genuine Sèvres vase still surviving, there are probably a thousand copies, all bearing fake crossed "LL" marks.

▶ Worcester plate, *c.*1772–5
Printed in underglaze blue with the "Gillyflower" pattern in the French style. Worcester exported much of its blue-and-white to the Continent in the 18th century. 20.5cm (8in) in diameter.
£140–180/$210–270

▼ Worcester coffee cup, *c.*1755
Painted with a somewhat individual interpretation of Chinese figure painting. Single coffee cups are highly collectable, and early examples can be surprisingly expensive. **£1,500–1,700/$2,250–2,550**

▲ Grainger miniature basket, *c.*1840–45
Painted with a view of Worcester from the North-west. Visitors to Worcester took home delightful porcelain souvenirs made locally. 10.8cm (4in). **£350–500/$525–750**

The Great Factories – Worcester

Worcester is an unlikely city to host a great porcelain industry, for it boasts no local clay or source of fuel. The factory was started in 1751 by an ambitious group of businessmen headed by Dr John Wall, and a local chemist, William Davis. Worcester's advantage over most of its English rivals was that its porcelain teapots and cups did not crack in contact with boiling water. Worcester was thus able to concentrate on fine tea sets and dinnerware, making very few figurines.

Early Worcester, made in the 1750s and 1760s, combines Chinese decoration with shapes borrowed from English silver. It excelled on a small scale, making delightful coffee cups, and tiny leaf and shell dishes for serving pickle, and its teapots are always superbly proportioned. Tea sets were made with enamelled decoration, and in blue-and-white with carefully painted Chinese-style patterns.

Worcester invented transfer-printing, facilitating a kind of mass-production. Although Chinese and Japanese patterns dominated 18th-century

Worcester, Meissen and then Sèvres were also influential. The value of the earliest Worcester has risen greatly, while prices for porcelain from the 1770s and 1780s have levelled and this now seems cheap. One Worcester speciality that is probably greatly undervalued is "scale blue" – a unique background created with tiny painted scales to break up the solid effect of dark blue. Reserved panels were painted with "Fancy" birds and crazy insects.

The complex story of Worcester involves several firms. The Flight family bought the original factory in 1783 and, in partnership with Martin Barr, traded as Flight and Barr from 1792, becoming Barr, Flight and Barr in 1804, and after 1813 Flight, Barr and Barr. No wonder collectors get confused. The Chamberlain family set up a rival factory in 1786 which made very similar porcelain to Flight's. It was of the highest quality – superbly painted and finished with the finest gold. The style was classical Regency, with coloured grounds and painted landscapes, birds, shells, and feathers. Meanwhile, from

▶ **"February"**
A Royal Worcester figure from the "Months of the Year" series modelled by Freda Doughty, c.1965. Her charming figures of children sold in large numbers. 16cm (6in) high.
£120–160/$180–240

◀ **Royal Worcester cup and saucer**
Painted with Highland scenes by Harry Stinton, c.1925. Sets of six similar cups, in fitted presentation boxes, were popular as wedding presents, although very few owners actually used them for coffee. **£500–750/$750–1,100**

▶ **Royal Worcester small box, c.1912**
Made of "reticulated porcelain", finely pierced by the craftsman George Owen, and just 9cm (3½in) in diameter.
£5,000–8,000/$7,500–12,000

c.1806, Thomas Grainger ran a third family china business that made porcelain in the Staffordshire tradition, aiming at a different end of the market.

Troubled times forced Chamberlain's and Flight's to amalgamate in 1840. New artistic direction was desperately needed, and came in 1852 when management of the firm was taken over by Kerr and Binns. The Worcester Royal Porcelain Co. was formed in 1862 and has been known as "Royal Worcester" ever since. Richard Binns led the company to its greatest triumphs in the Victorian era. Following his discovery of Japanese art, it produced stunning creations in the Oriental style, especially porcelain in imitation of ivory. James Hadley, England's finest figure modeller, was responsible for magnificent sculptures, notably his famous studies of children after the illustrator Kate Greenaway.

During the 20th century, models gave way to fine painting. The painters at Royal Worcester are today regarded as great British artists, their work changing hands for thousands of pounds/dollars.

Harry Davis was just 14 when he joined Royal Worcester, and he was still painting his landscapes and breathtakingly beautiful Highland scenes in his eighties. Charley Baldwyn drew the swans on the River Severn beside Worcester Bridge, and painted flocks of the birds in flight on his wonderful vases. Most famous of all, John Stinton and his son Harry painted Highland cattle in atmospheric mountain scenes, and John's brother James painted game birds. Porcelain paintings by the Stinton family are regarded as works of art, and deservedly so.

In the 1930s Royal Worcester followed Doulton and played a significant part in the production of figurines. Children modelled by Freda Doughty and charming animals by Doris Lindner sold well in the USA in the 1950s. In the 1960s and '70s the company made larger-scale "Limited Edition" bird, animal, equestrian, and figure subjects. As investments their fortunes have been mixed, but they are now enjoying renewed interest as it is realized that such superb workmanship is unlikely to be repeated.

◀ **A Derby basket from a fruit service, *c*.1765**
Painted with birds in distinctive style.
18cm (7in) wide. £800–1,000/$1,200–1,500

◀ **A Derby figure known as "The Ranelagh Dancer"**
A popular model *c*.1770–75, measuring 24cm (9in) in height.
£400–600/$600–900

▲ **A Derby cup and saucer, *c*.1795**
Painted with a bird and fruit in the distinctive style of George Complin.
£4,500–5,500/$6,750–8,250

The Great Factories – Derby

Derby produced some of the finest English ornamental porcelain, and also the most traditional. Established in the town around 1748, the factory initially struggled because hot liquid was apt to make its china body crack. As a result Derby chose to ignore teapots and instead specialized in making figures, as well as objects such as fruit baskets. The earliest Derby figures, pre-1765, are charmingly simple while at the same time sharply modelled, and it is hardly surprising that examples are expensive. The 1770s saw a massive increase in figure production; subjects were mostly issued as pairs, frequently with added candle nozzles.

In 1770 William Duesbury, Derby's principal manager, purchased the ailing Chelsea porcelain factory. The period up until the closure of the Chelsea works in 1784 is known as Chelsea-Derby, notable for its porcelain designed in the neo-classical taste. During the 1780s and 1790s Derby chose not to compete with the cheap tea wares of New Hall and Caughley. Instead it went up-market, specializing in fine hand-painting by skilled artists. Collectors seek the work of senior artists, such as figures painted by Richard Askew, landscapes by Zachariah Boreman, and flowers by William "Quaker" Pegg and William Billingsley.

During the Regency period, *Imari* patterns represented an important part of the factory's production. Extensive dinner and tea services were made in an improved china body, painted with stock patterns in Continental taste.

From 1811, the beginning of the Bloor period at the Derby factory, an increasing problem with crazing (fine glaze cracks) and resultant staining led to decline. A large number of figures were still made to 18th-century Derby models, and sets of urn-shaped vases with serpent handles sold in enormous quantities, judging by the numbers surviving today, but the quality was poor. Illness meant that Robert Bloor was unable to prevent Derby porcelain's almost total demise in 1848.

▼ A Derby vase, *c.*1900
Painted in the French style by Désiré Leroy,
who also applied the superb gilding.
£15,000–18,000/$22,500–27,000

Collecting
Derby Imari *Patterns*

▲ Derby vase, *c.*1820
With splendid decoration in the *Imari* style; these
patterns were easy and quick to paint, providing
customers with inexpensive decoration.
32cm (12⅝in) in height. **£500–700/$750–1,050**

Later in the Victorian period two essentially new china factories grew up in Derby, engaging former workmen and maintaining traditional forms of decoration. The King Street factory reintroduced many earlier Derby figures and *Imari* patterns. These were marked with the letters "SH" (for the director, Sampson Hancock) alongside a copy of the old Derby painted mark, and today they are frequently mistaken for early Derby specimens. The King Street works operated from 1862 until 1935. In 1876 a new factory, established in Osmaston Road, was given the name "Derby Crown Porcelain Co." and soon afterwards became known as "Royal Crown Derby".

Japanese and Persian styles in the Victorian period gave way to endless copies of old Derby *Imari*. The early 1900s are memorable for the work of Désiré Leroy who produced French-style vases, enamelled and jewelled with raised and tooled gold. This beautiful porcelain deserves the incredible sums that it commands at auction today.

After the 1730s Japanese porcelain in *Imari* colours (blue, red, and gold) was no longer exported to England, and Derby spotted the opportunity to supply this valuable market with English-made copies. Derby *Imari* patterns came into their own during the 1810s and 1820s. The influence was Japan, but Derby made very few direct copies. Instead they went one better and added extra flowers, additional panels, and coloured borders – filling up every available space with rich ornament, awash with brilliant gold.

Other factories also made *Imari*, but Derby examples became legendary. When the new Derby factories commenced production in the 1860s and 1870s they specialized in copying the famous old Derby *Imari* porcelain. Check Derby marks carefully, as many lesser factories copied Derby's most popular patterns. The most successful of the Royal Crown Derby patterns were given traditional Derby names, such as the "Old Witches pattern" and the "Kings pattern", as well as the "Cigar pattern", named after the decorative band that used to be wrapped around cigars. In the early 1900s a wide range of miniature shapes was made in *Imari* patterns. Royal Crown Derby still makes *Imari* today, and since the 1980s a whole new market has grown up for novelty animal paperweights in the *Imari* patterns.

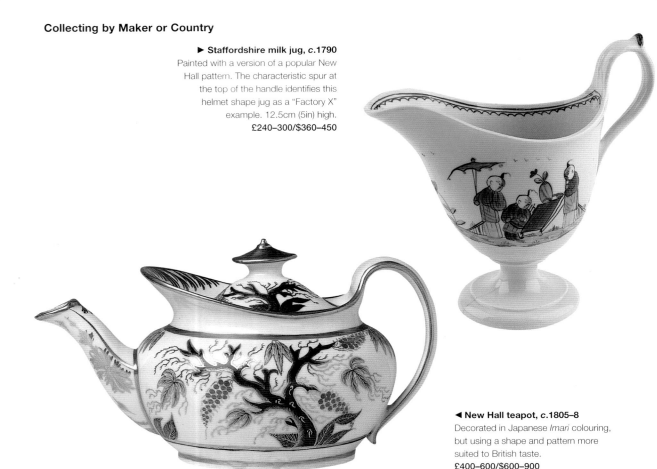

▶ **Staffordshire milk jug, *c*.1790**
Painted with a version of a popular New Hall pattern. The characteristic spur at the top of the handle identifies this helmet shape jug as a "Factory X" example. 12.5cm (5in) high.
£240–300/$360–450

◀ **New Hall teapot, *c*.1805–8**
Decorated in Japanese *Imari* colouring, but using a shape and pattern more suited to British taste.
£400–600/$600–900

Staffordshire Porcelain

Collectors of English porcelain mostly tend to concentrate on a single factory or type. As a result, surprisingly little attention is paid to the links between the many china factories operating side-by-side in "The Potteries" – the area around Stoke-on-Trent. This was Britain's most important porcelain-producing district. The separate factories made different kinds of wares for very different markets, and it is well worth collecting together pieces from various Staffordshire makers in order to learn what made the region special.

Stoke-on-Trent is known as the "Five Towns", for it comprises the separate communities of Burslem, Longton, Tunstall, Hanley, and Stoke. In a district long famed for its pottery, porcelain arrived around 1750 with the factory at Longton Hall established by William Littler. Exciting and individual porcelain was made there for just ten years, but while porcelain flourished in London, Derby, and Worcester, the industry in Staffordshire was a failure. The pottery industry continued, but

no significant porcelain was made around Stoke for more than 20 years. However, in the early 1780s a new china factory achieved huge profits by mass-producing tea wares, setting the course for the future of Staffordshire porcelain. The New Hall in Shelton was chosen as the location for the factory, which was managed by a consortium of Staffordshire pottery makers. Ignoring expensive ornamental vases and figurines, the New Hall factory concentrated on commercial tea services. It invented pattern numbers – a simple system enabling china shops to order differently designed sets identifiable by the number that was painted under each piece.

New Hall thrived for more than 50 years, and its success led to widespread copying. Several factories made their own versions of similar shapes and patterns, but in the total absence of factory marks not all have been identified. Collectors have designated three distinctive tea ware groups as "Factory X", "Factory Y", and "Factory Z". Various

▶ **"Envelope"-shaped Spode plate, *c*.1826–30**
So-named because of the delicate moulding that resembles folded paper. Marked "Spode" in red.
£150–200/$225–300

◀ **Miles Mason teabowl and saucer, *c*.1805**
With the so-called "Boy in a Doorway" pattern. A transfer-printed outline meant that teawares like this could be produced as cheaply as the Chinese imports they copied.
£100–150/$150–225

▲ **Spode ice pail, *c*.1825**
This impressive ice pail, which looks like a vase, was used to chill fruit as part of a dessert service. The panel depicts Pembroke Castle. 34.5cm (13½in) high. **£2,500–3,000/$3,750–4,500**

learned papers have been written in an attempt to put names to these makers, and some collectors are close to solving the riddle, although until we can be sure most of us prefer to use the anonymous letters. Factory X made good-quality teawares with distinctive spurs on the cup handles; Factory Z used an inferior china body but excelled in delicate transfer-printing. There is much satisfaction to be gained from recognizing a tea set as Factory X, and it can be a challenge to track down examples by unknown makers. However, in terms of collectability and value, New Hall remains way above the rest. Other people choose to collect a single shape – teapots, jugs, or coffee cans – belonging to as many different makers as possible.

Many little factories came and went. Established pottery manufacturers such as Neale & Co. and Turner had a brief stab at making porcelain, while a number of firms produced a range of different earthenware, stoneware, and porcelain bodies at the same time. Porcelain versions of Ralph Wood's

figures and Toby jugs are beautifully made and surprisingly inexpensive, for no one is too sure just who made them. Collectors of Staffordshire porcelain always favour pieces where the makers' names can be determined with certainty. This is where the detective work comes in. The factories grouped around Stoke shared many aims and, crucially, workmen and designs. If one firm made a successful range, another would copy it. All tried to keep up-to-date and produce the latest shapes. Their moulds varied only slightly, but enough to allow identification two centuries later.

From surviving design books we know the names that Spode gave to its various tea ware shapes. The factory replaced its "Old Oval" teapot shape with "New Oval", and in time the "London" shape became the most popular. Today's collectors use the Spode names even when the shapes were made by other factories. Learning the shapes is important, as very few Staffordshire firms used factory marks. China shops discouraged producers

▶ **Staffordshire porcelain comport, or centrepiece, c.1845**
Used for serving fruit as part of a dessert service. This is unmarked but identified by the shape and the pattern number as a product of John Ridgway's factory.
£200–300/$300–450

▶ **Large "Coalbrookdale" style vase, c.1840–45**
Although named after the Coalport factory's copies of Dresden flower-encrusted china, most English porcelain in this taste was made in the Staffordshire potteries.
£400–500/$600–750

◀ **Davenport plate from a royal service, 1830**
Made for the coronation of William IV. For an important royal commission such as this, the firm used its best painters and gilders. 25.5cm (10in) in diameter. £1,200–1,500/$1,800–2,250

from marking, and only a pattern number identifies most 19th-century tea sets. By linking the pattern numbers to surviving factory books and marked specimens, collectors have been able to recognize the Ridgway version of the "London" shape, the Minton version, and so on. Identifying unmarked ornamental shapes such as vases and inkstands is much more difficult.

Josiah Spode is credited with the greatest Staffordshire invention, bone china. A durable, thin and very white porcelain made from kaolin and animal bone, it proved ideal for making tea sets and plates. The Spode factory is famous for its blue-and-white printed pottery, but it also produced, from about 1797, a fine bone china decorated to the highest standards. Around 1810–15, having mastered the printing process, Spode used fine prints in black to decorate china tea sets.

Careful printing, both in black and in under-glaze blue, was a speciality of another Staffordshire maker. Miles Mason had been an important dealer in Chinese porcelain, involved in bulk imports from the Orient. When the supply from China dried

up, around 1800, he opened a factory at Lane Delph in Staffordshire to make copies of the Chinese porcelain he could no longer obtain. Mason's son later invented "Patent Ironstone China" – a type of pottery that was far more profitable.

Staffordshire porcelain-makers were in constant competition with pottery manufacturers, and firms generally survived by following one of two different routes. Some china-makers continued the ideals of New Hall and its imitators with the mass-production of cheap tea sets for everyday use. These tea services were usually unmarked and can be hard to identify. Some are referred to as "cottage sets" and are decorated with printed Chinese scenes or formal floral borders. Occasionally an edge of pink or copper lustre was used instead of gilding; it is the use of such gilding that sets apart the factories that chose to go up-market.

One of the biggest porcelain-producers was the Ridgway family, who potted at Cauldon Place in Staffordshire. From humble beginnings their business came into its own in the 1820s and 1830s, making tea and dinner ware copied from the

◄ **Simple pot-pourri basket, *c*.1830–35**
Floral-decorated porcelain in the rococo style was made throughout Staffordshire, and most examples are unmarked. 7.25cm (3in) high. **£75–100/$100–150**

Collecting Staffordshire Porcelain Figures

▲ **Turk figure by an unidentified Staffordshire maker**
Dated *c*.1845. These simple figures in exotic costume were popular novelties, made in large numbers, and as a result are generally inexpensive. 11.5cm (4½in) in height. **£60–80/$90–120**

▲ **Pair of Staffordshire spaniels**
Dated *c*.1850. Porcelain spaniels tend to be earlier in date than pottery ones. Separate front legs are also a good sign. 18cm (7in) high. **£450–550/$675–800**

latest French fashions. As the classical or Regency taste gave way to the rococo revival, Ridgway crammed as much ornament as possible into every cup and saucer. Other makers followed suit: the Davenport factory in Longport and Samuel Alcock in Burslem excelled in the rococo taste. Spode's senior decorators, Henry and Richard Daniel, set up their own factory in Stoke creating fanciful shapes and patterns. Minton made a smaller range of shapes and designs but decorated them to the very highest standards. There were also many other porcelain makers in Staffordshire. By the start of the Victorian era the amount of fine – and cheap – porcelain coming out of the Five Towns was simply breathtaking.

Many factories continued to produce fine porcelain during the second half of the 19th century, keeping the reputation of Staffordshire alive, although foreign competition hit the cheaper end of the business. Gradually a small number of the finest makers came to dominate the scene, with Minton the leader by a long way. At the Great Exhibition of 1851, Minton and Copeland (the

Although Staffordshire figures were cheap, and mostly made from pottery, a surprising number were made from bone china. Unlike Copeland's parian sculptures and Minton's copies of fine Meissen these were rather basic, but they have a naive charm that has appealed to generations of collectors. The best examples date from the 1840s, when figures of Queen Victoria and Prince Albert enjoyed obvious popularity. These shared mantelpiece space with a menagerie of birds and animals, especially pairs of spaniels, poodles, or greyhounds. The same makers produced models of houses, cottages, and castles, used as pastille burners that brought a breath of country air to the smelly towns of Britain. Figures of well-behaved schoolboys rubbed shoulders with priests and nuns, Turkish sultans, and Chinese mandarins. Collectors today usually prefer more sophistication, and as a result many delightful Staffordshire figures are ridiculously cheap. Look for well-coloured examples with deep blue coats and neat gilding on their bases. Choose dogs with separate limbs, well-defined coats and friendly features. Sadly Staffordshire figures died out in late Victorian times when German *bisque* figurines became cheaper still.

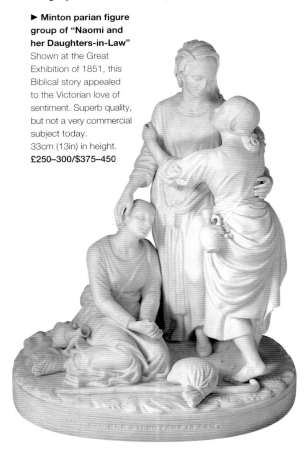

► **Minton parian figure group of "Naomi and her Daughters-in-Law"**
Shown at the Great Exhibition of 1851, this Biblical story appealed to the Victorian love of sentiment. Superb quality, but not a very commercial subject today.
33cm (13in) in height.
£250–300/$375–450

▲ **Large Wedgwood "Fairyland Lustre" vase**
Dated c.1925–30 and titled "Ghostly Wood with White Rabbit", this is one of Daisy Makeig-Jones' most impressive designs. 33cm (13in) high.
£15,000–20,000/$22,500–30,000

successor to Spode) both showed parian figures and busts. Parian, an unglazed white porcelain with the silky finish of marble, was Staffordshire's other great invention (*see* page 93). Elaborate parian groups were used as the supports for table centrepieces and fruit stands in extravagant dessert services. Minton specialized in wonderful dessert sets – each plate or comport painted with a detailed landscape, bird, animal, or botanical study. Made to be shown off, these dessert sets have spent a sad existence stacked in cupboards, and are frequently split up for sale. Collecting single, richly decorated dessert plates from Minton or any Staffordshire maker can be very rewarding, for the price today rarely reflects their great workmanship.

In the mid-Victorian period France had a direct influence on Staffordshire porcelain. Many top artists and potters left Paris to live in Stoke, mostly working at Minton under the art director Léon Arnoux, who came from Sèvres. Foremost among the decorators from Sèvres was Louis Solon, who introduced the *pâte-sur-pâte* technique. Works by Solon and his followers are Staffordshire's

masterpieces, and totally deserving of their high prices. Minton's use of external designers allowed them to dominate the 1870s and 1880s, when the Aesthetic Movement and Japanesque taste were at their height. It is strange, therefore, that the firm lost direction at the end of the century. Art Nouveau influenced Staffordshire pottery, but generally passed the porcelain-makers by. Doulton was the principal exception: the innovative stoneware potters from London established a porcelain branch in Burslem where vases were painted in new styles and original colour effects.

Wedgwood, the most important Staffordshire pottery firm, had little impact on the porcelain industry. Its bone china mostly copied that of others, but Wedgwood did create a unique style of its own in the 1920s. The local designer Daisy Makeig-Jones devised "Fairyland Lustre", a fantasy world peopled by elves and fairy folk realized in bright colours and gold against rich, pearl-like glazes. Doulton made some exciting Art Deco tea sets, as did Shelley (the name used by Wileman & Co. in Fenton), but these were exceptions. The

With *pâte-sur-pâte* panels by Alboin
Birks, and jewelled ornament by the
firm's Art Director, John Wadsworth.
Such quality will always be expensive.
27cm (10½in) in diameter.
£1,000–1,300/$1,500–2,000

► **Doulton figure of "The Sunshine Girl"**
Modelled by Leslie Harradine in 1929. This
proved too expensive at the time and
relatively few were sold, resulting in a high
value today. 13cm (5in) high.
£2,600–3,000/$4,000–4,500

◄ **Doulton vase, "The
Repose of Psyche", 1912**
Painted in the Burslem studio
by George White, the style is
influenced by Continental Art
Nouveau. 43.5cm (17in).
£5,000–7,000/$7,500–10,500

tableware departments of Staffordshire firms were
mostly set in their ways, and during the 1920s and
1930s they merely copied Victorian patterns.

Doulton really came to prominence by
reinventing the Staffordshire figure. Doulton's
figurines represent every artistic style, from Art
Deco sculpture and animal studies to copies of
Dresden crinoline ladies. Indeed it is the Doulton
figures of ladies that epitomize Staffordshire
porcelain in the 20th century. Doulton had been
encouraged by the British Board of Trade initially
during World War I, to undermine the German
economy. However, instead of merely copying
Meissen, Doulton created a range of figures that
were wholly British in style. Customers were keen
to remember the "good old days", and Doulton
dressed its china ladies in Victorian costume to
reflect this bygone era. Their spirit, though, was
modern and cheerful. These were no longer
"flatbacks" – the name given to crude Staffordshire
pottery figures modelled on one side only. Doulton
figurines, by contrast, were modelled in-the-round,
their swirling dresses full of movement.

Doulton is probably the single most collectable
Staffordshire porcelain, but there are many
others. W.H. Goss is famous the world over for
its crested china souvenirs, made with an
eggshell thinness that contrasts with most people's
image of industrial Staffordshire. Goss, and its
many contemporaries, made an enormous range
of crested china ornaments, bought at the time
as inexpensive souvenirs of seaside holidays.
Other miniature models of tanks, planes, and
field-ambulances were produced to raise funds
for wartime charities. Many examples still cost
just a few pounds today, and make an excellent
introduction to Staffordshire porcelain.

Hundreds of great, smoking bottle ovens
once dominated the skyline of Stoke-on-Trent.
Although very few of the old bottle kilns survive
today, Staffordshire remains very aware of its
heritage. A visit to the Potteries Museum in
Hanley, near Stoke-on-Trent, is thoroughly
recommended. Here the best products of the
area are beautifully displayed, giving Staffordshire
porcelain an identity of its own.

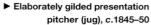

▶ **Elaborately gilded presentation
pitcher (jug), *c.*1845–50**
By the United States Pottery Co.,
Bennington. Special
decoration in gold is rare on
Bennington porcelain.
£335–465/$500–700

▲ **Blue-and-white moulded
pitcher (jug), *c.*1853–8**
Made by the United States
Pottery Co., Bennington.
The decoration copies a
Staffordshire jug of a similar date.
29cm (11in) high.
£335–465/$500–700

◀ **Moulded pitcher, *c.*1850–55**
By the United States Pottery Co., Bennington.
Moulded jugs of this type were usually sold in
sets of three, of graduated size.
£135–200/$200–300

American Porcelain

Porcelain manufactured in the United States is surprisingly rare, which is why auctions of "Americana" include porcelain *used* in the United States, such as Chinese exportware and Limoges made for the American market. The American porcelain industry didn't really get going until the late 19th century, and then largely copied European designs with surprisingly little originality.

The first soft-paste porcelain made in Philadelphia in 1770 was produced for less than three years. Only a few dozen pieces of Bonnin and Morris's blue-and-white survive today. The factory engaged English workmen, and its work looks very similar to that of Bow. Today, because of its great rarity, Bonnin and Morris pieces are among the world's most valuable porcelain.

Recognizing any early American porcelain is a problem. During the 1820s two Frenchmen, Decasse and Chanou, made porcelain in New York, while in New Jersey other French workmen helped William Shirley to make experimental porcelain.

Unfortunately their unmarked pieces cannot be distinguished from the products of Paris and Limoges. William Ellis Tucker opened a porcelain factory in Philadelphia in 1826, which was continued after 1832 by Joseph Hemphill. Tucker's pitchers follow the shape of Staffordshire jugs, and the painting is typically English, while the hard-paste porcelain resembles contemporary French tableware. Marked Tucker examples in American museums enable unmarked pieces to be identified, but the shape and decoration must correspond exactly. Vases with views of Philadelphia landmarks are Tucker's masterpieces, although they are poor relations of French Empire vases.

American porcelain-makers had trouble manufacturing plates and dishes, and specialized instead in moulded jugs or pitchers, copying models that were fashionable in England in the 1840s and 1850s. The most famous American jugs were made between 1848 and 1856 by Charles Cartlidge & Co. in Greenpoint (now Brooklyn), New York.

▼ Three oyster dishes, c.1880
From a set of twelve by the Union Porcelain
Works, Trenton, New Jersey. The shapes copy
Limoges pieces of a similar date. 21cm (8in)
wide. **£1,330–1,670/$2,000–2,500 (the set)**

**▲ Important hard paste porcelain
pitcher, c.1830** By William Ellis Tucker,
Philadelphia. The shape and decoration
exactly matches marked examples. 23cm
(9in) high. **£1,330–2,000/$2,000–3,000**

Cartlidge came from England and knew all about
Staffordshire productions. His heavily moulded
porcelain jugs were embossed with patriotic eagles
and American flags. When his business failed it was
incorporated into the other major New York factory,
the Union Porcelain Works (also in Greenpoint).
This produced hard paste from 1862 until 1890,
although it had been founded by William Boch &
Bros for the manufacture of bone china. Its
Centenary vase, embossed with presidential
portraits, was made for the 1876 celebrations, and
is an impressive piece of Americana.

The most prolific American porcelain firm is
better known for its pottery. The United States
Pottery Co. of Bennington, Vermont, is usually
referred to simply as "Bennington". It made parian
from 1843 using local New England raw materials.
Its basic relief-moulded jugs and simple vases were
initially sold only in plain white, although after
1853 the backgrounds to some moulded designs
were enamelled in "blue-and-white" to imitate

Wedgwood's jasper. Few pieces were marked,
and very similar wares were imported from
Staffordshire. As a result, a great deal is attributed
to Bennington in error, especially china poodles
and other dog models.

During the 1860s the discovery of a new source
of china clay transformed Trenton, New Jersey.
This clay made excellent parian, and the town
rapidly became a major porcelain centre. Trenton
was known as the "Staffordshire of America",
although Ireland had a far greater influence. The
Irish Belleek factory had exhibited its distinctive
lustrous glazed parian at the Philadelphia
Exposition in 1876, and its popularity inspired the
first "American Belleek". Around 20 American
china-makers copied the Irish porcelain, and many
added the Belleek name to their marks.

Ott and Brewer, in partnership from 1865 until
its closure in 1892, was the first maker in Trenton to
produce Belleek ware. This was thanks to William
Bromley, a senior workman from the Irish Belleek

▶ **"American Belleek" vase,** *c.***1895**
Made by Willets Manufacturing Co., Trenton,
using an innovative aerographic background
and finely applied silver-overlay decoration.
£465–600/$700–900

◀ **Ott and Brewer "Belleek" vase,** *c.***1890**
Of naturalistic form with twig handles and typical
painting. Such curious shapes left their Irish
roots far behind. **£400–535/$600–800**

factory, who, in 1882, helped Ott and Brewer to
perfect its parian formula. It made copies of popular
Irish Belleek tablewares, especially shell-moulded
tea sets. Other naturalistic shapes were inspired by
Limoges. While most Irish Belleek was white,
Ott and Brewer specialized in floral designs in
raised gold and platinum. Rare Ott and Brewer
parian figures include an imposing pair of baseball
players and busts of American presidents, modelled
by Isaac Broome.

Jonathan Coxon and Walter Scott Lenox
formed the Ceramic Art Co. in Trenton in 1889.
The porcelain is generally known simply as Lenox.
Inspiration came from Limoges, as well as Belleek,
Royal Worcester, and Japan. Many fine painters
enamelled landscapes, flowers, and distinctive
portrait panels, including an artist named Nosek,
and Lucien Boullemier, who came from Minton.
The Ceramic Art Co. name was dropped in 1906
when Walter Lenox became sole owner. Although
he had been blind and paralysed for ten years, he
continued to inspire his workforce. The Lenox
factory still thrives in Trenton to this day.

The firm of Knowles, Taylor and Knowles, in
East Liverpool, Ohio, made a fine bone-china body
in the Irish Belleek tradition. Its "Lotus Ware" is
some of the most delicate of all American painted
porcelain, although examples are rare. The Willets
Manufacturing Co. in Trenton was far more
prolific. This family business, established in 1879 by
brothers Joseph, Daniel, and Edmund Willets,
started making Belleek when the Irishman William
Bromley joined them in 1894/5 after the closure of
Ott and Brewer. Willets' Belleek was made until
1909. Willets is not as well known as Ott and
Brewer or Lenox, but its porcelain is far superior. It
produced particularly fine pierced porcelain,
decorated with raised gold and applied silver
decoration, some of it in the Art Nouveau tradition.

In 1929 the Irish Belleek factory was granted
an injunction stopping American firms using its
name, but by then the style was no longer in fashion
(although Lenox still made a Belleek-type parian
body). The Castleton China Co., established in 1940
in New Castle, Pennsylvania, concentrated, like
Lenox, on fine tableware, not ornamental shapes.

◄ American-decorated porcelain dish
This "blank" was made in Limoges, early 20th century; the amateur flower-painting is signed by the artist, M. Paterson. 24cm (9in) in diameter.
£70–100/$100–150

▲ Limoges cup and saucer
With a Haviland & Co. mark; celebrating the American Centenary in 1876, a copy of the White House china made for Abraham Lincoln. **£1,000–1,330/$1,500–2,000**

◄ Haviland & Co. Limoges dish
From dinner service ordered for the White House by President Rutherford Hayes; a highly individual set designed by local artist Theo Davis, 23cm (9in). Printed Presidential Seal and patent dated 1880.
£1,000–1,330/$1,500–2,000

Edward Marshall Boehm is the most celebrated 20th-century American porcelain maker. His lifelike *bisque* bird and flower sculptures, which were most popular in the 1950s and 1960s, have ensured him a place in ceramic history. The curious porcelain made by Taxile Doat and Adelaide Robineau early in the 20th century is also highly regarded. Their small kilns at University City, Missouri, and Syracuse, New York, produced crystalline and other special glaze effects that are both original and very expensive.

Amateur china-painting was a very popular hobby in the United States. Many towns had a china-painting guild where ladies would meet and enjoy recreational enamelling, making handicrafts to give to their friends. Not many of these amateurs were accomplished artists, although some had their own kilns and sold their work in art galleries. Some "non-professionals" painted on white American Belleek, but most of them purchased Limoges "blanks". A huge quantity of white Limoges porcelain was painted in the USA with floral designs copied from the instruction manuals that came with special sets of china paints. These pieces are rarely expensive to buy, and very decorative collections can be formed.

It was an American china dealer who established the biggest factory in Limoges. David Haviland found it was cheaper to make porcelain in France and import it than it was to manufacture fine porcelain in America. Vast quantities of Haviland and other Limoges china were shipped to the USA, and in 1880 Haviland & Co. received an important commission from the White House for a unique presidential dining set, which boosted the firm's reputation. A number of European china firms aimed their products solely at the American market. Almost unknown in their own countries, the firms of Royal Bayreuth and RS Prussia are household names in the USA, with active collectors' clubs and a host of price guides listing their wares. These firms specialized in fine lithographic printing and aerographic sprayed decoration. Although cheap at the time, their porcelain is thinly potted and of high quality, and justifies the reputation it has acquired among collectors.

Collecting by Object or Shape

Create impact and collect items from a variety of different manufacturers

◀ **A Chinese Dehua "blanc-de-chine" figure of a Bodhisattva, late 18th/early 19th century** Marked with the seal of Xu Yuquan Zhi. Fine Dehua porcelain is treated with true reverence. 46cm (18in) high. **£10,000–15,000/ $15,000–22,500**

Figures & Figurines

Every home displays a porcelain figure of some kind, loved almost as part of the family. Their origin dates back thousands of years to the time when ceramic idols played vital roles in archaic religions. Ancient Egyptian, Mexican, and Chinese tombs were filled with pottery armies and other clay figures destined to become servants in the afterlife. By the time porcelain was invented, most civilizations had given up burying grave goods. Instead these old traditions evolved, and all over Asia figures of gods and immortals were placed in shrines and accorded due reverence. The esteem in which porcelain was held meant this new material was ideal for the representation of these sacred beings.

When porcelain was first exported to Europe a few white figures were tucked into cargoes to make up weight. Ships' captains hoped to sell images of the Buddha and mythical lion dogs as novelties. In 1700 Chinese *blanc de Chine* figures of the goddess Guanyin were sold in London as "Sancta Marias" at a few pennies each. Nobody seriously thought the Chinese goddess looked like the Madonna, but the figures sold well because they were unusual. Wealthy collectors placed them in mock Chinese temples or on mantelpieces in country houses. The china figurine was born.

One keen collector of Chinese and Japanese porcelain figures was Augustus, King of Saxony. He also established the Meissen factory, so it is hardly surprising that among the earliest productions of Meissen were direct copies of Chinese Buddhas. These were sold as "pagods" or pagoda figures. They look so like the Chinese originals that it is easy to mistake valuable Meissen copies for much cheaper Chinese prototypes.

Augustus wanted a set of life-size porcelain animals to decorate his new palace. To complete the set in 1731 he engaged J.J. Kändler, an apprentice wood-carver from the court workshops who had never worked with porcelain before. His genius

Made at Capodimonte, or possibly Buen Retiro where the Royal Naples factory moved to around 1759, 22cm (8½in) high. The very subtle enamelling emphasises the beauty of the pure white soft-paste body.
£6,000–10,000/$9,000–15,000

▲ **A pair of Japanese Arita "Moon Viewing Boys", *c*.1700**
The rococo ormolu mounts were added in Europe fifty years later, when such figures were highly prized. 35cm (14in) tall.
£45,000–55,000/$67,500–82,500

► **A Meissen military bandleader, c.1765**
Bearing the insignia of Frederick Augustus of Saxony. A set of these porcelain soldiers, measuring 12.5cm (5in), was presented to Catherine the Great
£1,500–2,000/$2,250–3,000

soon became evident, and in a matter of months he was appointed master modeller at Meissen. Kändler can truly be called the father of the china figure, for he made the idiom his own. He turned his hand to absolutely any style, sacred or secular, rustic or regal, from figures of saints to the most basic representations of everyday scenes.

Meissen figures were sold in exclusive gift shops across Europe. In the 1750s you could buy single figures or matching pairs, and you could also build up complete sets to decorate your table at a banquet. Harlequin was joined by Columbine, Pierrot, Pantalone, and all the other characters from the Commedia Dell'arte series, playing out their slapstick routines for the amusement of dinner guests. Figures of tradesmen, artisans, and street vendors seem innocent enough, but these represent the *Wirtschaften*, a traditional pastime at the Saxon court based around role-playing. During high-society parties, members of the court, their wives and mistresses dressed in idealized peasant costume.

Roles were decided by drawing lots – the king could be a humble street pedlar, his mistress might be a shepherdess. Later, while seated at a fantastic banquet, the wealthy courtiers would be reminded by the figurines on the table of the fun they had had.

Kändler's figures were neatly placed along banqueting tables, grouped together in conversations. The *cris de Paris* brought to life street traders selling confectionery and trinkets on the streets of Paris. Soldiers lined up for battle with regimental precision, while singers and dancers performed to imaginary music played on china instruments by tiny musicians. Shepherds and farmers led flocks of sheep and cattle past barns, windmills, and dovecotes, all made of porcelain.

Kändler was not only incredibly prolific, he also taught a team of pupils. Peter Reinicke was immensely talented and is credited with many of the Commedia Dell'arte figures and street traders. Friedrich Meyer mastered the spirit of rococo and put great detail into his work. Johann Eberlein

▶ **Chelsea figure of a musician,**
*c.*1758-60 Marked with a red anchor. This is a direct copy of a Meissen model unavailable in England at the time. 17cm (6½in) tall.
£1,500–2,000/$2,250–3,000

▼ **Sèvres group of "The Flute Lesson",** *c.*1755–65
After Boucher, a delicate subject, ideally suited to the unglazed biscuit porcelain, 22cm (8½in) in height.
£5,000–7,000/$7,500–10,500

▶ **Derby figure of a tailor riding on a goat,** *c.*1830
A satirical model copied originally from Meissen. Derby had introduced this model 70 years earlier; the date of manufacture naturally affects the value.
12.5cm (5in) high.
£300–400/$450–600

◀ **Meissen figure of "Smell",** *c.*1870
From a set of the Five Senses modelled by Johann Schönheit. During the 19th century Meissen paid the closest attention to every decorative detail. £900–1,100/$1,350–1,650

and Johann Ehder similarly helped Kändler before they both tragically died, in 1749 and 1750. Sometimes it is difficult to distinguish master from pupil. As the demand for Dresden figures grew, the factory workforce rose from 218 in 1748 to 571 only three years later. Just imagine the size of the mould storerooms: thousands of different figures required separate moulds for bodies, limbs, and attributes. Every figure was a work of art, and quality was never compromised. Painting was applied with precision, with not a hair out of place. Any figures that failed stringent tests were condemned as "seconds", their factory marks cancelled by incisions cut across the blue crossed swords.

Meissen had many imitators, and each rival factory engaged the best modellers it could find. Konrad Linck and Karl Luck worked at Frankenthal along with Johann Peter Melchior, who also worked at Höchst. Simon Feilner made dramatic harlequins at Fürstenberg, and G.F. Riedel at Ludwigsburg designed a most charming set of miniature street stalls and costumed figures attending the local "Venetian Fair". At Nymphenburg the

rococo figures of Franz Anton Bustelli are regarded by many as the equal of those by Kändler. The work of Bustelli and Feilner is very expensive, but as a rule figures by the smaller 18th-century German factories are significantly cheaper than similar Meissen figures, an anomaly that is worth exploiting as great opportunities exist at present. Eighteenth-century Vienna porcelain figures are perhaps the best value of all.

When in 1756 Meissen was captured by Saxony's rival, Prussia, Frederick the Great forced some craftsmen to move to his Berlin factory, Freidrich Meyer among them. Kändler remained at Meissen, which was now run for profit. Quality declined, along with the fashion for rococo. Kändler was heartbroken, but continued his work until his death in 1775. The Meissen factory survived, and still produces Kändler's models today. Meissen figures were made throughout the 19th and 20th centuries, carefully moulded and always painted to the highest standards. For this reason the later figures are popular and expensive. Some mid-18th-century examples seem incredibly cheap by comparison.

▲ **Coloured *bisque* porcelain group by Gardner of Moscow**
This is decorative as well as historical, for it brings to life the colourful characters of 19th-century Russia. 25.5cm (10in) high.
£1,500–2,000/$2,250–3,000

Collecting Parian

◄ **Minton parian figure of "The Greek Slave"**
Dated *c.*1850, this is a miniature copy of the famous sculpture by Hiram Powers that caused a sensation wherever it was exhibited. 35.5cm (14in) in height.
£700–900/$1,000–1,350

In England the Chelsea, Derby, Bow, and Longton Hall factories all made close copies of Meissen figures. Soft-paste bodies and thicker glazes generally give English figures a very different feel from their German prototypes, but what they lost in detail they gained in a kind of primitive charm. Chelsea figures from the Red Anchor period in the 1750s are exciting and very expensive, but there are many 18th-century Bow and Derby figures available for just a few hundred pounds/dollars each, and interesting collections can be formed.

In France some of the greatest court sculptors, under royal patronage, provided models for the Sèvres factory. At Vincennes (forerunner of Sèvres) it was realized that thick creamy glaze hid the modelled detail, and so figures were issued without glaze – a state known as "biscuit". The designs were provided by artists, among them Boucher, and these were modelled with remarkable care, creating a most original art form. Sèvres biscuit figures were pure sculpture and were very influential.

Biscuit figures were made elsewhere in France, especially at Niderviller, which produced charming

Visitors to the Great Exhibition in 1851 could buy as souvenirs miniature porcelain copies of the sculptures on display. These were made in parian, a new porcelain named after the island of Paros where fine marble was mined in ancient times. Minton and Copeland had both developed parian, which was very different from Continental unglazed biscuit. A high glass content added to bone china meant it didn't need glaze to keep it clean. A parian bust in a smoky Victorian home didn't need a glass dome for protection. Works by the sculptors of the day were reduced in size and cast in parian as exact replicas for general sale or in special subscribers' editions. Visitors flocked to see sculptor Hyram Power's *The Greek Slave*, whose naked feminine beauty shocked the critics but meant no shortage of customers for Minton's parian version. Gentlemen could display it in their parlours without shame, for it was "art". Parian wasn't only naked flesh. Allegories of love and mortality, saints and Bible stories sold well, as did children and animals, literary and historical subjects, and busts of politicians and royalty. Today's value depends on the subject, while Copeland and Minton are most popular.

► Porcelain "fairing",
c.1880–1900
From Posnek, Germany. Many of these charming ornaments were won as prizes at fairgrounds, but they were also made for the British souvenir market. £60–90/$90–150

▲ **Royal Dux figural centrepiece in the Art Nouveau taste**
The colouring is inspired by traditional Viennese bronze and ivory sculptures. 28cm (11in) in height.
£1,000–1,400/$1,500–2,100

◄ **"Dresden" lace figurine, early 20th century**
Made at Volkstedt in Thuringia. Real lace was dipped in clay and applied to create the amazing dress. The lace burnt away in the kiln, leaving a perfect, delicate porcelain reproduction.
25.5cm (10in) high.
£400–600/$600–900

and detailed subjects early in the 19th century. Glazed and brightly coloured, Niderviller figures are distinctive pieces but curiously undervalued in today's market.

By the middle of the century enamelled biscuit figures had become fashionable. The idea originated in France, where superior examples were made in Paris by the firm of Jean Gille. Elaborate costumes were painted with textile patterns picked out in fine gilding, while the faces were given delicate flesh tints. Biscuit figures with enamelled colouring have become known as *bisque* (a term sometimes applied also to white biscuit pieces). A natural progression for the makers of coloured *bisque* figurines was the manufacture of *bisque*-headed dolls. One German doll maker, Heubach, also made an extensive range of *bisque* figures, including a series of sitting or crawling children – some almost lifesize. It was fashionable to place these children on the sideboard or the piano, and they are today known as "piano babies". Examples with impressed Heubach marks are keenly collected, but watch out for fakes made in the Far East.

The porcelain figurine industry declined in France, but flourished in Germany towards the end of the 19th century, where it was aimed at a rather different market. German *bisque* figures competed with Staffordshire pottery "flatbacks", selling cheaply on market stalls. The German pieces won hands down, for they were made of fine porcelain with pretty details, but the *bisque* finish attracted dirt and became grubby, so many figurines were sold with glass domes to keep them clean. Cheapest of all were small china novelties, which were known as "fairings" because they were often won as prizes at fairgrounds and carnivals. Charming groups, reflecting seaside or lavatory humour, were titled in English and exported in great quantities to Britain. Although keenly collected in the 1960s and '70s, the popularity of fairings has waned and they can now be bought relatively cheaply.

Royal Worcester was the best figure-maker in Victorian times, thanks to the factory modeller James Hadley, who was the equal of the great German sculptors from a hundred years before. He gave three-dimensional life to children's picture-book

▼ Suffragette figurine, c.1905–10
This cheap German *bisque* porcelain
Suffragette, calling for votes for women, is
now a sought-after political commemorative.
£300–400/$450–600

◄ German porcelain Buddha, c.1900
A "Nodder" figure, with separate head and hands
carefully balanced so that they nod gently. This
happy Chinese Buddha derives from a Meissen
prototype and was made cheaply in Dresden.
10cm (4in) high. **£200–300/$300–450**

► "Darling", a Royal Doulton figurine
Modelled by Charles Vyse, and introduced
in 1913, this proved an immediate best-
seller. As a result it is a common figure, and
among the least expensive to buy on
the collectors' market. 19cm (7½in) high.
£120–150/$180–225

illustrations by Kate Greenaway. James Hadley's children are typically prim and proper, impeccably dressed, and perfectly behaved. They clearly all belong to the same family, for a James Hadley face is unmistakable. Like Kändler before him, Hadley was very versatile and also modelled Japanese, Indian, and Arab subjects – fine sculptures that were decorated in imitation ivory and bronze.

Charles Noke, a pupil of James Hadley, introduced figure-making to the Doulton factory. During World War I, English factories were encouraged to copy the Dresden figurines previously imported from Germany. Doulton's crinoline ladies and other costume and character figures were hugely successful in the 1920s and 1930s. Royal Worcester followed Doulton's lead, replacing Hadley's children with more natural child studies by Freda Doughty. Between them, Doulton and Worcester exported vast numbers of figures to the United States. Some sold well, and these are common today. Other models were unpopular at the time, and these rarities are now much sought after by collectors, commanding incredible sums.

Meissen still made Kändler's 18th-century figures, but in addition it introduced Art Nouveau and Art Deco subjects, including delightful children modelled by Konrad Hentschel. Rosenthal also made some wonderful Art Deco figures, many of which were sold with just a pure white glaze. Royal Copenhagen became one of the largest European porcelain-makers thanks to its extensive range of figures. Underglaze colouring gave the figures a sculptural feel while it also kept production costs down. More recently the Spanish maker Lladro has built up a keen collectors' following for its figures that follow similar traditions.

Many porcelain figures today are made as "Limited Editions" – a clever marketing technique started by Royal Worcester half a century ago. Worcester's Limited Edition figures from the 1960s rose to dizzy heights within ten years, but values have since fallen dramatically. There has never been a better time to buy fine Limited Edition figures if they can be found on the secondary market, for most command just a fraction of their original manufacturing costs.

► **Cheap German bisque swan, *c.*1900**
Light in weight, and hollow, this was designed to sit on water, with floating flower petals.
4.5cm (1½in) high. £15–20/$25–30

▲ **Japanese Hirado porcelain group of two fighting dogs of Fo**
Finely detailed and a wonderful porcelain sculpture in miniature. 30.5cm (12in) high.
£2,000–3,000/$3,000–4,500

◄ **Derby miniature group of a cat and kitten, *c.*1825**
Tiny models of cats and dogs have always been popular, and it is worth seeking out examples by the major makers.
7cm (3in) tall.
£400–600/$600–900

Birds & Animals

Amazing dogs, elephants, and tigers were made in early Japanese porcelain at the end of the 17th century. These cartoon creatures had great presence and are enormously valuable. In contrast Chinese white porcelain "lion dogs", or *kylin*, in *blanc de Chine*, of similar date, are surprisingly affordable today as huge numbers were imported into Europe at the time, leading to a fascination with china animals. A life-sized menagerie of Meissen animals and birds was made in *c.*1730 for Augustus the Strong's Japanese Palace in Dresden. This ambitious project proved difficult to fire and could not be made commercially, but it was followed 20 years later by a great range of small Meissen animals made for table decoration, with dogs, cats, chickens, cows, and sheep – all charming models tended by china farmers and shepherdesses. Meissen also made a veritable aviary of birds. In the 1740s J.J. Kändler modelled a large set of life-sized birds with brightly coloured plumage – parrots and pheasants, oriels, magpies, and hoopoes, each as a matching pair on a leafy stump. These were placed in china cabinets or on gilded wall brackets in the homes of the wealthy.

Meissen animals were extensively copied across Europe, especially in England at Chelsea, Derby, Bow, and Longton Hall. Sheep were very popular, as well as simple songbirds such as chaffinches and canaries. Some of the copying throws an interesting light back to the Orient, as Chinese porcelain-makers produced *famille rose* copies of Meissen animals in the 1750s and 1760s. All 18th-century porcelain animals are expensive, but 19th-century animals are more affordable and are collected in a different way – usually according to a single type of animal or breed, rather than by individual maker. Thus you get collections of china cats, pug dogs, or spaniels, and here the detail and realism are important.

The specific maker is certainly unimportant as far as Staffordshire is concerned, as virtually no examples are marked. A very extensive range of animals was produced in Staffordshire. Many were

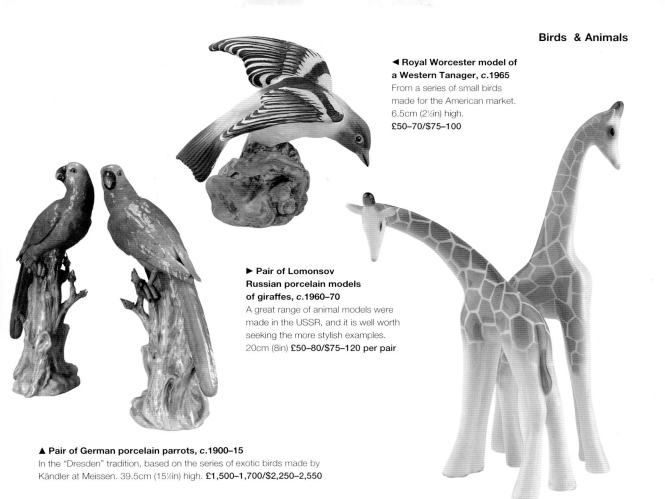

◄ **Royal Worcester model of a Western Tanager**, *c.*1965
From a series of small birds made for the American market. 6.5cm (2½in) high.
£50–70/$75–100

► **Pair of Lomonsov Russian porcelain models of giraffes**, *c.*1960–70
A great range of animal models were made in the USSR, and it is well worth seeking the more stylish examples.
20cm (8in) **£50–80/$75–120 per pair**

▲ **Pair of German porcelain parrots**, *c.*1900–15
In the "Dresden" tradition, based on the series of exotic birds made by Kändler at Meissen. 39.5cm (15½in) high. **£1,500–1,700/$2,250–2,550**

made from pottery and so fall outside of the scope of this book, although collectors normally display porcelain alongside earthenware examples. In the 1840s the most delightful range of bone china animals, dogs in particular, was made at Samuel Alcock's factory in Burslem. Although Alcock's sheep and poodles can be positively identified from impressed model numbers, most are still known by the name of a very different factory. The works at Rockingham in Yorkshire made few animals, but an enduring misunderstanding has meant its name is used incorrectly to refer to a wide range of porcelain animals with fur made "fluffy" by pushing clay through a sieve. Many Staffordshire animals are still incorrectly called Rockingham today.

During the 19th century Meissen continued its extensive range of birds and animals. The quality of decoration is generally superior to that of the 18th century, a fact that is rarely reflected in the value. Meissen was much copied by smaller German makers who produced ornaments known as "Dresden".

Pug dogs in a range of sizes replicate the Meissen pugs first made in the 1740s as disguised emblems of a secret Masonic-like society, although by Victorian times they were purely decorative. Dresden parrots with brilliantly coloured plumage sold very well, and today are more popular than ever. During the Art Nouveau and Deco periods Meissen made an exciting range of new animal models with a sculptural feel. Further highly original animals were made by Rosenthal and other German makers. In Denmark, Royal Copenhagen and Bing & Grondahl specialized in carefully observed animals and birds in distinctive underglaze colours. Their success led Royal Worcester and Royal Doulton to produce similar sets of dogs and birds. Collectors can buy single models of favourite breeds, or else build up full sets. Rare examples are expensive, but most Danish or English 20th-century models are reasonably priced. Porcelain animals made in Russia since the 1960s are even better value, and the more stylish examples show much potential as collectables.

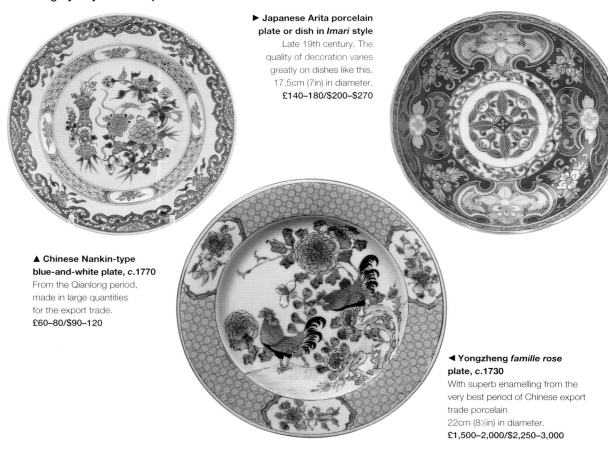

▶ **Japanese Arita porcelain plate or dish in *Imari* style**
Late 19th century. The quality of decoration varies greatly on dishes like this. 17.5cm (7in) in diameter.
£140–180/$200–$270

▲ **Chinese Nankin-type blue-and-white plate, *c*.1770**
From the Qianlong period, made in large quantities for the export trade.
£60–80/$90–120

◀ **Yongzheng *famille rose* plate, *c*.1730**
With superb enamelling from the very best period of Chinese export trade porcelain
22cm (8½in) in diameter.
£1,500–2,000/$2,250–3,000

Plates & Dishes

Plates have been used since ancient times, not just for serving food but also for decoration and display. Long before porcelain was available in Europe, finely painted majolica plates were made in Renaissance Italy. These were displayed as works of art alongside gold and silver plates, not as crockery to eat off for they were far too expensive to use. The tradition of treating plates as an art form is therefore deeply rooted in ceramic history.

In the 16th century Chinese porcelain dishes that had been traded along the Silk Road were hung on the kitchen walls of the Topkapi palace in Istanbul by the Ottoman sultans. Blue-and-white from the Yuan or the Ming dynasty was greatly prized in the West, and fine dishes are still very expensive today. However, many simple examples from the Ming period have been recovered recently from shipwrecks, and some can be as cheap to buy as modern china. It is amazing just how inexpensive Chinese plates can be. Marvellous "Kraak" porcelain dishes from the 17th century can fetch just a few

hundred pounds/dollars, while many 18th-century blue-and-white plates are as little as £40/$60. It is therefore not difficult to reconstruct a typical 18th-century china room by hanging Chinese plates in rows around the walls. Simple enamelled *famille rose* plates also cost only £60–100/$85–140, although rarities from the Yongzheng period can set you back £1,000/$1,500. Watch out for fine hairline cracks, as these are commonly found on the rims of Chinese plates and can devastate the value.

Many people are surprised by the thinness of Chinese porcelain plates, for potters in Jingdezhen were able to fire stacks of plates without any kiln distortion. No wonder they were in such demand in 18th-century Europe. However, they were readily available, so there was little need for European alternatives. Some Chinese plates were copied at Meissen, but mostly the German potters imitated more precious Kakiemon wares from Japan. Finely drawn in bright colours on pure white porcelain, Kakiemon designs were copied at Meissen,

► **Meissen plate from the Academic or "Dot" period, c.1765**
With a simple floral pattern in the classical taste, crossed swords and dot mark. 20.5cm (8in) in diameter.
£150–200/$225–300

▼ **Viennese dish, c.1870**
A fine large dish painted by D. Wagner, one of the best independant Viennese china-painters. The original painting by Titian hung in the Vienna Picture Gallery. 55cm (21½in) in diameter.
£5,000–8,000/$7,500–12,000

◄ **Chinese plate in the Canton tradition, c.1930–40**
Although decorative, the quality is very poor and this plate is consequently inexpensive. 17.5cm (7in) in diameter.
£10–15/$15–22

Chelsea, and Worcester, while cheaper versions were made at Coalport and Derby, and in Staffordshire. The same basic designs were made everywhere, and for display purposes this doesn't greatly matter. Plates can be mixed and matched according to colour and style, to suit the taste of any porcelain collector.

European factories made two principal sorts of plate – for the table, and just for display. The latter are known as "cabinet plates", for they were placed in china cabinets and admired as art. "Service plates", on the other hand, formed part of dinner, dessert, or tea sets and were meant to be used. In reality, of course, many service plates were much too costly for this, and their owners only brought them out on special occasions just to show them off.

Dinner sets usually include dinner or table plates (about 22–25cm/9–10in), deeper soup plates of similar size, and dessert plates (around 20–22cm/ 8–9 in). Extensive sets also included smaller side plates, cheese plates, and salad plates – the latter

sometimes of a curious crescent shape. A tea service normally includes two large plates for serving cakes or slices of bread and butter. After the mid-19th century, tea sets contained small side plates or tea plates (about 15cm/6in) to accompany each cup and saucer. Some early Victorian tea sets included tiny plates (7–10cm/3–4in); these are "cup plates", on which you stood the empty cup while you drank from the saucer, a custom particularly popular in the USA between about 1830 and 1860.

The idea of a separate dessert service originated at Meissen before the 1740s. Dessert was the most important course of a dinner, so a dessert table would be richly dressed with ornamental centre-pieces and serving dishes piled high with fruit, cakes, and pastries. Dishes shaped as leaves and flowers were placed among novelty fruit and vegetable tureens. By around 1800 a typical dessert set comprised two small tureens for sugar and cream, with four differently shaped dishes for serving fruit – oval, square, heart, and shell. Plates

▲ **Worcester dessert dish painted with "Fancy" birds in the French style,** *c.*1780
Painting of this quality from the 18th century can sometimes be excellent value.
£700–1,000/$1,000–1,500

▲ **"Cigar Pattern" Royal Crown Derby plate,** *c.*1975
This was a popular *Imari* design. Earlier 20th-century examples would be more expensive, as they are painted with greater care. 25.5cm (10in) in diameter.
£40–50/$60–75

► **Swansea plate,** *c.*1815–20, **with exotic decoration added in London**
Welsh porcelain is always expensive, but this comes from the famous Gosford Castle service and so is especially costly. 23cm (9in) in diameter.
£4,500–5,500/$6,750–8,250

came in multiples of 12, 18, or 24. The decoration on dessert services was usually much more lavish than that on dinner or tea services.

Over the years a great many dinner and dessert sets have been split up. Few homes still entertain on a grand scale, and there is a general reluctance to place antique family services in a dishwasher. Displaying a large set takes a great deal of room, and so many wonderful services sit unused in cupboards. Old sets are often bought by dealers, who sell the pieces individually to collectors looking for single display plates or pairs of dishes for the mantelpiece. In many ways it is a shame so many complete sets have been split up, but this does mean there is enormous scope for people to form varied and decorative collections.

Some fortunate plates have always been kept on display in cabinets, but many plates and dishes have spent much of their time stacked up in cupboards. When they were made, to prevent plates sticking together in the kiln the footrims were not normally glazed. These rough "feet" have caused enormous damage over the years, and not

just to polished tabletops. "Stacking wear", as it is known, is the result of plates rubbing against one another when stacked in a pile. Severe rubbing to the decoration usually corresponds with the position of the footrim, each one in the pile having rubbed against the plate beneath. Rubbing like this, especially to gold borders, severely affects the value of fine porcelain, and it could have been prevented so easily. Some Victorian ladies lovingly embroidered linen plate separators for their best chinaware. Other careful homes cut circles out of old sheets or scraps of cloth, and placed these between each plate. Sets of plates looked after in this way can remain a joy for years. Unfortunately I see all-too-many tragic sets where every single plate is worn in the same place around the centre.

Unlike the Chinese, European factories had trouble making plates. Even Meissen initially had problems keeping them flat in the kiln. The centres of hard-paste porcelain plates tended to sag during the firing, so extra supporting ridges were built underneath to keep them level. Soft paste was actually easier to fire, so Chelsea copies of Meissen

▶ **Selection of Minton sample plates**
Showing a range of different tableware patterns, *c.*1905–15. Individual plates from dinner services can make attractive and inexpensive displays.
£10–20/$15–30 each

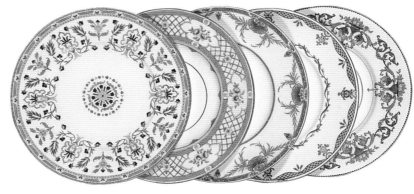

▼ **"Painted Fruit" Royal Worcester display plate, *c.*1960**
Signed by the painter Harry Ayrton. The value depends on the artist and the date of manufacture. 22.5cm (9in) in diameter.
£250–300/$375–450

▶ **Staffordshire plate with Art Nouveau-style border, *c.*1900**
From a simple Staffordshire teaset that can be dated by its border. Single antique plates like this are cheap enough for everyday use.
£2–4/$3–6

retained their shape more successfully. Worcester managed to make thin plates, but they were often misshapen. The best European plates, made at Sèvres, were thin and smooth, with a distinctive creamy glaze. Sèvres made many, very individual table services, every one a perfect exercise in elegant design.

Many plates just have smart border designs, with plain centres that are practical for serving food. For display, decorative centres are much more popular. Meissen introduced a fashion for a range of central paintings – varied landscapes, different birds, assorted flower specimens, or scattered ripe fruit. The purpose was to provide a topic of conversation over dinner. The question "What have you got on your plate?" will have broken the ice at many a formal banquet.

The dessert service really came into its own during the 19th century. The porcelain factories of Europe competed for commissions to make great services with fantastic painted decoration. After the victory of Waterloo, the Duke of Wellington was presented with complete sets of Meissen, Sèvres,

and Berlin porcelain, every plate with a different, finely painted scene framed by rich borders with tooled gilding. Each piece was an individual work of art, actually far too precious for the Duke to put in front of his guests. The centres were canvases upon which porcelain artists painted their very best work.

Every Victorian family wanted to emulate great households such as the Duke of Wellington's. Dessert services were ordered to suit the pockets of different customers. Top firms such as Minton and Royal Worcester engaged skilled artists to paint plate centres with scenes copied from travel books, or with reproductions of famous paintings by Turner or Landseer. Cheaper sets were made by smaller manufacturers in Staffordshire and Limoges. Simple flowers or idealized lakeland scenes were painted so quickly that they are often little more than doodles. Needless to say, the value of these services today is in proportion to their original cost. When not in use, dessert sets were often displayed around a room on a plate rack – a strip of wood running around the wall, with a groove to stop the plate slipping. Plate racks became standard

► **Royal Doulton commemorative plate**
To celebrate the sesquicentenary
of Australia, made in 1938.
£150–250/$225–375

▲ **Russian plate, dated 1920**
Designed by Sergei V. Chekhonin, with
the bold calligraphy associated with the
post-Revolutionary period, and marked
with the hammer, sickle, and cog mark
of the new State factory. 23.5cm (9in) in
diameter. £500–700/$750–1,000

◄ **Royal Copenhagen
Christmas plate**
For the year 2001,
continuing a long
tradition of annual
plates given as gifts.
Such designs would
usually be mass-
produced.
£35–45/$50–65

in many Victorian and Edwardian homes. The
Doulton factory even sold single pictorial plates as
"rack plates" to use purely as decoration in this way.

The china factories that produced rich dessert
services also made single plates of similar quality.
Cabinet plates were not parts of sets but stood on
their own, representing the best workmanship
available. Enamellers in Dresden and Vienna
painted plate centres and fine large dishes with
detailed copies of the masterpieces hanging in art
galleries, and their work was intended to be framed
and hung on a wall in place of a painting. Top china
painters signed their work and certainly deserve
recognition, for their plates were sold for enormous
sums in galleries rather than china shops. Taking
into account the value of money in the 19th century,
most cabinet plates cost more then, in real terms,
than they are worth today. However, certain china
painters have since become sought after in their
own right. Royal Worcester plates by senior artists
Harry Davis and the Stinton family (*see* pages
76–77) fetch enormous prices, for their work is
now regarded as fine art.

Cheaper alternatives to hand-painting became
available. A hundred years ago lithographic
printing was used to make very decorative plates for
a fraction of the cost. Bohemian factories produced
inexpensive printed copies of Vienna and Dresden
plates to hang on the walls of ordinary homes. Some
cheap plates bear fake signatures of well-known
Vienna artists, but under close examination these
"paintings" are revealed to be made up of tiny dots
of printed colour, rather than fine brushstrokes.
Nevertheless, these plates provided extremely good
decoration for a fraction of the cost. Around 1900
a range of very cheap German plates with pierced
borders was made, and it was common practice to
hang these up by tying ribbon through the cut-out
rims. They consequently became known as "ribbon
plates" and are popular with collectors because they
are still inexpensive to buy today.

By the 1960s colour photography had been
perfected, and plates could be printed with photos
of original paintings. Vast numbers of identical plates
could be made very cheaply, and this revolutionized
the porcelain industry. The fashion for "collectors'

▲ **Modern porcelain plate**
Commissioned from china-painter James Skerratt, showing the cruise ship *Oriana*. **£100–140/$150–200**

Using Wire Plate-Hangers

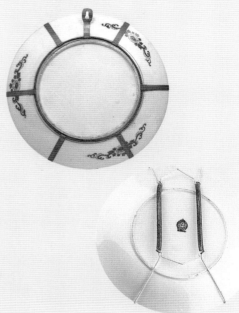

▲ **Hanging wires**
Many plates have been harmed by old hanging wires, such as these tight metal clamps (top). Plates can be hung safely on plastic-coated wires secured by springs (below), but they mustn't be too loose or too tight.

plates" started with Royal Copenhagen Christmas plates more than a hundred years ago. During the 1970s manufactured collectables were popular investments. Sets of cheap pictorial plates, issued as "Limited Editions", sold in unbelievable quantities. Some were made by major European companies, while others were manufactured even more cheaply in the Far East. The market became saturated, and values plummeted when collectors realized that the cost of making the plates was less than the cost of the magazine advertisements that promoted them.

A few plates do sell for substantial sums, but most can now be bought for very little on the secondary market. These plates are just colour photographs printed on porcelain. In contrast, it is still possible to commission plates painted entirely by hand, for a number of skilled artists work as independent china painters. However, large china factories practise very little hand-painting. When you investigate the cost of modern porcelain plates, it soon becomes apparent that superb cabinet plates from the 19th century represent wonderful value for money.

Few subjects evoke more discussion among porcelain lovers than plate-hanging. Some experts say plates should never be hung, but I have lots of plates hung on my own walls. It is all a question of safety and the type of hanger used. My hangers are made from two long springs linking shaped pieces of wire coated in soft plastic. They are exactly the right size for each individual plate: too loose and the plate could fall out, too tight and the plate might crack. For added safety I place a piece of felt between the springs and the plate to cushion against vibrations, and I use hooks rather than nails, secured in the wall by the correct size of wall-plug. This way I am confident my plates are safe.

Old wires, which can rust and snap, or stain the plate, should always be replaced by modern, plastic-coated spring hangers. Never force the old wire off the rim, instead, lay the plate on a soft cushion and cut through the hanger at the back using wire cutters or a hacksaw. Finally, never use the kind of hangers that are glued onto the back of a plate. These hide important makers' marks and can affect unstable glaze.

▼ **Chinese tea kettle, *c.*1880**
Painted in blue-and-white, in traditional style. The late
date means that this is decorative but not expensive.
£40–60/$60–90

▲ **Early Chinese teapot, late 17th century**
The shape derived from a traditional wine vessel, decorated in
famille verte enamels. A curious and rare object from the Kangxi
period. 10cm (4in) high. **£3,000–4,000/$4,500–6,000**

Teapots

The craze for collecting teapots started as early
as the 18th century, as the painter François
Boucher was known to be a keen collector. Today
this is one of the most popular areas of collecting.
Philip Miller, who wrote the standard book on teapot
shapes, put together an extraordinary assemblage
of more than 2,000 teapots, many of which are
displayed in Norwich Castle Museum. It is certainly
a sight to behold – row upon row of containers
for brewing and serving a curious beverage, the
origins of which are shrouded in Asian antiquity.

Tea, of course, came from China, but it is
seldom appreciated that the Chinese themselves
did not, initially, use teapots. In China and Japan
the taking of tea was as much a religious as a
social occasion. Different forms of tea ceremony
were developed, most involving boiling water
poured from a kettle onto powdered tea in a cup
or bowl. Early European visitors to China described
the medicinal and magical qualities of the infusion
known as "cha". A valuable export trade developed,

and by the late 17th century tea was regularly drunk
in England and The Netherlands, using whatever
Chinese porcelain vessels were available. Wine was
served in China from a variety of spouted vessels,
some with separate covers, and Europeans used a
number of these wine pots for brewing tea to the
right strength before pouring the clear liquid into
teabowls. In this way the teapot was invented.

From about 1680, pots specifically for tea were
ordered from China. Their popularity increased as
the demand for tea escalated. Teapots arrived in the
West packed inside chests of tea. Most were sold as
part of a tea "equipage", with matching cups and
saucers, jugs, and sugar bowls. Paintings of 18th-
century families taking tea were popular, and show
clearly how teapots were used at that time. A
servant filled the teapot from a metal kettle of
boiling water. The teapot was placed on the "tea
table" – a new piece of furniture devised for the
purpose. Chinese teapots did not pour smoothly,
and to protect the table from drips the pot was

► Sèvres teapot
Of small size and simple shape,
the painted royal cipher mark
dates this to 1768.
10.5cm (4in). high.
£1,300–1,500/$2,000–2,250

▲ Meissen monkey teapot or coffee pot
Dated *c.*1740–45, this is attributed to J.J. Kändler.
It was impractical to use, but was aimed at
collectors as a novelty. 20cm (7½in).
£8,000–12,000/$12,000–18,000

◄ Eccentric Naples teapot
From a presentation set painted
with topographical views, *c.*1815; a
"Grand Tour" souvenir. This would
have been enormously expensive
when it was made. 13.5cm (5½in)
high. **£4,000–6,000/$6,000–9,000**

placed on a silver tray. Soon teapot stands made of
matching porcelain were ordered from China. The
teapot stand became an integral part of a tea service,
and most teapots were sold with stands at least until
the 1850s. However, a great many teapots have
subsequently become separated from their stands.

Hard-paste porcelain is durable, and Chinese
teapots stood up well to boiling water. Soft-paste
porcelain teapots, on the other hand, were prone to
cracking when hot liquid was poured inside. The
early French soft-paste factories made very few
teapots, whereas Meissen, with its fine hard-paste
material, specialized in fine vessels for serving and
drinking tea. Early Meissen teapots from the 1720s
are exciting but impractical: master-modellers
created their shapes, and their designs were great
to look at, but Meissen pots never poured at all
well. Instead they were placed in china cabinets
and admired for their workmanship, while the lady
of the house served her guests from a cheaper
Chinese porcelain teapot on which she could rely.

Realizing that customers bought teapots for
show as much as for actual use, Meissen made some
teapots just for collectors. Around 1720 a teapot
was made in the shape of a grotesque helmeted
man, while another had an eagle with outspread
wings instead of a normal spout. Twenty years later
teapots as chickens, a monkey, and a squirrel could
be found. In theory these novelties were functional,
but few were ever used. To accompany everyday tea
sets Meissen developed a spout that was shaped as
a bird's head but that poured well. The handles
were remarkably thin, yet strong enough to take the
weight of a pot full of tea. Meissen teapots were
certainly durable, for a surprising number from the
18th century are available to modern-day collectors.

In England the Meissen teapots were copied
at Chelsea, Derby, Bow, and Longton Hall.
Unfortunately, without kaolin English soft-paste
porcelain was vulnerable to cracking during use.
Indeed, the Derby factory is said to have warned its
customers not to use their teapots for making tea.

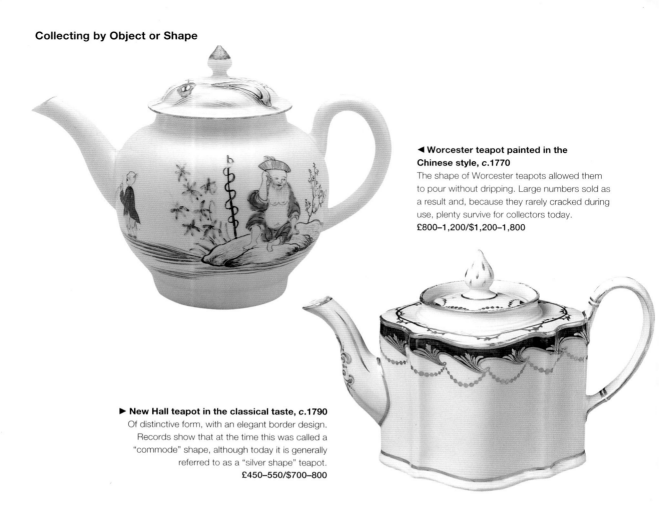

◄ **Worcester teapot painted in the Chinese style, *c*.1770**
The shape of Worcester teapots allowed them to pour without dripping. Large numbers sold as a result and, because they rarely cracked during use, plenty survive for collectors today.
£800–1,200/$1,200–1,800

► **New Hall teapot in the classical taste, *c*.1790**
Of distinctive form, with an elegant border design. Records show that at the time this was called a "commode" shape, although today it is generally referred to as a "silver shape" teapot.
£450–550/$700–800

Soft-paste porcelain cracked when heated too quickly, but the problem was avoided if the teapot was warmed gently, first with lukewarm water and then with hot water, before the boiling water was finally added. This process has been widely used in Britain to protect ceramic teapots, and led to a long tradition known as "warming the pot". Many tea-drinkers today swear that warming the pot makes tea taste better, but in reality we do it only because in the 18th century our teapots would otherwise have cracked.

This weakness wasn't a problem if your teapot was made at Worcester, for a special ingredient called "soaprock" gave Worcester porcelain a unique durability. Worcester teapots rarely cracked and, in addition, a brilliant design meant that they poured beautifully without dripping, while the lid always stayed in position. Worcester created the perfect teapot, and as a result far more survive than from any other English 18th-century maker. Teapot collectors like to get examples from as many different factories as possible, but Worcester teapots outnumber all the rest many times over.

In the 18th century tea was an expensive commodity, within the reach of only the wealthiest households. It was drunk in quite small quantities, and consequently the teapots imported from China before 1740 were small. The size of teapots remained in proportion to the price of tea, and the capacity increased only slightly during the 18th century. However, there are exceptions: some cabaret or dejeuner sets, on matching china trays, came with only two cups and saucers and didn't need large teapots; and at the other extreme, some teapots from the 1760–80 period are of exceptional size. A few of these will have been for tea, but evidence suggests that most oversized examples were for serving punch. Instead of taking a hot punchbowl out to the riders at a fox hunt, a "punch pot" was used to fill stirrup cups with a warm alcoholic punch as riders sat in their saddles. Some were inscribed with the cry "Tally-ho", confirming their hunting association.

Families replaced their tea sets regularly, in order to keep up with the latest fashion. China factories could not afford to be left behind, and

▶ **Coalport "Coalbrookdale" tea kettle, *c*.1830**
A fancy design epitomising the rococo revival. This was
surely made for the china cabinet, as it was too fragile
to survive a tea table. **£1,200–1,500/$1,800–2,250**

▲ **Derby teapot, *c*.1785**
From what would have been a costly cabaret set.
The flower festoons in the border are painted
by the factory's top artist, William Billingsley.
It has a painted mark in blue. 12cm (4½in) tall.
£1,500–2,000/$2,250–3,000

▶ **Berlin teapot, *c*.1805–10**
From an "Egyptian" cabaret set. The decoration
is eccentric and also very rare, accounting for
the high price. **£7,000–9,000/$10,000–13,500**

followed closely on the heels of silversmiths. The
shapes of new silver teapots led the way. In the
1780s round teapots were replaced by oval shapes in
the neo-classical taste, and then oblong teapots
took their place after 1810. Each new shape
introduced by a porcelain-maker can be matched
exactly to a slightly earlier silver prototype. In order
to identify the various teapot shapes, collectors of
English porcelain tend to use Spode factory
names. Extensive archives survive at Spode, and we
therefore know the name given to each new shape
as it was introduced.

Of course, everyone copied everyone else.
Between 1815 and 1825, every principal maker
issued the shape that Spode called "London", which
was an oblong teapot with angled shoulders.
This popular shape was not restricted to Britain –
French, German, and even Russian versions of
the London teapot are known, and we will never
know who made it first. Most teapots are
unmarked, but fortunately there are minor
differences in detail that distinguish the London-
shape teapots made by each porcelain factory. It

takes a while to become familiar with these
differences, but it is worth persevering, for then it
is possible to recognize a rare Swansea example
masquerading as Staffordshire for a fraction of
its real value.

During the 1830s and '40s cheaper tea meant
that teapots were larger and fancier, although few
designs from this period are noted for good taste.
Coalport made an elaborate scrolling shape with
a bird-head spout, inspired by early Meissen,
while Rockingham created a splendid shape on
scroll feet with a crown as the finial. However, there
followed a curious decline in china teapots as the
Victorian era became instead the heyday of the
silver teapot. Fashionable families would show off
by using a silver (or cheaper silver-plated) teapot.
Good Victorian porcelain teapots are therefore
hard to find. Many totally original teapots were
made in majolica by leading pottery makers, but
porcelain novelty teapots are rare. Some very
special china teapots were made, richly jewelled or
with fine piercing, but these were intended for the
display cabinet, not the tea table.

▼ **English porcelain teapot, c.1812–15**
From an "ordinary" tea set, attributed to the Grainger factory in Worcester, with inexpensive black-printed scenes. £150–180/$225–270

▲ **Japanese "eggshell china" teapot, c.1920**
Made at Noritake. The hand-painted geisha girls appealed to customers all over Europe and the USA, and several million sets were exported. £20–30/$30–45

► **Grainger & Co. Worcester "reticulated" teapot, c.1880**
The double-walled construction involving a pierced outer layer and solid interior, means that this could have been used for making tea, had it not been incredibly expensive. £1,400–1,600/$2,000–2,400

Cheap imports arriving from China and Japan in the later Victorian period brought about the revival of the porcelain teapot. Admirers of Japanese art, which was available in Europe in the mid-19th century for the first time for two hundred years, headed a reaction against the over-decorated shapes of the Victorian period. Plain teapots – Chinese red stoneware and traditional blue-and-white forms – became fashionable once more. Some tea connoisseurs used Oriental teapots instead of silver ones. British porcelain tea sets came with cups and saucers, milk jugs, and sugar bowls, but a teapot was still an optional extra: it was regarded as perfectly normal to use a teapot that didn't match the rest of the service.

Most European porcelain teapots made in the 20th century were staunchly traditional, copying antique forms. Meanwhile tea drinkers preferred Japanese eggshell china teapots, and these were imported in overwhelming quantities during the 1920s and 1930s. Modern designs were generally made in pottery, not porcelain. With just a few exceptions, no significant developments were

made in the shapes of porcelain teapots until the 1960s, and then it was the Scandinavian and German factories that led the way.

Rosenthal made some stylish shapes, and in due course Royal Worcester and Wedgwood also made elegant forms. The shape of some 1960s and '70s teapots are very attractive, Wedgwood's "shape 225" in particular, but their success was short-lived. The custom of using a teapot to brew tea went into decline as soon as the teabag was invented, and teabags have now replaced loose tea in just about every nation. A teabag on a string with a tag attached can be dunked straight into a cup or mug, making the teapot sadly obsolete.

While many teapots sit in cupboards today unloved and unused, collecting teapots has never been a more popular hobby. There is, understandably, a strong preference for antique examples, although cheap Asian teapots are also popular because they represent such good value for money. At large antiques shows there are plenty of teapots from which to choose, so it is

▲ **Southampton Pier teapot, *c*.1910**
A cheap, printed souvenir. On the bottom
it is clearly stamped "Made in Germany".
£30–40/$45–60

▲ **Rosenthal teapot by Walter Gropius, 1966**
This is a reissue of an earlier design by Walter Gropius, the
important modernist designer. If it had been original it would be
much more valuable. £300–500/$450–750

often best to specialize in a particular type or
period in order to scale down the search.

When buying teapots always make sure that
the lid matches. The pattern must link up in some
way – if there is a border design on the lid and not
on the teapot itself, this is a reason to be suspicious.
Some element of the decoration used on the teapot
should always be repeated on the lid. The lid must
not be either too loose or too tight, and there
must always be a tiny hole pierced through
somewhere in the lid. The purpose of this vent
hole is nothing to do with firing in the kiln,
but instead allows tea to pour from the spout
without spurting. Sometimes the lid of a teapot
and a sugar box have been mixed up and a teapot is
sold with a sucrier lid instead. This often happens
with larger oval teapots, and so the absence of a
vent hole is an important clue. Also, wherever
possible, avoid teapots with chipped or broken
spouts. As the most vulnerable part of the vessel
the spout is frequently chipped, and ingenious
restoration to disguise such damage is all too
common these days.

Collecting
Coffee Pots

▲ **Royal Worcester kookaburra coffee pot, *c*.1914**
Made for the Australian market, lightly moulded and
painted; signed by the artist. £500–700/$750–1,000

Since the mid-17th century, coffee and tea
have been served in different shaped pots.
The earliest silver coffee pots were tall with
long, low-set spouts. Potters followed silver
forms, and it became traditional for coffee to
be served from a tall pot. English tea services
normally included sets of coffee cups, but it
is rare to find a porcelain coffee pot, as silver
coffee pots were used instead. The situation
was different on the Continent: early German
porcelain coffee pots were as common as
teapots, and tea sets usually included both
shapes. Continental coffee pots normally have
pointed lips, like a jug, and are sometimes
referred to as "coffee jugs".

Coffee pots' generous size presented
decorators with excellent opportunities, and
wonderful examples were made at Meissen
from the 1720s to '30s. After 1760 the price
of coffee fell, and coffee pots became even
larger – some Worcester examples after 1770
can be surprisingly large. English coffee pots
are generally scarce. In spite of the popularity of
coffee cans in the early 19th century, coffee pots
vanished almost completely in English porcelain.
They came back into fashion in the 20th century,
generally small and part of separate coffee sets.
Compared with teapots, the number of coffee
pot-collectors is relatively small.

▲ Meissen tea and coffee service, c.1770
Painted with Cupids in clouds and a "mosaic"
border. The shapes include a coffee pot,
teapot, milk jug, slop bowl, spoon tray, and
tea canister. £3,500–4,500/$5,250–6,750

▼ Coalport part tea service, c.1800–05
With very simple "Picturesque" landscapes.
The teapot sits on a matching stand.
£500–600/$750–900

Tea Services

A great many tea services have been split up over the years, so it is satisfying to come across an entire set still intact after maybe two centuries. They sometimes survive simply because they cost so much money and their original owners were afraid to use them. Kept for best in china cabinets, tea services were displayed and admired. The standard components of a porcelain tea service developed out of shapes imported from China in the 17th century. Potters in France and Germany, who were strongly influenced by silver forms, adapted these to suit European customs and traditions.

Since the 1740s the composition of tea sets has changed surprisingly little. A teapot for brewing the tea was accompanied in deluxe services by a teapot stand to protect the table. Lumps of sugar chipped off a sugarloaf were kept free from flies in a lidded sugar box, generally known as a sucrier (its French name). In cheaper sets an open sugar bowl replaced the covered sucrier. A small milk jug was occasionally also protected by a lid.

Teacups with handles (or teabowls without) were provided in sets of six or twelve with the same number of saucers. Coffee cups or straight-sided coffee cans were also included in the majority of tea services until the mid-19th century. As tea and coffee were never served at the same time, the coffee cups and teacups usually shared the same saucers; either six or twelve coffee cups would accompany a set of twelve teacups and saucers. Coffee pots were normal additions to a Continental tea service, but in English sets coffee pots are rarities, as silver was the preferred material.

A single large bowl was included in most sets made before 1900. This was a slop bowl, or waste bowl, into which the dregs were poured before the cups were re-filled. Two large plates on which were served cakes or savouries are sometimes known as bread-and-butter plates, for it was usual to serve slices of buttered bread with tea in the 18th century. These plates are also sometimes called saucer-dishes because of their shape. One is

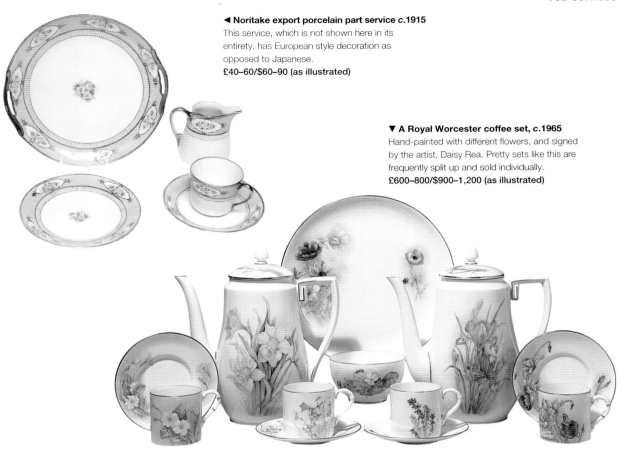

◀ **Noritake export porcelain part service** *c.*1915
This service, which is not shown here in its entirety, has European style decoration as opposed to Japanese.
£40–60/$60–90 (as illustrated)

▼ **A Royal Worcester coffee set,** *c.*1965
Hand-painted with different flowers, and signed by the artist, Daisy Rea. Pretty sets like this are frequently split up and sold individually.
£600–800/$900–1,200 (as illustrated)

normally bigger than the other, and the smaller of the two occasionally functioned as a stand for the slop bowl. Eighteenth- century tea services usually included a small oval spoontray, used to pass a single teaspoon among the guests. A tea canister, or sometimes a matching pair of canisters, was a common addition to an 18th-century tea set, although these are not found after 1800. Tea plates or side plates, one for each cup and saucer, were not introduced until the mid-19th century, when fancy cakes replaced simple bread and butter.

Large households usually replaced their tea services with each generation, selecting a more fashionable design and condemning the previous set to the attic or the back of a cupboard. Particularly delicate sets, such as those made in Noritake eggshell from Japan, were too fragile to use, and most often ended up shut away in boxes. Families with lots of space are now unpacking their sets and putting them on display, but few homes have the room to spare. Hardly any old

sets are used any more, as today most homes use mugs that can go in the dishwasher.

Some collectors of a single pattern go to enormous lengths to bring together all the parts of a matching tea service. Other tea-set owners are concerned if a few pieces are missing, and engage in desperate searches to replace any missing cups. For every enthusiast who believes a tea service should be complete, there are many others who feel it is far more practical to split sets up. Today there are surprisingly few buyers for complete tea sets. In almost every case, when a set is sold a dealer will buy it and break it up straight away. The teapot will be offered to a teapot collector, the spoontray to a spoontray collector, and likewise for the sucrier. Cups and saucers are normally sold separately, or as "trios" of a coffee cup, teacup, and single saucer. Dealers who have the patience to sell the pieces separately can often make a considerable profit, as the component parts of complete tea sets are amazingly good value.

▶ **Chinese Export porcelain beaker, c.1740–50**
Held in a "trembleuse" saucer. The decoration is typically Chinese, while the shape was probably made for the French market.
£300–400/$450–600

▲ **Meissen teacup and saucer, c.1770**
From an everyday teaset painted with simple flowers, with the Meissen crossed swords and dot marks.
£130–160/$200–240

▶ **Doccia cup and saucer, c.1760**
With very intricate relief-moulded and enamelled decoration depicting figures from mythology. Many later copies are recorded.
£800–1,200/$1,200–1,800

Cups & Saucers

Afternoon tea should be served in dainty china cups and saucers, but this centuries-old tradition is at risk of dying out, to be replaced by the modern fashion for drinking tea out of mugs. A mug may be practical for dishwashers and microwaves, but it's just not the same. Sipping tea from a delicate china cup is a way of bonding with porcelain – a unique pleasure and a special treat for an unashamed porcelain enthusiast such as myself.

Small shallow bowls were used in Chinese tea ceremonies in the days of the Song dynasty (960–1279). The first teabowls were not placed on saucers or plates but were held with both hands, the fingers supporting the bowl beneath the rim, or sometimes with just one hand. When tea arrived in Europe, Chinese teabowls were provided to patrons who were unaccustomed to the use of porcelain. Europeans were reluctant to place hot teabowls directly onto fine furniture, and preferred to put them down on the little Chinese porcelain dishes that they used for pickles or sauces (which is how

they came to be known as "saucers"). Orders were sent to China for matching stands for the teabowls and beakers.

In Germany teabowls and saucers (which were there called *untertassen*, for they literally sit under the cup) were first made in milk-white glass that mimicked porcelain, but it was hard to hold a hot glass teabowl. Instead tea was poured into the wide saucer to cool, and soon people started drinking tea directly from it. Some parts of society looked down on this custom with disdain, while in other households it was deemed perfectly acceptable to slurp from the saucer. Tea-drinking certainly brought out different customs in different places: the English and Dutch coped with teabowls, but in Germany they were disliked. So the Meissen porcelain factory developed handles on teacups, just like those on coffee cups. This fashion spread across the Continent through Austria and France, although handles on teacups were not common in England until much later, in the 19th century.

Collecting Teabowls

▼ **Chinese "ruby ground" teabowl and saucer, c.1730**
Made during the Yongzheng period, these are of almost eggshell thinness. Although made for export, this dainty decoration is very much in the Chinese taste. £700–900/$1,050–1,350

▲ **Liverpool porcelain teabowl and saucer, c.1785**
Attributed to Seth Pennington's factory. The larger size of this example is typical of the later 18th century.
£150–180/$225–270

Coffee had always been drunk from taller, handled cups that were normally passed round on a tray and did not need saucers. In 17th-century England these were called "capuchines" and were often made in silver or stoneware. Porcelain coffee cups became popular in France early in the 18th century. They were made at the St Cloud factory, and placed in deep saucers with raised central ridges for stability, which became known as "trembleuse" saucers. After 1730 Chinese tea sets copied Meissen by including coffee cups alongside teacups and saucers. The coffee cups were still served on silver trays without their own saucers, but if hosts did want to give their guests saucers for coffee cups they would use the ones provided with the tea-cups, for it was never the custom to serve tea and coffee at the same time. Of course today there are usually insufficient saucers left in an old service to match all the surviving cups. Instead they are displayed or collected as "trios" comprising a teacup (or teabowl), a coffee cup, and a single saucer.

The Chinese custom of drinking tea from small porcelain bowls was widely adopted in Europe. Many fine 18th-century paintings show families taking tea, and it is clear from these that there was no uniform way to drink from a teabowl. Some ladies and gentlemen held the rim firmly between the thumb and forefinger of one hand, while others used two hands to hold both sides of the bowl. Some elegant ladies held the foot of a teabowl daintily in their fingertips, others held just the saucer while sipping from the bowl balanced in its middle. Etiquette seems to have been left to the individual.

Curiously, there are very few teabowl collectors. Cups are more plentiful, as I suppose they are easier to display. Odd teabowls usually cost far less than single cups, and they are also much cheaper than when sold with their saucers. In terms of potting, Chinese teabowls are far superior to coffee cups; many teabowls are of eggshell thinness. Cups and saucers provide a wonderful opportunity to start an exciting collection. Teabowls can best be appreciated when they are held in the hand, although for showing a collection of teabowls a high shelf is an advantage, as more of the decoration can be seen. Placing teabowls on small Chinese turned-wood stands, or individual Perspex blocks, can make an enormous difference to the overall effect.

▼ **Noritake eggshell cup and saucer, *c.*1920**
Superbly potted and hand painted. Many of
the huge numbers made were moulded with the
head of a geisha girl in the bottom of the cup.
£5–10/$8–15

▲ **Coalport coffee cup and saucer, *c.*1812–15**
This popular, so-called "London" shape
was made by a great many manufacturers.
£70–100/$105–150

◄ **Russian "Imperial Porcelain" cup and
saucer from the "Raphael Service"**
Ordered by Tzar Alexander III, and dated
1894. Although stylish, the real value
is in the historical importance of the service.
£2,500–3,500/$3,750–5,250

Just as the shapes and uses of cups and saucers
followed different traditions in different countries,
attitudes to collecting also vary greatly today. In
England coffee cups are often thought of as single
items worthy of collecting by themselves, and
indeed some early cups can be very costly. Coffee
cans – straight-sided cups made in the early 1800s –
are particularly popular with collectors, many of
whom actually prefer them without saucers. On the
Continent things are different, and single coffee
cups are regarded as seriously incomplete. Single
Meissen or Sèvres coffee cups without saucers are
positively cheap in comparison with English cups,
and it is possible to collect examples of single
cups from different German or French factories
for quite a modest outlay.

The custom of drinking from the saucer waned
in Europe, although in the United States it lingered
on with the use of "cup-plates". These were usually
made of glass, on which the empty cups were placed
while the tea was drunk from the saucer. This
tradition finally died out in the 1850s when saucers
became shallow and flat. The saucer was now held
in one hand and the cup in the other. For stability a
slightly sunken well was moulded in the centre
of the saucer so that the cup would not slide
about. A well in the saucer is therefore indicative
of post-1850 manufacture.

There are other kinds of cups and saucers.
Chocolate cups are traditionally like coffee cups,
only larger. Some chocolate cups have two handles
and are often called "caudle cups", as caudle (a
sweet medicinal broth) was served in similar
vessels. Another very different kind of tea service
became popular in Victorian times, although it
originated in the 18th century. Breakfast sets
included cups that were of exceptional size, for
at the breakfast table it was usual to drink tea
in copious quantities. These oversized breakfast
cups and saucers are surprisingly unpopular with
collectors today. On the other hand, moustache cups
are highly collectable curiosities: some Victorian
and Edwardian breakfast cups were fitted with a
little bridge below the rim, to stop a gentleman's
moustache falling in his tea. Many large cups and
saucers were never intended to be used at all. For

instance, a "cabinet cup" was for display only, usually given as a present for some special occasion. Cabinet cups are art objects, representing the greatest skills of the porcelain decorator.

In the early 1900s a set of coffee cups and saucers became especially popular as a wedding gift. These were normally sold in fitted presentation boxes, complete with six matching silver spoons, and most have remained unused in their boxes ever since. When sets are boxed in this way they are more valuable when complete. However, aside from these boxed sets, these is surprisingly little advantage in keeping sets of cups and saucers together. As they are no longer used for practical purposes collectors don't want six or a dozen all the same, and prefer variety. When tea services are sold by auction the buyer is very often a dealer, who will make a significant profit by selling the cups and saucers separately to individual collectors.

Collecting cups and saucers has been a popular hobby since the late 19th century, especially in Germany and the USA. It was common to give a single small cup and saucer as a present when visiting a friend. Known as "*demitasses*", these half-sized cups were also never used, and instead looked pretty on display. Today collecting cups and saucers is more popular than ever. Collectors can buy special stands to display a cup with its saucer standing up behind. Alternatively you can set out cups on their saucers, but if you do it is terribly important to cut out a circle of cloth and put it under the cup foot-rim to prevent abrasion.

Recently there has been a particular interest in cups and saucers from buyers in Japan. In a country where the tea ceremony is deeply rooted in native tradition, collectors like to use special teacups for drinking tea. This is a wonderful development, as it has been a tragedy that so many porcelain tea services have never been used – the Japanese eggshell tea sets especially. Some Japanese buyers even enjoy using valuable early Meissen and Worcester cups and saucers, which is perhaps stretching things a bit far. However, I do think that many more 19th- and 20th-century cups should be used for their intended purpose. It makes a lovely change from drinking tea out of a thick pottery mug.

▲ Sèvres milk jug of distinctive shape, c.1765
This example is by the sought-after painter André-Vincent Vielliard, and is raised on three twig feet. 9.5cm (3in) high.
£1,200–1,600/$1,800–2,400

▲ New Hall "Helmet"-shaped milk jug, c.1785–90
So-called because it resembles the shape of an ancient Greek helmet when turned upside down.
£350–450/$525–675

◄ Worcester "sparrow beak" milk jug, c.1765–70.
This shape, named after its neat, pointed lip, is enormously popular with collectors.
£350–400/$525–600

Milk Jugs & Cream Jugs

The custom of serving milk in tea and cream in coffee is essentially European; the Chinese rarely diluted their beverages in this way. A range of jugs of various shapes has been made at different times to accompany tea sets, and there remains much confusion as to how each was used. The earliest Meissen porcelain tea equipages, from the 1720s and 1730s, contained smaller versions of the coffee-pot shape, for use with either hot or cold milk. In Germany jugs were almost always provided with separate covers or lids, and Chinese export porcelain milk jugs were normally covered too, whereas most early French or English tea sets had open-topped jugs instead. The origin of many porcelain milk jugs is contemporary silver, for it is possible to find silver prototypes for most popular porcelain forms.

If a china jug is small, it is popularly called a cream jug, whereas larger jugs are known today as milk jugs. However, in surviving records from the 18th century even small jugs were normally noted as being for milk. Cream was usually served in a creamboat, which was a smaller version of a sauceboat (*see* pages 118-119 for examples). Milk jugs can be surprisingly small and rather dainty, so it is easy to understand their appeal to collectors; the smaller examples are the most desirable. Condition matters a great deal, for the lip of a jug can chip easily. A milk jug should end with a tiny point on the lip, and if this is broken the whole form is spoilt. The most popular 18th-century English shape was the "sparrow beak" jug – so-called because the neat, triangular lip looks like the beak of a garden bird. Derived from Chinese shapes and larger, early Meissen jugs, the sparrow beak jug was popular at Worcester from the early 1750s until 1790, and comes in a huge variety of patterns. Many other English china factories made sparrow beak jugs, which provides great scope for collectors.

Some English sparrow beak jugs were aimed at the Continental market and were sold with

◄ **Staffordshire porcelain milk jug painted with roses, *c.*1830**
This popular pattern was made by many different factories. As most sets were unmarked, a positive attribution to the maker is generally impossible.
£90–130/$130–200

► **Royal Worcester "flat-backed" jug, 1886**
Decorated in imitation of old ivory. This was the most popular jug shape at Worcester, and was made in at least seven different sizes. This one is 10cm (4in) high.
£150–200/$225–300

◄ **French jug, possibly Samson**
Although in the "Empire" style of the early 19th century, this French jug, painted with fable subjects, is a 20th-century copy. £200–300/$300–450

matching lids. Gradually lids were made for jugs in some English services too. It is important to look for signs that tell you a jug once had a lid. Many milk jugs are complete without lids, while others cry out for a missing cover. If a pattern on a jug includes a border design around the inside lip, then the jug had no lid as it would have covered up the decoration. If a jug did have a lid, the border was usually placed around the outside rim of the neck so it could be seen. There are some exceptions, but this observation can help prevent a costly mistake, for nobody wants to pay as much for a jug that is missing a lid and is thus incomplete.

The milk jug was always modelled so that it was in proportion to the size of the cups in a tea service. As tea became cheaper, cups got larger and more milk was needed to dilute the tea. Nineteenth-century tea sets can include fairly large jugs. Popular shapes were oval and then oblong from *c.*1800–25, but jugs returned to circular forms again as tastes changed over successive decades. Subtle differences

in the shape of the jug can enable identification in some cases, although it is surprising how few jugs were marked by the maker before the latter part of the 19th century. In many Victorian households porcelain jugs in teasets were replaced by silver or silver-plated examples, or else by glass jugs. Sets of three large pottery jugs were used for storing and serving milk in many homes. Luxury versions were made in porcelain, while many ornamental jugs were made, more for display than for serving milk. Twentieth-century coffee sets often include very small jugs for cream, rather than milk, and these can form a delightful and inexpensive collection.

Naturally these are execptions, and some of the finely decorated jugs by major manufacturers will be costly, especially when painted by top artists. Royal Worcester, for example, specialized in pretty jugs that were often sold on their own as ornaments. A series of these, from the 1920s–'30s, were shaped as tiny barrels, painted with birds by William Powell. Many very tiny jugs were made as miniatures.

▲ **Worcester "high-footed" sauceboat, c.1755**
The shape is copied from contemporary English silver, while the decoration is painted in blue in the Chinese style. £800–1,200/$1,200–1,800

◀ **Chinese double-lipped sauceboat, c.1750–55**
With armorial decoration, made for the Export market. This was probably intended just for display, as if the original owner had ever used it the contents would have covered up his coat of arms. £500–650/$750–975

Sauceboats & Creamboats

In the 18th century sauces were a very important element in otherwise fairly tasteless cooking. Thick gravy and creamy sauces were poured from vessels that would really impress dinner guests. Before the 1740s this meant fine silver in England. The Chinese copied many European silver shapes, but for some reason the supply of porcelain sauceboats from the Orient never matched the demand, leaving the market wide open. All of the early English china-makers produced sauceboats in great variety, some in the most exciting forms. Sauces and gravy were mostly served very hot, and sauceboats were sometimes kept warm by setting them down in hot water. Worcester's durable "soaprock" formula was at a great advantage here. More Worcester sauceboats survive than from all other makers, which is indeed fortunate as Worcester made such innovative shapes. Its "high-footed" sauceboats were very popular in the 1750s, and no wonder, for these are exciting rococo shapes. They replaced a rather different shape made at Bow and

Limehouse from the late 1740s, which was raised on three lion's-paw feet, inspired by silver sauceboats of similar date. A different sort was made with a flat base or a low foot. These were cheaper, and so gradually replaced the more interesting high-footed versions. All sauceboats were sold as pairs to begin with, and we know from contemporary price lists that they were very expensive. Consequently, grand households looked after their sauceboats, and plenty survive, offering a great deal of scope for collectors.

Despite the attraction of these pieces, collectors have traditionally avoided sauceboats in favour of smaller objects, which means that many super examples are surprisingly affordable. However, this situation is slowly changing, and there are now a number of specialist sauceboat collectors. English porcelain dominates this field – Worcester and Bow made beautiful pieces that today cost upwards of £1,000/$1,500, although they should cost far more. Some fantastic shapes are also available from Continental makers, and these too are

◄ **Very fancy sauceboat and matching stand in the "Empire" style**
By a leading Paris maker such as Dagoty or Darté Frères, *c*.1810–12.
£4,000–5,000/ $6,000–7,500

▼ **Small cream boat, *c*.1756–8**
Made at the Vauxhall porcelain factory. Early English cream boats are always expensive.
£3,500–4,500/$5,250–6,750

◄ **"Dolphin ewer", *c*.1770**
Derby cream boat with two dolphins moulded beneath the shell-shaped lip. Versions were made by various English makers. **£400–450/$600–675**

underpriced. For example, Meissen made some wonderful creations to accompany important services, and some of these are sculptural triumphs. On the Continent a double sauceboat shape was popular, with two handles and two pouring lips. These were imported from China in fair numbers, although they never really took off in England.

Cream was served in vessels that resemble sauceboats but are much smaller. Collectors rarely agree at which point a small sauceboat can be classified as a creamboat, but the distinction is important, for while sauceboats are often reasonably priced, creamboats are far more expensive. These delightful little objects are unique to Britain. Often called "cream ewers" when originally made, they were a speciality of Worcester and its forerunners at Bristol and Limehouse. Early examples were often hexagonal or octagonal in section, with delicate rococo moulding. They combine shapes of English silver with Chinese painting in blue-and-white, or simple scenes in *famille rose* filling the reserved panels. During the 1760s and 1770s a range of distinctive creamboat shapes was made by many factories. They copied each other, so that it is possible to collect the same basic forms made at Worcester, Derby, Liverpool, and so on. The "Dolphin Ewer" has embossed shell motifs and a fish-like handle; the "Chelsea Ewer" was derived from an earlier shape made at Chelsea with embossed spiralling leaves, while the "Gadroon Boat" was a simple lobed shape with moulded gadrooned rims. Some of the most pleasing creamboats were made at the Vauxhall factory in simple blue-and-white patterns. Caughley, New Hall, and the Pennington Liverpool factories made creamboats until *c*.1790, when the fashion died out. It is curious how few sauceboats and creamboats were made after the 18th century. Double sauceboats continued on the Continent, usually fixed onto stands that replaced handles, and later 19th-century sauceboats on fixed stands can be decorative and rarely cost much money.

▼ **Pair of Chelsea vases, *c*.1762**
Painted with allegories of The Elements, probably by John
Donaldson, with gold anchor marks. These were inspired by
Sèvres examples of similar date. **£6,000–10,000/$9,000–15,000**

▶ ***Imari*-decorated Japanese vase** Painted in the
distinctive *Imari* palette with an unfolded screen zig-zagging
around the vase, late 17th or early 18th century. 93cm
(36in) high. **£10,000–15,000/$15,000–22,500 (a pair)**

Vases

There is a mistaken belief that vases were
originally intended for holding flowers. While
this was occasionally the case, the finest porcelain
vases were far too precious ever to use in this way.
Rather, vases were art objects, often as the focal
point of a room display – a fine set of vases can look
stunning. Vases developed from the clay vessels
used for storage in ancient times. The best Greek
and Roman vases survive from the tombs in which
they were placed as precious offerings. The Chinese
did the same with their pottery storage jars, and by
the Ming period really wonderful porcelain jars
were placed in tombs – the kinds of vessel that were
used as sacred objects in shrines.

Fine Ming blue-and-white jars and vases are
incredibly valuable – they can fetch several million
pounds/dollars – for they are perfect in form and
decoration, as befits the emperors for whom they
were made. At the other extreme, some small vases
from the Ming dynasty, especially those made in
provincial kilns, are today curiously inexpensive.

The reason for this is the proliferation of shipwreck
cargoes from which great quantities have been
recovered (*see* page 33). This is particularly true
of "jarlets" – in effect, miniature vases used for
offerings in shrines and temples. Examples dating
back 500 years can be bought for as little as
£30/$45 – a real bargain for a genuine Ming vase.

From the later 17th century, Chinese porcelain
vases were made specifically for export to Europe.
Some were placed in sets on top of fine pieces
of furniture, while others were intended for
mantelpieces in great homes. They became known
as *garnitures de cheminée* (which translates as
"decoration of chimneys"), and would be displayed
in sets of three, five, or seven matching vases.
These mantelpiece garnitures usually combined
sets of covered vases or jars with open-topped
beaker-shaped vases. Many have been split up
over the years, so it is wonderful and rare to see a
set that has survived intact for three centuries as
a complete garniture.

▼ **Spode trumpet-shaped vase, *c*.1820**
Decorated in Japanese *Imari* style, intended for spills of wood or paper for lighting the fire. 15cm (6in) high. **£350–400/$525–600**

▼ **Chinese vase, Jiaqing period**
Dated 1797–1820. Moulded and pierced with dogs of Fo among clouds picked out in *famille rose* enamels. The shape, intended as a joss stick holder in a Chinese shrine, was exported to Europe as a spill vase. **£300–400/$450–600**

◄ *Famille-rose* **Chinese vase, *c*.1900**
A large vase enamelled in Canton for the export trade. The traditional *famille rose* scenes were popular in Britain where pairs of these vases sold in great numbers and in many different sizes. 51cm (20in) high. **£400–550/$600–825**

Some vases imported into Europe in the Kangxi period, early in the 18th century, were of truly monumental size – suitable for display in palaces and grand halls. Augustus the Strong, King of Saxony, collected Chinese blue-and-white vases for his china rooms, and on one occasion he swapped a whole battalion of dragoons for a set of massive Chinese porcelain vases. These survive in Dresden today, along with copies of Chinese vases that were made in Augustus's porcelain factory at Meissen.

Japanese porcelain vases were even more precious than Chinese. Hexagonal jars and covers in delicate Kakiemon porcelain are today known as Hampton Court Vases, for in the 1690s a set of these was treasured by Queen Mary II in her royal apartments at Hampton Court. Augustus loved them too, and set his Meissen factory the task of making imitations. Direct copies were made, as well as original designs that combined Japanese and Chinese decoration in wonderful colours on powerful shapes. Marked with the King's personal

cipher, "AR" for "Augustus Rex", these Meissen vases from the 1730s–40s are breathtaking examples of the art of porcelain. Today they can fetch up to £100,000/$150,000 a pair, but beware of the many copies made much later in Dresden. Popular vase shapes remained in production for a very long time and a great many 19th-century vases were derived from these shapes from the previous century.

Copies of Chinese and Japanese vases were made in France at Chantilly early in the 18th century. Later, at Vincennes and Sèvres, the fashion for rococo resulted in a very different appearance, quite unlike anything that had gone before. Striking turquoise, pink, and green grounds suited the reserved panels of birds, fruit, and flowers, and the intricate tooled gilding, while the modelled shapes were superbly designed to match the latest rococo interiors. Sèvres vases were conceived to form garnitures, the central vase flanked by a pair of a different, but complementary, shapes in the same colours. Eighteenth-century Sèvres vases are very

Painted with panels of classical figures on a richly gilded, multicoloured ground, with a pseudo Vienna shield or "beehive" mark. 33cm (13in) in height. £800–1,200/$1,200–1,800

◄ **Minton vase decorated in _Pâte-sur-pâte_ technique**
By the important decorator Louis Solon, made c.1876–8. The design is essentially Roman, adapted to suit the High-Victorian taste. £10,000–15,000/ $15,000–22,500

expensive, but you only have to see the examples on display in great museums around the world to understand why.

Meissen influenced, as well as other German makers, the earliest English porcelain factories – for direct copies of Meissen vases were made at Chelsea and Worcester in the 1750s. These were followed by very original exercises in English rococo, an area in which Chelsea excelled during the Gold Anchor period of the 1760s. In spirit these Chelsea vases copied Sèvres, but in shape they were even more eccentric. Many rococo vase shapes had pierced shoulders or cut-out lids that released into the room the sweet scent of pot-pourri. Some pot-pourri vases had inner covers that preserved the odour of the perfumed dried flower petals kept inside. The alternative name of "scent jar" was used for these early air fresheners. In addition, Meissen vases with applied china flowers were sprinkled with perfume to make the room smell sweet.

Vases were rarely used for cut flowers. In grand homes bulbs were cultivated in greenhouses and then brought into the house when in bloom.

Bulbs were grown in metal containers that fitted inside porcelain vases and could be replaced with fresh bulbs as each flower faded. With the cultivation of new varieties of bulb, different vase forms were introduced to show them off to best advantage. Small jardinières, also known as cachepots, were filled with soil and drained through a hole in the bottom into separate bases. Larger rectangular or semi-circular "bough pots" became fashionable from the late 18th century, to sit on mantelpieces in the formal classical style. The idea originated in Paris and was copied in England, where many fancy examples were made during the Regency period. Some bough pots and jardinières survive with their original metal liners. Today it is fashionable to fill antique vases with dried flowers and use them for their intended purpose as great decoration.

A different kind of vase also sat on mantelpieces in Regency times. Spill vases held long sticks of rolled-up paper or thin wood, used to light pipes or candles. They were also known as "match pots", as a match was another name for a spill. Small

► **Royal Copenhagen vase in Art Nouveau style**
Dated *c.*1915–20 with underglaze decoration. The size is unknown, but a 30cm vase would have a value of **£600–900/$900–1,350**

◄ **Dresden "Augustus Rex" vase**
Dated *c.*1870–80, this was decorated in Helena Wolfsohn's workshop and marked with a copy of the "AR" cipher used in early Meissen. Vases like this were always sold in pairs.
£650–800/$1,000–1,200 (the pair)

▲ **Meissen vase, late 19th century**
One of a pair based on a design from 1750 but using the bright "gloss gold" popular at the end of the 19th century. It has a crossed swords mark.
£1,000–1,300/$1,500–2,000 (the pair)

cylindrical or trumpet-shaped spill vases were sold in pairs for the mantel shelf, or as single spill vases to accompany desk sets or writing sets, for spills were also used to light tapers for melting sealing wax. Spill vases are very popular with collectors, as they are neat and small in size, and, being luxury objects in their day, they are usually decorated to a very high standard.

In Victorian times highly decorative vases were made to add colour and ornament to ordinary homes. Many were inexpensive, and rarely cost much even over a century later, so they can be good value, although cheap quality should be avoided. At the other extreme there are many very costly vases that represent extraordinary workmanship. A few could, in theory, hold flowers or pot-pourri, but in reality these were cabinet pieces, made for display only. In Dresden and Limoges all manner of vases were made to reproduce the old styles of Meissen, Sèvres, and Vienna. They copy the patterns of the best 18th-century masterworks, but they were not made as fakes deliberately to deceive – they are simply sumptuous decoration intended to brighten

up the well-to-do homes of more than a century ago. Their high price-tags today reflect the lavish workmanship, nothing more.

Alongside these copies of the past, a great many modern porcelain vases were made early in the 20th century. Some were avant-garde in the Art Nouveau taste, followed by others in the Art Deco style of the 1920s. The major Continental makers, especially Meissen, Sèvres, Berlin, and Copenhagen, created wonderful and totally original vases inspired by nature and geometry. In England, on the other hand, surprisingly few really modern vases were produced. The established china factories headed by Royal Worcester and Royal Crown Derby stuck to traditional vase shapes, painted by fine artists and finished with exquisite gilding. Expensive at the time, these are very collectable today when signed by top painters and in perfect condition. A small chip devastates the value, so be sure not to use precious porcelain for displaying flowers. Value is also affected if a vase has lost its original lid – it is important to check factory records to see if the vase had a matching lid when made.

◄ **Madonna plaque, c.1870–80**
A German porcelain plaque, probably decorated in Florence with a copy of Raphael's Madonna. A very faint outline print was used as a guide to the painter. £200–300/$300–450

▲ **Berlin KPM Plaque, c.1890**
Painted in the Wagner workshop in Vienna. The quality is very high and the subject is popular. It measures 26.5 x 20cm (10½ x 8in)
£6,000–8,000/$9,000–12,000

► **Vienna plaque, 1825**
Signed and dated by Joseph Nigg, who is regarded as the finest of all porcelain flower-painters; his work sells for astronomic sums.
£40,000–60,000/$60,000–90,000

Porcelain Plaques

Painting a plaque was an enameller's dream as it was creating a work of art that could be framed and hung on a wall like a canvas. While collectors regard porcelain-painting as a legitimate form of fine art, china-painters working in the china factories saw themselves as merely humble craftsmen, doing a job of work simply to earn wages. Some top china-painters were well paid, of course, and occasionally were even permitted to sign their work. As a result a few painters aspired to greater things, and rather than trying to squeeze their compositions onto teacups or vases, they relished the opportunity to paint on flat plaques. Although some porcelain factories allowed their decorators to paint plaques in their own time, most regarded plaques as frivolous objects that merely encouraged painters to show off.

Making china plaques was a skilful business, for thin slabs of porcelain tend to distort in the kiln. Totally flat plaques were very expensive, and few china-painters could afford the luxury. A popular alternative was to create a plaque by cutting a circle or a rectangle of white china from the centre of a faulty plate or dish. Painters were allowed to practise their skills on plaques made from chopped-up plates, to give to friends and family. When these were placed in frames, it was not immediately apparent that the rough rims had been nibbled down with a pair of pliers. Porcelain plaques that are roughly cut out from larger slabs have usually been painted by china artists out of their usual work time, and this is why many are signed and dated. Factories rarely let their painters sign otherwise.

Talented artists bought blank plaques from specialist manufacturers, and the finest were enamelled by independent painters working in their own studios. The best plaque-maker by far was the German state factory in Berlin, for it was able to fire massive slabs of glazed porcelain without blemish or distortion. As a sign of quality, Berlin plaques were marked with the impressed royal stamp (a sceptre), and the initials "KPM". From 1840 to 1870 vast numbers of KPM plaques

▲ English bone china plaque, c.1880
Signed by Frederick Sutton, an independent china painter.
Decorated blank Staffordshire plaques are rarely as expensive as
plaques from major manufacturers. £1,500–1,800/$2,250–2,400

▼ Royal Worcester oval plaque, dated 1924
By Harry Davis, who is famous for his original studies of sheep.
The colouring is typical of the 1920s. 24.5cm (9½in) wide.
£6,000–8,000/$9,000–12,000

were painted in enamelling studios in Dresden, Vienna, and even Rome. China-painters copied the works of famous old masters displayed in art galleries. Framed porcelain plaques were sold to wealthy tourists, who admired the smooth shiny surfaces and seemingly invisible brushstrokes.

The best plaque painters used KPM blanks, and proudly signed their work. Many survive with paper labels still attached giving the address of the decorating studio. The Wagner workshop in Vienna was responsible for stunning portrait plaques in the style of contemporary artists. R. Dittrich, Otto Wustlich, and other fine German enamellers faithfully reproduced the old masters. Joseph Fischer and Joseph Nigg specialized in flower compositions at the Vienna state factory, where some of the finest plaques were made. Plaques of exceptional quality were also made at Meissen and Sèvres, and sold to appreciative connoisseurs. Porcelain plaques need to be examined closely, for cheaper examples were made all over Dresden. Watch out for signs of a

printed outline used to reduce the costs of freehand painting. Photography and lithographic printing were used to make cheap, decorative plaques later in the 19th century, and recently clever fakes of KPM plaques have been made in the Far East, using modern colour-reproduction methods.

It is much harder to paint fine detail on English china than on Continental porcelain, and English makers also had great difficulty producing large plaques. But in the mid-19th century Davenport patented a method of making very thin china plaques that could be sold to independent artists. Subsequently Minton, Doulton, and Royal Worcester made plaques signed by their own top artists. Some can be very valuable, but large numbers of amateur china-painters also decorated plaques, so it is important to judge the quality as well as the maker. Recently Bronté Porcelain has produced English plaques of exceptional size painted by Tony Young and Milwyn Holloway. These are surely destined to be highly collectable in the future.

▼ **A Mennecy bonbonniere shaped as the bust of a lady, *c*.1762–8**
With original silver-hinged mounts. Many novelty boxes were made by French soft-paste porcelain factories, and these are always highly collectable. 6cm (2½in) high.
£1,600–2,000/$2,400–3,000

▼ **Sèvres-style box, *c*.1890–1900**
Possibly made by Samson, or else in Limoges. Although ostensibly a fake with a spurious 18th-century Sèvres mark, this 14-cm (5½-in) diameter box is very decorative and valued accordingly.
£600–750/$900–1,125

▲ **German porcelain snuff box, *c*.1770**
With delicate rococo moulding and panels of Watteau figures, attributed to Berlin. The mounts are gilt metal rather than gold, which affects the value.
£2,000–3,000/$3,000–4,500

Snuff Boxes & Other Small Boxes

Acollection of china boxes set out on a table attracts a great deal of attention, so it is little wonder that these porcelain luxuries have always been expensive. However, even though some snuff boxes cost their original owners more than fine jewellery, plenty of cheap, decorative, and novelty boxes can also look very pretty displayed together.

While painted boxes of enamelled copper were produced in Germany and France from the 17th century, the earliest porcelain boxes were made in St Cloud early in the 1700s, combining the shapes of French silver with *Chinoiserie* decoration. The French *pâte tendre* has a very soft glaze, so the brightly painted decoration may be worn after centuries of handling. Some of the most appealing snuff boxes are, therefore, those made just in white – shaped as animals, chinamen, or baskets of flowers. The tradition continued at Chantilly and especially Mennecy, where a great many novelty boxes were made in the 1740s. A few superb snuff boxes were made at Sèvres, with richly coloured grounds and lavish gilding. Authentic Sèvres examples are incredibly rare and very valuable today, while Mennecy boxes remain undervalued.

Meissen made many exceptional snuff boxes from the 1720s. White porcelain was ornamented in Augsburg by court jewellers, using bright gold and applied jewels. Hinged mounts of finest gold were added, and the King presented the completed boxes to favoured courtiers and diplomats. The finest enamelling was carried out at Meissen where, under the direction of J.G. Höroldt, breathtakingly beautiful boxes were created. The painting on Meissen snuff boxes is usually superb, and their gold mounts are of the highest quality. They were sold at the time for enormous prices, so it is little wonder they are so collectable and expensive today.

Identification can be a problem, for very few snuff boxes carry makers' marks. Frankenthal, Berlin, and other German factories all made very similar boxes between the 1750s and the 1770s, while others were made in Vienna, Copenhagen, and Italy.

► **Royal Worcester cosmetics box from a dressing table set**
The decoration, known as "blush ivory", was very popular in Edwardian times. Date mark for 1903, 6cm (2in) in diameter.
£60–90/$90–135

▼ **Coalport trinket box, c.1910**
Made simply for show, with remarkable gold and turquoise jewelled decoration; every tiny jewel was individually applied. 15cm (6in) in diameter.
£800–1,100/$1,200–1,650

▲ **Meissen box decorated with the "Green Dragon" pattern**
First made in the 1720s, although the mark dates this example beween 1926 and 1939; the box measures 6cm (2in) in diameter.
£50–70/$75–105

Most 18th-century hard-paste porcelain boxes are referred to as "Meissen" today, although clearly other makers were also responsible. In England a range of fine, soft-paste porcelain boxes was made at Chelsea, and another, now known as "Girl-in-a-Swing", at the St James' porcelain factory. However, examples are very rare as customers favoured the enamelled metal boxes from Battersea and Bilston.

While gentlemen had snuffboxes, ladies had smaller, dainty porcelain boxes. Bonbonnières were containers for tiny, very concentrated sweets that disguised bad breath, and these could be fitted inside an evening bag, or tucked discreetly inside a muff. Bonbonnières frequently took the form of animals, birds, or everyday objects. Distinguishing between snuff boxes and smaller bonbonnières is far from easy; in theory they had a different purpose, although only a few were ever actually used. They were too costly to risk carrying around in a pocket, and most were kept safe at home, to be brought out only to show off to guests.

Porcelain snuffboxes and bonbonnières went out of fashion in the early 19th century, and it is almost impossible to find Regency or early Victorian examples. But plenty were made later in the century, and in the early 1900s, specifically for collectors. The Paris firm of Samson made huge numbers of fakes in the style of Meissen, Sèvres, Naples, and Chelsea. These were generally sold as pretty decoration rather than with any intention to deceive, but some of the best Samson copies do fool many collectors.

Collecting little boxes became a popular hobby, and since 1900 all manner of china pots have been made. Some contained cosmetics on dressing tables, others were only there to look pretty among other knick-knacks; prices reflect maker and quality. The great range of novelty bonbonnières made in Limoges is particularly popular, although care needs to be taken as vast numbers of china boxes are still made in Limoges and in the Far East. Very few examples that you see at antiques fairs are actually of any great age at all.

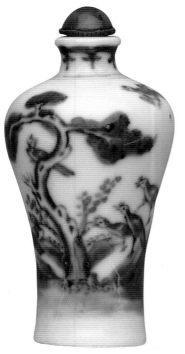

► **An early English porcelain "toy" scent bottle, c.1750–55** Made at Charles Gouyn's factory in St. James. The head forms the stopper and the gold collar mounts are finely enamelled. 6cm (2½in) high. **£5,000–7,000/$7,500–10,500**

▲ **Chinese blue-and-white snuff bottle in shape of a miniature vase, 18th century** Qing period, Yongzheng mark (1723–35) in blue script. 8.5cm (3½in) tall. **£2,000–3,000/$3,000–4,500**

◄ **Chinese snuff bottle with traditional enamelled decoration, c.1821–50** Chinese taste, with the Daoguang four-character iron-red seal mark in a line. 6cm (2½in) tall. **£2,000–2,800/$3,000–4,200**

Scent Bottles & Snuff Bottles

Snuff bottles and scent bottles are very different, although the terms are frequently confused. In Europe snuff was kept in a snuff box, whereas in China a bottle was used. The snuff was taken from the bottle with a tiny spoon-like applicator, usually made of ivory, attached to the underside of the stopper. Some Chinese snuff bottles were exported to Europe in the 18th century and were converted, by the addition of silver mounts, to be used as bottles for perfume, but this was not their original purpose.

Some Chinese snuff bottles were made from natural hardstones such as jade, agate, or rock crystal, while many others were made of glass. By comparison, porcelain snuff bottles were generally uncommon until quite recent times. Because snuff bottles were made for the Asian market rather than for export to Europe, the decoration is always in Chinese taste – principally dragons, formal patterns, and emblems. Blue-and-white decoration is usual, as well as a combination of underglaze blue and iron red. Plants, birds, and figure subjects were often painted in *famille rose* enamels, executed with great care to suit the small size. Flattened oval or globular shapes were copied from popular forms in hardstone. Others were made as miniature copies of well-known porcelain vase shapes. It is sometimes difficult to tell whether certain bottle shapes were intended as tiny toy vases or as containers for snuff.

Some very special porcelain snuff bottles were made for the imperial court, bearing the reign marks of Yongzheng or Qianlong, and enamelled in the palace workshops. The rare authentic examples are worth incredible sums, but in practice very few marks painted on snuff bottles relate to the actual period of manufacture. Endless copies of 18th-century porcelain snuff bottles have been made ever since, and it takes practice to date them. This may be one of the reasons why porcelain snuff bottles are generally inexpensive, thereby offering a good opportunity for a very attractive collection.

The distinction between scent bottles and perfume bottles is also ambiguous. Some collectors

► A Chamberlain's Worcester scent bottle, c.1800,
Painted with souvenir view of Gloucester, with contemporary gold top. An original stopper always adds to the value of a scent bottle. 9.5cm (4in) tall.
£400–600/$600–900

▼ Coalport scent bottle and matching porcelain stopper, c.1895–1900
Decorated with tiny enamel jewels, the mounts are in silver-gilt, 12cm (5in) high.
£500–800/$750–1,200

◄ Rockingham scent bottle with modelled flowers in Meissen style, c.1831–42
Condition of the flowers is important, as every chip is costly to repair. With puce factory mark, 11cm (4in) high. **£700–1,000/$1,050–1,500**

feel a scent bottle should be small enough to carry around in an evening bag, while a perfume bottle is a larger, free-standing container that could sit on a dressing table. The terms are open to different interpretations, of course, and it doesn't really matter, except that generally there are far more collectors of little scent bottles than of larger scent or perfume containers. Scent bottles were made in many materials, glass and silver in particular, but there are a large number of porcelain bottles still available.

Understandably, the finest 18th-century bottles are expensive. Meissen made plain shapes that were finely painted, and in the 1740s and 1750s they introduced a range of novelty, miniature figurines that contained separate stoppers, often disguised as a flower or a detachable head on a shepherdess or pug dog. These inspired a tradition of figural scent bottles at Chelsea and St James' in the 1750s.

With such a variety available, collectors of scent bottles are spoilt for choice. Selection will be determined by price as much as anything else, as fine early scent bottles are very expensive – indeed, all scent bottles are costly. Such is the popularity of these pretty little pieces that copies have been made for a long time. Fake Chelsea and Meissen bottles were made in Dresden and France 150 years ago. Some Samson copies of Chelsea figural bottles sell for £500/$750 – an extraordinary price for a fake, but they are highly decorative pieces in their own right.

Some of the best porcelain scent bottles were made in Victorian England. Royal Worcester specialized in bottles with painted flowers or birds, as well as some very fine double-walled bottles with intricate pierced decoration cut into the outer shell. Coalport made a range of richly enamelled scent bottles with very distinctive jewelled decoration. An original, matching porcelain stopper is always important. So too is a high-quality silver or gold mount. Collections of snuff bottles or scent bottles can be displayed in very attractive arrangements, but it is always important to lay bottles down on soft cloth only, to avoid rubbing the surface decoration.

▶ **A complete English porcelain desk set in the "Coalbrookdale" style, *c*.1840**
With modelled flowers copying Meissen. The two covered inkwells sit either side of a taperstick.
£550–700/$825–1,050

◀ **A Berlin pounce pot in the shape of a celestial globe, *c*.1775-85,**
The matching inkwell from the desk set would be formed as the companion terrestrial globe. 8cm (3in) tall.
£1,000–1,400/ $1,500–2,100

▲ **A Vauxhall inkwell, *c*.1758-60** Copied from a Chinese blue-and-white example of the Kangxi period; English 18th-century porcelain inkwells are rare and valuable. 8cm (3in) in diameter. **£6,000–8,000/$9,000–12,000**

Inkwells & Desk Sets

This is a very popular area of collecting, for the art of writing has inspired many wonderful objects. Letter-writing is a personal craft, and desk sets are equally individual. Ink required a robust and impervious container, but pottery wasn't really suitable as surface crazing encouraged unsightly staining. Soft-paste porcelain also stained, and to preserve their beauty porcelain inkwells were usually provided with separate liners, as well as lids to stop the ink drying out. Early porcelain inkwells have often lost their covers, but are wonderful when they are complete and in original, clean condition.

Porcelain inkwells were very much luxury items, and all 18th-century examples are rare. Most surprising is the lack of Chinese porcelain inkwells. The Chinese didn't use inkwells themselves, for their calligraphy called for brushpots and ink stones instead. This is the most likely reason why so few Oriental porcelain inkwells survive. Early French examples are also very rare. German pieces are more plentiful, made by a number of factories,

although in a limited range of shapes. The most popular form was a simple cube, with a central hole in a recessed top. Two or three little cubes were sometimes placed on a dish, and this forerunner of the inkstand led to the curious name "inkstandish", which is still sometimes used. The most common form of inkstand was a shaped tray with recesses for an inkwell and a pounce pot, usually fashioned as matching pairs. Pounce was an absorbent powder mixed with sand that was sprinkled on a letter to dry ink, an important aid when writing on an impervious surface such as parchment. Pounce pots are sometimes mistaken for salt cellars or sugar sifters, but usually they have no separate filling hole underneath. Instead they were filled, with difficulty, through the tiny holes in the recessed top.

Some very special inkstands were made. Sèvres created a fabulous design for the desks of royalty, with an inkwell disguised as a miniature globe – an idea copied at Berlin. Fancy shapes originated in

▼ **A Meissen paperweight,** *c.*1870
Designed to lie across papers on a desk, encrusted with delicate china flowers, and a cat forming the handle, crossed swords mark. 20cm (8in) long. £800–1,000/$1,200–1,500

▼ **A Meissen blotter,** *c.*1875 With scenic view and flower panel, finely gilded. Porcelain-mounted blotters took the place of the pounce pots found with earlier desk sets. £500–600/$750–900

▲ **A Staffordshire porcelain pen tray,** *c.*1830
With simple flower painting. Pen trays would make a charming collection, although they are rare in porcelain. 22.5cm (9in) long. £150–200/$225–300

the age of rococo. Derby copied Meissen with a scroll-moulded inkstand set, with a taperstick in addition to the inkwell and pounce pot. A taper-stick was a tiny candlestick, too small to provide much light but used instead to melt a stick of sealing wax. The Derby sets were exceptional in England, for other early British porcelain inkwells were surprisingly plain. All inkstands are rare and expensive today.

Some exciting novelty inkstands were made at the end of the 18th century, especially in Paris. Sèvres developed a combined inkwell and inkstand in a plain drum shape with a central well surrounded by quill holes. The applied carrying handle had a nozzle for a taper set into the top, while pouches around the outside held pounce or spare nibs. This circular shape was copied all over Europe until the 1820s, when elaborate inkstands became fashionable again. Two different inkwells and a taperstick were usually set in the middle of a large tray, on which pens could be rested. Many also

incorporated spill vases, to hold the wooden spills with which the tapers were lit from the fire. The rococo revival in the 1830s and 1840s saw some particularly fancy combined inkwells and pen trays, especially in England in the Dresden style.

Tapersticks were also sold separately, and these delightful objects are highly collectable as they can be formed into very attractive displays. Some pen trays were made as separate desk items and, although uncommon, these are popular today with collectors of fountain pens. In the Victorian era other shapes were made in porcelain to decorate writing desks. Engraved seals were given porcelain handles, and unusual porcelain blotters were made at Meissen, often beautifully painted. Glass paper-weights are familiar to everyone, but it is seldom appreciated that many paperweights were also made in porcelain. Shaped as dogs or other animals, they are rarely recognized for what they are. Some figurines of children reading or writing letters were intended as functional paperweights.

◀ One of a pair of Derby
double candlesticks, c.1775
With a shepherd and shepherdess
seated next to delicate flowering
bocage. Original candle nozzles
are always an advantage.
25.5cm (10in) high.
£1,600–2,000/$2,400–3,000

▼ Chamberlain and Co. Worcester
taperstick from a desk set, c.1840
Painted with a topographical view
and "weed" gilding. Their small size
gives tapersticks an obvious appeal
to collectors. 6.5cm (2½in) high.
£450–550/$675–825

▲ Chinese porcelain candlestick, Qianlong period c.1750
Armorial decoration in *famille rose*; the shape copies a silver
prototype. 17cm (6½in) high. £4,000–5,000/$6,000–7,500

Candlesticks & Candle Snuffers

In the days when candles provided the only illumination, households needed an extensive range of candleholders, both fixed and portable. For practical reasons most were made of brass or silver plate, but a great many luxury candlesticks were of porcelain. Recently candles have enjoyed a massive revival, and porcelain candlesticks are no longer just bought by collectors – in many cases they are actually used to provide delicate lighting once more.

Perhaps more than any other porcelain object, candlesticks follow the shape of silver prototypes. This is certainly true of Chinese examples, for these were copied exactly from Dutch or English metal versions taken to China by European sailors. However, the decoration, in blue-and-white or *Imari* colours, was refreshingly different from silver or brass. Kangxi candlesticks from the early 18th century are rare and wonderful pieces. Chinese armorial candlesticks were real status symbols in the 1750s for, with the family crest in *famille rose*, they cost more than the best silver-gilt.

Candlesticks in baroque or rococo style sum up the strengths and beauty of Meissen porcelain. The master modeller J.J. Kändler took inspiration from the great silver candelabra of the courts and palaces, but he went one better. His stunning figures support writhing arms of pure white porcelain heightened in gold. Imagine them lit only by their own candlelight, casting shadows that emphasize every modelled scroll and flourish; in 1740 they must have seemed magical. Some 18th-century Meissen candlesticks, while not exactly cheap, seem excellent value today, sometimes costing little more than 19th-century copies. The same is true of many Chelsea, Bow, and Derby figural candlesticks from the 1760s to the '70s. In Germany the traditional Meissen/Dresden style was very popular in the 1880s and '90s. Vast numbers of fancy candelabra were made, encrusted with cherubs and china flowers, and these remain popular. Their price depends on the maker and the quality of workmanship, which can vary greatly.

▲ Royal Worcester candle extinguisher
or snuffer in the shape of cartoon character Mr Punch, 9cm (3½in) high, factory mark dated 1882. Relatively few were made, and as a result they are costly today.
£3,200–4,000/$4,800–6,000

▼ A Royal Worcester candle snuffer
Also called an extinguisher, in the shape of an owl wearing a nightcap; the owl proved popular and sold well, so it is now fairly common. Factory mark dated 1901, 8cm (3in) tall. **£350–400/$525–600**

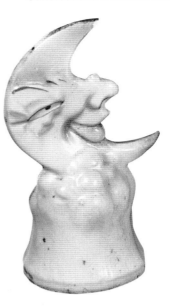

▲ A German candle snuffer in coloured bisque porcelain, c.1880
A wide range of snuffers were made on the Continent and these have a keen following, but they are worth far less than snuffers by English makers.
£80–120/$120–180

Small candlesticks are most popular with collectors. Chamber candlesticks were portable versions with carrying handles and wide saucer-like bases to catch dripping wax. Miniature versions went with desk sets and were used for tapers to melt sealing wax. Fine Regency chambersticks and tapersticks are always costly. By contrast, 100 years ago little candlesticks were very popular seaside souvenirs, and Goss and other crested chambersticks cost little; German versions for dressing-table sets cost still less.

A few early chambersticks were made with matching conical extinguishers, or "snuffers". These became popular in early Victorian times, with finely painted examples made at Berlin and Meissen. In France in the 1830s some conical snuffers were modelled as novelty figurines, especially as priests, monks, and nuns. Similar figures were made in Staffordshire in the 1840s, and Minton made a small number of finely decorated candle snuffers of theatrical subjects, sold on matching bases. Kerr and Binns of Worcester expanded the idea in the 1850s, making further comical monks and priests. Subsequently Royal Worcester produced a great range of humorous and finely observed subjects, the best modelled by James Hadley.

Royal Worcester extinguishers have recently become hugely popular and can be extraordinarily expensive, if rare. Some snuffers sold well when they were made and are fairly common today, fetching £100–200/$150–300 each. Others did not prove popular, or were too expensive for the 1880s, and very few were made. Some rare Royal Worcester snuffers are now worth over £5,000/$7,500, making them among the most expensive porcelain collectables. Plenty of snuffers by other makers are much cheaper, including German *bisque* porcelain novelties and Goss crested china cones or modelled hats. Known in the USA as "candle crowns", snuffers are enjoying new popularity thanks to Bronté Porcelain's extensive range marketed in the USA by Department 56. Their high quality guarantees future collectability.

◄ **Selection of Nankin-type scallop shell pickle dishes, c.1730–50**
Blue-and-white 18th-century Export pickle dishes are much rarer than their English-made counterparts, and yet curiously these Chinese examples are far less expensive. **£120–160/$180–240 each**

▶ **Bow pickle dish in the shape of a vine leaf, c.1755-58**
Overglaze enamels were affected by the vinegar used in pickles and consequently coloured examples are great rarities.
10cm (4in) wide. **£600–700/$900–1,050**

▲ **A Worcester shell-shaped pickle dish, c.1758-60** Painted in blue with a popular pattern, marked with a workman's sign. English pickle dishes were mass-produced and the quality of painting varies greatly.
10.5cm (4in) long. **£450–550/$675–825**

Pickle Dishes & Spoon Trays

Dear little shapes are often exactly that – dear. Tiny dishes are proportionally much more expensive than large porcelain pieces, for in the smaller homes of today collections need to be of manageable size. It is important to stay focused and to stick to particular fields of collecting, as there are so many little dishes to choose from. Pickle dishes and spoon trays are without doubt the most popular kinds, for they provide so much scope for attractive and representative collections.

The first pickle dishes were actual seashells. Empty scallop shells were used to serve preserved fruits and pickled condiments in many European homes. Silver would have been more fashionable, but the vinegar in most pickles reacted with the metal. Following the invention of porcelain, pickle could be served to guests in smart, blue-and-white containers. They were vital additions to the dining table as without refrigeration meat tasted stale, and strongly flavoured pickles and condiments provided a badly needed disguise.

Early porcelain pickle dishes from China were modelled on the shape of the scallop shells that they replaced. Sets of Chinese pickle dishes were imported into Amsterdam or London 300 years ago, and sold as "nests" of three or more shell dishes in graduated sizes. These were either in blue-and-white or in the Imari colours that proved so popular in The Netherlands. However, it soon became clear that vinegar affected enamel colours and gilding. Underglaze blue was impervious to the acid, and so blue-and-white pickle dishes became the norm.

Curiously, Chinese blue-and-white pickle dishes are hard to find, but they are not particularly expensive as they tend to be avoided by collectors of English blue-and-white. Instead, it is rare early British pickle dishes that are very costly indeed. This is a very British collecting field, for pickle shells and leaves were not made in any quantity in any other country. The reason is probably the English love of blue-and-white. Around 1750, as enamelled pickle dishes were not practical,

▶ **Chinese porcelain spoon tray, *c*.1750-60**
With an original underglaze blue border and coloured flowers that were added in London. 11.5cm (4½in) in width.
£500–600/$750–900

▲ **Meissen spoon tray from a tea service, *c*.1745**
Painted with landscape panels. This example has a rare, coral red-ground on the underside, not visible here, which makes a big difference to the value. **£4,500–5,500/$6,750–8,250**

▼ **A Caughley spoon tray, *c*.1788-90**
Printed with a Chinese Willow-type pattern in underglaze blue; the gilding was added by Chamberlains, Worcester. Impressed mark "Salopian", 15cm (6in) long. **£300–400/$450–600**

English china-makers seized the opportunity to make a popular item that wasn't readily available from the Orient. Bow and Limehouse produced leaves and shells in large numbers, although in nothing like the quantity subsequently made at Worcester. Some dishes were made by taking moulds from actual shells and leaves, and it is that which gives them such a wonderful feel.

English porcelain pickle dishes remained popular until the 1790s, when they were replaced by Spode's blue-printed pottery versions. For 40 years every porcelain factory made its own dishes, creating the great variety now available to collectors. Worcester leaves are the most plentiful, and in terms of quality also the best. In the 18th century they cost just a few pennies each – today prices start from about £250/$375, rising to £5,000/$7,500 for the rarest early Limehouse shell dishes. Enamelled dishes are always more expensive than blue-and-white. Rim chips are common, of course, but they do make a surprising difference to the value.

After stirring your tea it was considered ill-mannered to place your teaspoon on the saucer. Deluxe tea sets were provided with a single spoon tray instead, passed around among the guests. Not every tea service had a spoon tray, and so these have always been regarded by collectors as special objects. Meissen spoon trays were surprisingly large, whereas Chinese export porcelain spoon trays were small. Shapes vary from ovals or pointed lozenges to octagons and rectangles. China factories all over Europe made them with every kind of tea ware pattern, and their manufacture was as varied as porcelain itself. It is possible, therefore, to form a wonderfully mixed collection, although most collectors limit their range to either English or Continental spoon trays. Worcester examples are the most plentiful, and, although they were made in only a limited number of shapes, every one is a charming object. Spoon trays went out of fashion in the 1780s. All are quite expensive today, but spoon tray collections are exciting and very beautiful.

► **Caughley miniature coffee pot,
c.1785-90** Painted with the "Island"
pattern in underglaze blue. Caughley
made a wide range of miniature or
"toy" tablewares in this pattern, all
of which are keenly collected.
£800–1,200/$1,200–1,800

▼ **Spode miniature jug with coloured
print of Chinese figures, c.1830-35**
Just 4.5cm (1¾in) high, marked Spode
with a pattern number in red.
£150–200/$225–300

◄ **Bow miniature teabowl, coffee cup
and saucer, c.1760-65** Painted with vines
in underglaze blue. The saucer is just 5cm
(2in) wide. All miniature porcelain from this early
date is scarce. **£1,000–1,200/$1,500–1,800**

Miniature Porcelain

The appeal of dolls and dolls' houses extends far beyond childhood. Some grown-up children are fanatical collectors of toys, games, and the tiny playthings they enjoyed when they were little. Miniature ornaments have an obvious appeal, and as a result very tiny pieces of porcelain can be surprisingly valuable. Miniature porcelain was collected as long ago as the mid-18th century, and fine-china shops and jewellers sold "toys" of all sorts. Porcelain "toys" were small luxury goods, such as scent bottles and bonbonnières, and, of course, miniature chinaware. These expensive novelties make delightful presents.

The fashion for collecting miniatures became something of an obsession in The Netherlands, where tiny silver models of furniture and other household objects were popular from the late 17th century. Miniature tea sets in Japanese and Chinese porcelain were imported. Children would have played with some of these, but mostly the miniatures were far too precious to be touched by

small hands. The Meissen factory was the first in Europe to make miniature porcelain part of its regular production. Tiny vases and tubs of china flowers were made as ornaments for banqueting tables. These were displayed alongside miniature figurines, and animals as small as 2cm (⅜in). A porcelain model of the "Venetian Fair", with hundreds of tiny figures milling about among the stalls and sideshows of this local street carnival, was commissioned by the Duke of Württemberg and made by the Ludwigsburg factory.

Miniature tea sets and dinnerware became increasingly popular. Around 1750, china factories throughout Europe made tiny teapots, and cups and saucers. Many English toy tea sets were made for the Dutch market, and included special shapes of kettles and tea-stands that were in general use in The Netherlands at the time. Around 1760, Worcester made particularly fine miniature tea sets in blue-and-white. Delightfully small, and with the most superb thin potting, they are understandably

◀ **Royal Crown Derby miniature saucepan, c.1910** In the *Imari* "Old Witches" pattern; one of the rarer shapes found in this popular pattern
£400–500/$600–750

▲ **A Chinese export "toy" teapot, c.1880**, With Canton-enamelled *famille rose* decoration, 7cm (2¾in) high; this was made as an inexpensive novelty.
£35–45/$52–68

Collecting Limoges Miniatures

▲ **A suite of Limoges porcelain miniature furniture, c.1970**
With coloured decals or lithographic prints, and gold edges. The piano is 3.5cm (1¼in) long, and marked "Limoges France". This is just a small selection of the many shapes that are available.
£30–40/$45–60 (as illustrated)

expensive. All early porcelain miniatures cost more than their full-sized counterparts, for in general they appeal to very dedicated collectors.

The Caughley factory in Shropshire specialized in miniatures during the 1780s. A century later Caughley's successor at Coalport was to revive the tradition, making a variety of cups and saucers, and tiny teapots. The Crown Staffordshire factory made an extensive range of miniature tea wares in the early 1900s, and Royal Crown Derby is the best-known English maker, famed for its *Imari*-pattern miniatures that include saucepans, coal scuttles, and a flat iron on a stand. In Germany a great many miniature porcelain items were made in Dresden. Collectors prefer the smallest sizes, and examples from named factories where possible. Since the 1970s sets of porcelain miniatures have been specially created as collectables. These are mostly made in the Far East, and sold with their own display stands. However, few have yet to develop any secondary market.

Collecting miniature porcelain became a popular hobby in France between the two World Wars. Several manufacturers in Limoges took advantage of inexpensive photographic colour printing and produced a new kind of souvenir. Famous paintings by Fragonard and other traditional artists were reduced in size and applied as lithographic transfers, or decals, which were printed onto an extensive range of miniature novelties.

During the 1960s every gift shop in France was selling Limoges miniatures. Tiny plates were made as menu holders and brooches. Miniature tea sets were sold on little china trays, small enough to put in a doll's house and cheap enough for children to play with. Two main patterns were popular: coloured prints were placed on a white ground with a gold trim, or, alternatively, gold prints were used on a deep blue glazed background, which produced a very rich effect.

Following the success of miniature teapots and plates, Limoges china-makers introduced an extensive range of novelty shapes, from tiny furniture, and other household objects, to miniature models of the Eiffel Tower, and gondolas from Venice. Small and lightweight, Limoges miniatures are easy to collect via the Internet. Typical prices, ranging from £4/$6 to £20/$30, won't break the bank, but watch out for many modern productions – not all of these are made in Limoges.

◀ **Samson group of dancers, *c*.1880**
After a famous Meissen original. The
style and colouring of the Samson fake
is surprisingly convincing and pieces like
this have fooled many experts. 15cm (6in)
in height. £300–400/$450–600 as
a Samson fake, £7,000–10,000/
$10,500– 15,000 if genuine Meissen

▼ **Early Sèvres dish, *c*.1760** "Doctored" to
improve its desirability. The decoration was added
entirely in the 19th century, probably in London,
c.1840. £250–350/$375–525 as a re-decorated
forgery or £4,000–6,000/$6,000–9,000 if original

◀ **A Samson figure of a Turkish
girl, *c*.1900** Copied from a Bloor
Derby original, 7.5cm (3in) high, with
spurious Derby red mark in red.
£60–80/$90–120 as a Samson fake
or £220–250/$330–375 if genuine

Fakes & Forgeries

As a keen collector of porcelain I visit a lot of antiques fairs and flea markets, and love to rummage in boxes at car-boot sales. In doing so I am shocked by just how many fakes I come across. Ingenious deceit is everywhere. There is not a single type of antique that has not, at some time, attracted the attention of the forger, but the sheer number of fakes at present circulating is both staggering and alarming. Every so often the market is hit by a new kind of fake, sometimes so clever that even the experts are taken in. I have to admit that several of the pieces illustrated on these pages fooled me when I encountered them for the first time. It was only after I had seen three or four, all exactly the same, that I realized what I was looking at.

Potters in the Middle East copied Chinese Ming porcelain back in the 14th century. In 1690 Queen Mary II hung Dutch Delftware in her royal palaces, while Augustus the Strong displayed his Meissen copies alongside his treasured collection of Chinese and Japanese porcelain. Nobody regards

early Delft and Meissen as "fakes", but when they were made this is exactly what they were – deliberate reproductions. It is important to distinguish between an honest reproduction and a fake. The term "genuine reproduction" is a real oxymoron, but how else do you classify a Bow porcelain dish in the "Quail" pattern, made in the 1750s as a copy of the Kakiemon porcelain that was no longer available from Japan? Most Bow and Derby figures were copied from Meissen originals, sometimes complete with the crossed swords marks. And what about a Minton *Japanesque* vase with flying cranes, made in 1872 in imitation of the latest porcelain brought back from the Orient? The latter does say "Minton" on the bottom, but plenty of Victorian copies of Chinese and Japanese prototypes were not marked, except with copies of Oriental seal marks.

The dictionary definitions of the words "fake", "forgery", and "reproduction" have been quoted *ad infinitum* in celebrated court cases where art

▲ **French part dinner service, *c*.1920** In the style of a "Chinese *Imari*" original from *c.*1720, probably by Samson. The set is very decorative if you can't afford the real thing. **£80–100/$120–150 each French copy plate or £1,000–1,400/$1,500–2,100 for Chinese**

Samson
The Master Forger

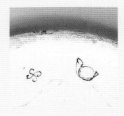

▲ ▶ **Samson copy of a Chantilly tureen in the Japanese Kakiemon style** With fake Chantilly horn mark and Samson's SS mark, late 19th century. The copy is in hard paste. **£150–200/$225–300 the copy or £3,000–4,000/$4,500–6,000 original**

forgers have been tried for counterfeiting. I don't believe that it is possible to define fakes quite so straightforwardly. For instance, a Samson copy, made in 1870, of a Meissen figure is thought of as a fake, but a Derby copy of the same Meissen figure, made in 1770, is regarded as highly collectable. This is nonsensical, but excusable. Some simply decorated Chinese and Meissen porcelain was, some years later, enhanced by independent enamellers in Augsburg and The Netherlands. This decoration (termed *hausmalerei* in Germany) is today very desirable. Some rather unexciting Sèvres porcelain from the 18th century has also had rich decoration added at a later date. Old Sèvres porcelain redecorated in the 19th century with lavish coloured grounds is now regarded not as outside decoration but as a particularly devious kind of fake, which of course it is.

It is very easy to copy famous factory marks such as crossed swords and gold anchors; it is much harder to copy the porcelain glaze. Many experts

In the world of antiques the name of Samson is synonymous with fake porcelain. Edmé Samson, who founded the firm in 1845, and his son, Émile, originally worked as decorators in Paris, specializing in "china matchings" – replacements for old china services, copying any china pattern required. They soon realized that there was a huge market for reproductions of old porcelain designs, and the factory grew to an enormous size. The Samson firm always claimed that it was making not fakes but instead honest reproductions, made for decoration. These sold for a fraction of the price of real old Meissen or Chinese porcelain. Even so, there was nothing to stop unscrupulous china dealers buying Samson copies wholesale and re-selling them as the real thing. A century later Samson's fakes are in collections everywhere, and in many cases are still regarded as authentic. Samson's own mark – the letters SS conjoined – rarely appears, and in its place were used versions of every great china mark from the past.

Samson porcelain is now fetching good money in its own right, simply because it is extremely well made and highly decorative. Today the work of many lesser fakers is frequently mistaken for the famous Samson – an ironic state of affairs in view of Samson's own notoriety.

◀ ▼ **A Thuringian figure, c.1780** Altered to improve its desirability. The Russian imperial cipher of Catherine the Great has been added in gold to the base. **£250–350/$375–525 (£5,000/$7,500+ for a real Russian figure)**

▲ **Plaque "signed" by the artist, James Stinton** With a Royal Worcester mark for 1924. This is an English forgery – a number of these fake Worcester plaques appeared on the market in the late 1980s. **£2,000–2500/$3,000–3,750 for a genuine Stinton plaque, but the forgery is worthless**

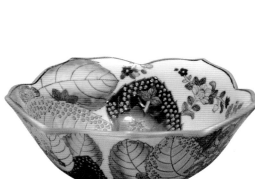

◀ **Chinese bowl of "Tobacco Leaf" design** Bearing the reign mark of Qianlong, purporting to be c.1770. The decoration was, in fact, transfer-printed in Canton less than ten years ago. 21cm (8in) in diameter. **£10–20/$15–30 for fake or £3,000–£5,000/$4,500–7,500 for genuine 18th century bowl**

will tell you that the best way to avoid falling for fakes is to learn the proper feel of the real thing, but this is clearly easier said than done. Samson's hard-paste porcelain is very different from that of Chelsea or Worcester, but its body is very like old Paris porcelain, and also similar to Meissen. I have seen many Samson pieces on display in great museums masquerading as the real thing. Also I can't pretend that I have always got it right and have never been fooled by clever Samson fakes myself.

The most sophisticated porcelain fakes, and the hardest to detect, originate in China. In the 18th century potters in the imperial kilns at Jingdezhen made exact copies of precious old Ming porcelain from the palace collection, just to prove that the skills of their illustrious ancestors still existed. In the 19th century the same kilns made copies of 18th-century porcelain, complete with Yongzheng and Qianlong reign marks. The best of these can be very, very misleading. Recently I have seen some modern fakes of valuable Chinese imperial porcelain that have left me breathless with fright. With fakes that are this

ingenious coming on to the market direct from the Far East, most collectors now will not even consider touching any piece unless it has a provenance that cannot be disputed.

Many fakers try just a little too hard, and overdo the signs of age – this unconvincing surface-wear gives the game away more than anything else. A lot of modern copies have abrasion marks scarring the surface in places that would not have been scratched through natural usage. These scratches, probably made with sandpaper, are often enhanced with boot blacking so that you can't miss them. I have been shown many modern porcelain fakes, bought in regional salerooms or antiques markets. Their owners proudly tell me: "This was black when I bought it, but I have spent hours scrubbing off the dirt and see how nice it looks." I have to break the sad news to them that instead of the natural dirt of centuries, all they have washed off is liquid shoe polish. One clever faker, Reginald Newland, worked at Torquay in the 1950s. When he sold his fake Rockingham animals and Staffordshire cottages he instructed

► **Porcelain figurine bearing mark of Worcester factory Flight and Barr, used *c*.1790-95** This figure was made in East Germany or Taiwan less than 20 years ago. A permanent marker pen and varnish have been used to add the mark. £10–20/$15–30 for modern figure, but no price for original as Flight and Barr did not make figures!

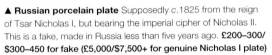

▲ **Russian porcelain plate** Supposedly *c*.1825 from the reign of Tsar Nicholas I, but bearing the imperial cipher of Nicholas II. This is a fake, made in Russia less than five years ago. £200–300/ $300–450 for fake (£5,000/$7,500+ for genuine Nicholas I plate)

his customers to rub gum Arabic into the corners and shake them in the vacuum-cleaner bag! Every few months someone shows me one of Newland's fake Derby or Bow figures that they have bought believing it to be the real thing.

One sort of forgery is very hard to detect, and that is "redecoration". This term describes the procedure of altering a genuine piece of antique porcelain at a later date to increase its desirability. A great deal of genuine 18th-century Sèvres and Worcester porcelain, with original factory marks, was doctored a century later by adding rare ground colours, dates, and inscriptions. A lot of collectors were fooled at the time, and many people are still caught out today. To spot redecoration you have to look out for anomalies in the painting style and tell-tale signs of burning, which affects porcelain that has been re-fired after a gap of 100 years.

Now that porcelain from the industrial age is keenly collected, a new kind of fake is emerging. The moulds from which Royal Worcester and Doulton figures were made were not always destroyed, and some modern castings are indistinguishable from those made in the 1930s. Other 20th-century Doulton figures have been re-painted in rare "colourways" – unrecorded colour variations that are worth a fortune if authentic. Some Royal Worcester vases, originally just in the white, have recently been enamelled with paintings done, supposedly, by top artists. In spite of fake signatures, these shouldn't fool anyone familiar with the real work of Harry Davis and the Stinton family, but they are often sold via the Internet to novice collectors attracted by an apparent bargain.

Modern advances in colour photography can create the most sophisticated fakes. Colour photos of real Berlin plaques are now used to make fakes in the Far East, which are put into old, dusty frames. Few people viewing an auction examine every lot with a powerful magnifying glass, and you need a very strong lens to see the tiny dots that make up the colour photographs. These fake plaques have sold for several thousand pounds.

An experienced dealer once gave me sound advice: "The cleverest fakes are the ones no one knows about". Be warned.

Care & Display

▲ **A Victorian watercolour of a connoisseur's porcelain collection, by Benjamin Walter Spiers, dated 1879**
Among fine Meissen, Chinese, and Japanese porcelain is a fake Worcester tea canister – just a few years old when the painting was done.

Living with a Porcelain Collection

All collectors like to show off their antiques when friends come to visit. A collection is also a very personal thing and the pleasure it gives to you, as the owner, is paramount. How you choose to display your antique porcelain is terribly important. Properly displayed, simple pieces can look wonderful. At the same time, a wonderful piece in the wrong place can look like nothing at all.

Chinamania

The first porcelain collectors couldn't get enough of the precious stuff as it arrived by sporadic trade from China. Some was indeed used for dining, but a great deal was collected for display. "China rooms" were built in grand homes, where porcelain formed the wall decoration. Dozens of delicate teabowls and saucers sat in rows above the chimney breast. Plates were hung in sweeping fan shapes or formed rainbows of *famille rose*. Vases stood in ranks like soldiers on parade, and mock Chinese temples were built to house figures of Quanyin and Buddha. Queen Mary II filled her palaces in The Netherlands

and London with blue-and-white, and spawned similar obsessions among the nobility and gentry of Europe. Society ladies would flock to the docks when a china-trade ship returned from its voyage. They literally fought on the quayside for the chance to buy any special porcelain brought back by the ship's crew. "Chinamania" in the 18th century created an extraordinary rivalry between obsessed collectors, and vast sums, for the time, were spent in pursuit of rarities from old Japan.

By the 1800s there was no longer any shortage of porcelain in Europe, but a new kind of collector became equally obsessive. The wonderful soft paste of Sèvres, made before the French Revolution, was collected by George III and the Prince Regent, and prices spiralled ever higher. The crazy Oriental interior of the Royal Pavilion in Brighton included old Japanese *Imari*, and every grand home wanted the same fashionable look. By the Victorian period, collecting porcelain had become a popular hobby. Old blue-and-white from China was extraordinarily expensive in the 1870s and '80s, while modern

▲ The Watney collection of early English porcelain
The collection was photographed in Bernard Watney's dining room before it was packed up for sale. Different factories and types were grouped together systematically on a series of open shelves.

porcelain from Japan was also popular. Collectors were mostly interested in the pieces for decoration. The Japanesque interior was the height of fashion, and porcelain was displayed along with other curios from the East in imitation Japanese rooms.

There has been a revival of interest in china rooms since the discovery of the "Nankin Cargo" and other such shipwrecks (*see* page 33). Old Chinese porcelain is plentiful today, and affordable too. If you are buying purely for display, chips or cracks don't matter all that much. A whole wall of blue-and-white porcelain, set out in a decorative pattern, will create a stunning effect. Contrary to popular opinion, it is perfectly safe to hang most porcelain on a wall, as long as you use the right variety of hanger (*see* page 103).

Collecting to Learn

Dr Bernard Watney was a true scholar who formed one of the most important collections of English porcelain. He once wrote that "nothing can replace the knowledge gained by forming, cataloguing and living with a really representative collection". When he died I was privileged to be asked to sell his collection of nearly 2,000 pieces, in a series of memorable auctions in 1999 and 2000. The picture above illustrates just one corner of Bernard and Mavis Watney's collection as it was displayed in the dining room of their home. The collection was started in the 1950s and '60s, when it was possible to buy interesting porcelain quite cheaply, for the knowledge needed to identify most of it didn't then exist. Many of the pieces were unidentified, but Bernard realized, of course, that certain pieces looked similar to one another and were probably

by the same maker. He grouped related pieces together on shelves, so that each shelf was likely to be from a different factory. His research then put names to most of the groups he had isolated. He continually moved pieces around as new purchases suggested sub-groups. As the collection grew, the laden shelves in the Watneys' dining room became the basic classification for English blue-and-white porcelain as we know it today.

It is no longer possible to collect rare and interesting porcelain in such quantity, but Bernard Watney's methods of sorting and displaying porcelain as a learning tool can be applied to far more modest collections. Bernard studied by continually revisiting his collection, picking pieces up to learn the feel of different glazes, and comparing each piece with another. A beginner's collection, with examples from as many different makers as possible, presents endless opportunities to learn. Damaged and broken pieces cost far less than perfect ones, but provide just as much knowledge. It is even worth buying a few well-chosen fakes to study alongside the real thing. Once you have gained sufficient knowledge, it is then possible to progress to a really specialized area of collecting.

Displaying Your Collection

Every collector seems to have a different attitude to the way in which porcelain should be displayed. Tightly packed or spacious, traditional or modern: clearly there is no right or wrong way.

▲ A collection of rare blue-and-white porcelain
From John and Jane Pennington's Liverpool factory, the collection includes dated pieces painted by William Jackson, 1779–85. Displayed here on a set of ornamental shelves of the period.

▲ **A collection of Meissen figures from the *Cris de Paris* series, modelled by Peter Reinicke, *c*.1757**
Displayed on a German rococo table of the period, the central figure has original French Louis XV-period ormolu mounts and Sèvres flowers.

The important thing is that, as far as is practical, everything should be on view. Porcelain should always be seen, and handled too, wherever possible.

It is always satisfying to display your antiques on furniture of the same period. Authentic display cabinets from the 18th century are hard to come by, but good-quality reproductions from the Edwardian era can make excellent substitutes. Sets of hanging wall shelves in rococo or Chinese Chippendale style are usually expensive, but special pieces of early porcelain can look wonderful on such shelving. Larger pieces can be displayed on top of cabinets, chests or side tables to create an authentic antique interior. Elaborate Victorian porcelain looks even more impressive set out on appropriate cabinets, and Art Deco furniture can also be a stylish way to display 20th-century porcelain and figurines.

Asian hardwood furniture has enjoyed a revival worldwide, and Chinese cabinets and shelf units are an excellent way to show Oriental porcelain. It is possible to buy purpose-made cabinets for small items such as snuff bottles. Chinese hardwood stands have been made for several centuries, and the right kind of stand transforms the appearance of a Chinese porcelain vase. Sales of Asian art regularly include boxes full of wooden stands, and it is well worth buying examples that can take a good wax polish. Modern stands are made today throughout the Orient and can be bought from import suppliers, but do avoid cheap, low-quality ones.

There are, of course, drawbacks to using period furniture (apart from the price). It is not always easy to add lighting to antique cabinets, and porcelain does need plenty of light. Also, old furniture is not always a secure way to store valuable porcelain. With any display cabinet it is vital to check that the shelf fixings are totally safe. Antique furniture can look out of place in a modern-day home. Instead, modern display cabinets and shelving units are fine for displaying traditional as well as contemporary ceramics. Modern cabinets have clean lines, and very often they come with built-in lighting. Lighting is everything. Porcelain comes to life when it is properly lit, although you have to make sure there is sufficient ventilation to stop the porcelain cracking from overheating. There are plenty of spotlights and fluorescent strip-lighting systems that can be adapted for use in your home, and these are worth the investment.

Glazed doors protect the contents of a display cabinet, but reflection off the glass detracts from the porcelain. For a very effective display, modern open shelves or *étagères* are preferable. Open shelves really enable you to see your collection, and also to handle it whenever you want. However, dust can be a nuisance, and if you have lively pets, or inquisitive children, open shelves are never a good idea.

Choosing the right kinds of display stand is of vital importance. Traditional dark-wood stands for plates or cups and saucers are fine in a Georgian-style cabinet, but look quite out-of-place in a contemporary display. An extensive range of modern display stands is available in clear Perspex, and others are made from plastic-coated wire. The correct size of stand must always be used, as large plates can easily fall over if the stand is too small. Always discard any bent or misshapen stands. Where space is limited, a very effective display can be made by using blocks of wood or Perspex to raise pieces to different levels. Always check any arrangement for stability, and anchor stands that could slip or slide.

Keeping Records

Provenance is incredibly important. Records of past sales and previous ownership become part of the history of a piece of porcelain, for if an item comes from a well-known collection it will always sell at a premium. Whenever a memorable collection is sold, acquisition details add an extra dimension to the interest generated. Personal collection labels are a very good idea, as they provide a permanent record of ownership. All labels should be as small as possible. Also, care needs to be taken to make sure they do not hide any interesting features, such as workmen's marks.

Most collectors like to keep catalogues of their porcelain collections. Computer software is available to help collectors record their purchases and log full details for insurance purposes. An up-to-date inventory and accurate appraisal are essential, as the insurance value of fine porcelain changes on a regular basis. A good photographic record is also imperative, and much easier now with the advent of digital cameras. Insurance companies and police forces encourage detailed recording of collections. Some also advocate marking your antiques with your postcode or zip-code written in a special

colourless ink visible under ultraviolet light. Property marking is sensible, but you should only ever mark an unobtrusive, plain white glazed area. Also, never mark porcelain where the glaze is crazed, as chemicals can penetrate right into the body and in extreme cases can affect the value.

Upgrading a Collection

Most collectors love to buy more and more pieces and hate selling anything. Sadly, this means that a lot of collections are in danger of getting out of hand. Unless space is unlimited, and funds too, most collections will benefit from a regular cull. It is natural to have a sentimental attachment to your first purchases, but as your collection progresses and your knowledge grows with it, certain pieces will seem out of place. When starting out it is sensible to buy as wide a range of pieces as possible in order to learn from them. After a while preferences develop and it is time to specialize. An important part of collecting is upgrading. Sell anything that is clearly inferior, and use the funds to buy new and better pieces. A spacious display of the best that is available will give far greater pleasure than a display cabinet crowded with average examples. While you should not buy porcelain merely for financial gain, a selected collection of better pieces will always prove to be a far wiser investment in the long term.

▲ **A collection of porcelain on modern, open shelving**
When space is limited, a porcelain collection can be displayed on different levels using stable Perspex blocks to give height. Pieces from different periods can be mixed together in a modern display.

Conservation & Restoration

Nothing incites more controversy in the world of fine porcelain than the subject of restoration. The practice is widespread, and there are as many arguments in its favour as there are against. Attitudes have definitely changed, as have the skills of the china restorer. Restoration *can* improve the appearance of damaged porcelain, and even simple cleaning can also make quite a difference.

Cleaning Porcelain

Porcelain that was repaired long ago can look a dreadful mess. However, it can be cleaned and restored again far more sympathetically. I can think of many pieces that were bought cheaply, on the assumption that they were very damaged, before removal of the old over-painting revealed that there was very little actually wrong with them.

A good clean alone can make a huge difference. Many owners are nervous about doing this, but as long as you are careful there is no reason to be afraid. Always use a plastic bowl instead of the hard kitchen sink, and steer clear of taps. Water should be slightly warm, but never too hot or cold. A mild detergent – ordinary soap or washing-up liquid – will not harm the majority of porcelain. A soft toothbrush or a child's paintbrush will gently remove dirt from complicated shapes such as figurines. If the enamels are shiny and there is no gilding, you can give your porcelain a gentle scrub without any worries, but some enamels can oxidize and become unstable. If the colouring is matt or blotchy at all, or if there is any flaking, use only a soft cloth and clean water, and take very great care.

Never use metal polish to bring the shine back to gilding. I know this sounds obvious, but I have seen plenty of pieces that have been ruined by abrasive creams rubbed over the gold decoration. Stable gilding can be polished very gently with a soft, dry duster, but that is all.

If there is no enamelled or gilt decoration, you can be more aggressive in your cleaning. Plain white or underglaze blue porcelain can be cleaned using a non-abrasive cream, preferably diluted. This will lift dirt from surface scratches and can make an incredible difference to scruffy-looking pieces, but make sure you rinse thoroughly with clean water afterwards. If you have porcelain that is stained, never attempt to clean it yourself. China restorers use concentrated peroxide to draw the discoloration of ages from under the surface of stained porcelain, but this should always be left to

▲ **Damaged Chelsea "goat and bee" creamjug, *c.*1745–48**
A famous model from the Trangle period, this example, from the Watney collection, lacks its handle and sold in 1999 for £900.

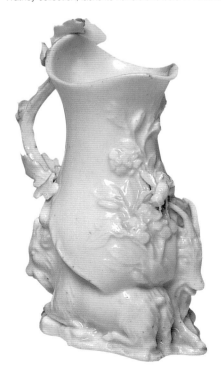

▲ **Perfect Chelsea "goat and bee" creamjug, *c.*1745–48**
A perfect example sold in 1999 for £9,000. Restoring a new handle is advised, although the value will never match that of a perfect jug.

► **A Tournai plate**, before cleaning (left) and after (right). The decoration is in underglaze blue and so was completely unharmed by gentle chemical cleaning to remove dirt from the surface scratches.

professionals. Never use bleach or any other caustic agent to clean your porcelain – these can make the staining worse, and cause glaze flaking.

Restoration

Ceramic restoration is an ancient craft. Some of the famous "terracotta warriors" of China had been repaired before they were buried, while Egyptians and Romans mended broken pots with metal rivets. Nobody wanted to throw away a precious pot if it could be salvaged. Traditionally the Chinese mended chipped porcelain with gold or with gilded lacquer, making a feature of the repair. In Europe as early as the 17th century, porcelain that had broken on its journey from China was bought by dealers who paid menders to stitch it back together.

Many of today's porcelain collectors despise restoration. If they buy a damaged piece for its rarity, the first thing they do is to pour on paint-stripper and remove all traces of old repair and restoration. This was very much the opinion of Dr Bernard Watney, the porcelain expert and legendary collector. He had bought most of his 2,000 pieces in a damaged condition, and never had any porcelain restored, no matter how rare or how defective. He liked chips, as they helped him to understand the nature of the china body.

When the Watney collection was auctioned there was enormous competition for the rare pieces. The specialist dealers and collectors who fought it out in my saleroom realized that they would not see the like again. They also knew that modern restoration methods would transform the appearance of some of Watney's noble wrecks. Specialist china restorers were kept busy for months afterwards. When certain pieces re-emerged on the market they were barely recognizable. Chips and cracks had vanished and even missing handles had magically reappeared.

Cosmetic and sympathetic, this relatively modern phenomenon restores without deceiving, and enhances rather than detracts. I am very much in favour of this type of work. My own attitude to restoration has certainly changed.

Traditional Restoration

Before modern glues and epoxy resins, the only way to mend broken china was by riveting. This was a skilled craft, passed down from father to son. It involved drilling tiny holes each side of a crack or break and inserting a red-hot metal rivet. As the metal cooled it contracted and pulled the porcelain together like a series of strong stitches. Riveting is remarkably resilient. Some porcelain mended in this way, such as the bough pot pictured below, is still strong and firm two centuries later.

One other method was practised in the 18th century. The firm of Coombes operated as "china

▲ **Coalport porcelain bough pot by Thomas Baxter**
This pot was severely broken in the 19th century. Skilful riveting, as seen on the base, salvaged the pieces so it could be displayed.

burners" in Bristol. It used an enamel paste, rather like melted glass, fired in a kiln to fuse the broken parts together again. We know of the firm's work from signed pieces, for when Coombes mended your china it proudly wrote its name and address in lustre on the bottom. Some of these repairs have remained intact since the 1780s. Old repairs by early china-burners, as well as fine examples of the riveter's craft, make an interesting area for collecting in their own right.

More severe damage, to the handle of a mug or the spout of a teapot, required a different kind of repair. In the 18th century fine porcelain was more precious than silver, and some china repairs were carried out by silversmiths so that the vessel could still be used. Many Chinese porcelain teapots were given completely new silver spouts, and broken lids were replaced entirely using silver. Teapots with 18th-century silver spouts rarely cost much money today, and yet this is part of their history, revealing how much their original owners loved their teapots.

Once strong glue was discovered, professional china-restorers took on a very different role. Previously, broken plates had been mended so that they could be used, but now collectors wanted broken pieces to look perfect again. The repairer's job was to hide any evidence that damage had ever occurred. Initially this meant slapping paint over the entire surface to match, as closely as possible, what lay beneath. Gradually the technology developed to match porcelain glaze synthetically. Transparent varnishes were sprayed and fired for a smooth finish.

▲ **A Chinese teapot with London enamelling, *c.*1750–55**
The spout was broken off by the original owner, but a silver replacement was made to continue using it for making tea.

During the 1970s china restoration became very fashionable. Evening courses, books, and videos taught amateurs how to mend their own porcelain. Skilful firms did very good work, but the reputation of the profession suffered through the botched efforts made at china-mending classes. One big problem is that restoration does not always stand the test of time. Pieces that looked fine when they first came back from the restorer would gradually discolour. Over-painting and surface sprays changed colour like gloss paint on a doorframe, turning from white to cream and then yellowy-brown. Synthetic gold in particular does not last. Worn gilding retouched with artificial gold can look horrible and brown just a few years later.

▲ **Unfortunate and unsightly damage to this English porcelain spill vase** has been professionally restored so that the beauty of the form and decoration can be appreciated once more. The vase is no longer perfect, but it looks 100 per cent better.

Modern Conservation

There is nothing worse than a crack in a porcelain plate, except maybe a chip on a saucer, or perhaps a broken teapot spout. All irritate me beyond belief. Damage can ruin the splendour of a fine piece of porcelain. Instead of admiring the beauty, your eye is drawn to the crack or break. If all you notice is the damage, then something needs to be done. If damage is hard to see, and therefore not disfiguring, then there is no need to restore it. Leave it well alone. But if the imperfection bothers you every time you look at the piece, it is time to call in a restorer. Finding a good restorer is not easy. Some are registered members of professional bodies, and museums often carry lists of registered conservators.

The role of the modern restorer is not to pretend a piece is perfect, but to stabilize the damage so it can't get any worse. Cracks and breaks are cleaned up and sealed so they cannot deteriorate or extend. Any missing pieces are made up and coloured to match, and visible cracks are colour-filled so they do not detract from the beauty. Some over-painting and spraying is necessary to disguise certain imperfections, but in museum-type restoration this is kept to a minimum. Before restoration can be undertaken, it is important to keep an eye on the cost. Experienced conservators are expensive, for the whole process takes a long time, so don't spend a lot of money repairing an object of only modest value. Rare porcelain, on the other hand, usually benefits from sympathetic restoration, and its value can be increased. I am much in favour of this kind of repair, and have had several pieces of my own restored, although without extensive spraying.

Some restorers lack sufficient skill to disguise damage without a lot of over-painting. Their botched repairs may have cost their owners considerable fees, and pieces that have been over-restored can be extremely difficult to sell. There are many instances where pieces have sold at auction for less than the cost of their repair, and they would have fetched a higher price if they had been left well alone.

Detecting Conservation

A large number of restored pieces are on sale at auctions and antiques fairs. Unfortunately many of these are not listed as restored in the catalogues or on their price tags. In many cases the dealers bought them in good faith and simply did not know they were selling restored pieces. However, some dealers are quite aware of the fact but choose to say nothing. I find it heartbreaking to have to inform a collector that an expensive purchase is in fact damaged and sprayed all over.

Modern professional restoration is designed to be invisible. Never be afraid to ask a seller to describe any repair in detail. Always examine any purchase very closely, if possible in natural daylight. Look particularly at danger spots – the neck and fingers on a figurine, the spout on a teapot – for signs of later painting. Poorly matched gilding is usually the giveaway. Ultra-violet lights ("black lamps") are useful tools, as different surface textures fluoresce at different intensities. Repaired areas can show up as yellow or white patches against untouched porcelain glaze that glows dark purple. Portable UV-lamps are available but need to be used in pitch darkness. However, lamps are not infallible, as some synthetic glazes fluoresce to the same colour as the original. Also, if a piece has been sprayed all over, the extent of the repair will be hidden. In extreme cases X-rays or tomograms (a medical technique that photographs slices through an object) are used to show the full extent of restoration. If you are unsure about the extent of a repair, ask the dealer, and never use a pin or coin to scratch the surface. Scratching can ruin a very expensive restoration.

▲ **A Derby figure of a boy viewed under ultraviolet light**
Restoration to the neck and arm fluoresces to a different, brighter colour than the remainder of the figure that has no overpainting.

Porcelain Marks

Factory marks are an indispensable guide to identification, although they cannot always be taken at face value. It is easy to copy a maker's sign, and fake marks have been applied to porcelain since the early 18th century. Fortunately, most markings are authentic, and they enable us to learn a great deal about makers, dates, and workmen.

In China, marks mostly paid homage to the emperor or had other religious meanings, while the purpose of European marks was primarily to identify individual factories. Actual names were rarely used in the 18th century. Important makers had a symbol, such as a heraldic device relating to a king or other patron. These were usually painted in blue, or sometimes in enamels. A few factory marks were impressed into the soft clay before firing.

Royal patronage gave way to private commerce in the 19th century. With makers in competition with one another, individual factory names were used, often with a city or street address. China dealers discouraged factories from marking, and a large quantity of porcelain was unmarked except for pattern numbers that enabled shops to reorder. After 1850 most important porcelain-makers used clear printed or impressed marks, and by 1900 almost every china factory put its name clearly on every piece. Printed factory marks are very rarely faked.

Workmen's marks enabled individual craftsmen to get the credit for their work, and payment as a result. When factory archives survive, these marks tell us a great deal about the potters. Other porcelain bears factory codes relating to the pieces themselves. Model and pattern numbers assisted china shops with stock control. Date codes were used by various factories to help with the rotation of their wares and prevent undecorated porcelain from sitting around too long before firing. Many factories used their own code sequences, and these are listed in specialist reference books. A number of different books list factory marks, although no single book could possibly include them all. A representative selection of marks is shown here.

Asian Marks

▲ Ming dynasty six-character reign mark of the Emperor Chenghua (1465–87).

▲ Qing dynasty six-character reign mark of the Emperor Yongzheng (1723–35).

▲ Qing dynasty Imperial seal mark, reign of Jiaqing (1796–1820).

▲ Japanese printed mark, Fukagawa factory, c.1900.

Painted Factory Marks

▲ Chelsea, anchor mark painted in red, 1752–56.

▲ Chelsea-Derby, conjoined gold anchor and letter D, 1770–84.

▲ Derby, crown, painted blue crossed batons and D, c.1790–95.

▲ Worcester, square mark in underglaze blue, 1765–75.

Painted Factory Marks continued

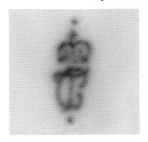

▲ Frankenthal, crowned CT cipher for Carl Theodore, c.1765.

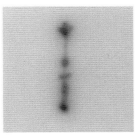

▲ Berlin, sceptre mark in underglaze blue, c.1780.

▲ Tournai, crossed swords with additional crosses, c.1775.

▲ Ludwigsburg, crowned conjoined C mark, c.1770.

Printed Factory Marks

◀ Rockingham, griffin mark printed in red, 1826–30.

◀ Sèvres, reign of Louis Philippe, dated 1846.

▲ Royal Worcester, printed puce mark with date code for 1926.

▲ Royal Copenhagen, printed and painted, c.1890.

▲ Russian Imperial & Soviet marks, decorated after the Revolution, 1922.

▲ Lenox, printed wreath mark, 1906–30.

Impressed Marks

▲ Seal of He Chao Zong, 17th century.

▲ Worcester, initials of Flight, Barr and Barr, 1814–40.

Workmen's Marks

▲ Meissen, crossed swords with painter's initial G, c.1745.

▲ Worcester, IH workman's mark in underglaze blue, c.1755.

Glossary

Acid Gold
The glazed surface of the ware is etched with hydrofluoric acid and coated with burnished gold; popular at Minton at end of 19th century

Aesthetic Style
Further development of the Japanesque style, 1880–85 – direct copies of Japanese art adapted to suit English taste

American Belleek
Name used by several US porcelain makers, c.1880–90, for their glazed parian body based on the Irish porcelain method

Arita
Area of Japan famed for its blue-and-white and Imari-coloured porcelain

Armorial Porcelain
Porcelain with decoration involving heraldic crests or coats-of-arms

Art Deco
Distinctive style of the 1920s and '30s – bold colours and geometric shapes

Art Nouveau
Literally a "new" style in art, developed by 1900, with extreme asymmetry, flowing curves and plant forms; little direct influence on English porcelain

Artificial Porcelain
Alternative name for soft paste porcelain

Baroque
Art style inspired by architectural and sculptural influences on a grand scale, arranged with dramatic symmetry; popular from 17th century, until superseded by the lighter and more frivolous rococo style

Bat Printing
Use of a "bat" of glue to transfer the design in oil from an engraved copper plate to the surface of porcelain, before dusting with fine powdered colour; produces a delicate, finely stippled effect

Biscuit Porcelain (Bisque)
Ware fired once but not glazed, with dry, slightly rough surface

Blanc de Chine
Glazed white porcelain, mostly associated with Chinese porcelain made at Dehua in the Fukien province

Blue-and-White
Porcelain decorated in underglaze blue; a popular collecting field

Blush Ivory
Decoration developed at Royal Worcester using a strongly shaded ivory and peach-coloured, semi-matt ground; much imitated during 1890s

Bocage
A modelled flowering tree, or other leafage, placed at the back of a figure group as decoration; also adds support during manufacture

Body
Mixture of raw materials; basic ingredients of the ware, excluding glaze

Bone Ash
Alternative name for calcined bone

Bone China
Porcelain body containing up to 50 per cent animal bone, used by most English manufacturers from about 1810; quantity of bone can vary greatly

Botanical Decoration
Naturalistic flowers used as ornament, originally adopted at the Chelsea and Derby factories in 18th century

Burnishing
Process of polishing gold after firing with fine sand, or hardstones such as agate or bloodstone; patterns in the gold can be created in this way

Calcined Bone (Bone Ash)
Animal bone reduced by heat to a powder – an ingredient of bone china

Casting
Forming a piece by pouring liquid clay or slip into a porous mould; any surplus is emptied out and the cast left to dry slightly before it's removed

Celadon
Green-tinted glaze used on Chinese stoneware and some porcelain in the Song and Ming dynasties

China
Generally any white porcelain, so-called as the first porcelain was Chinese

China Clay
Fine white clay, rich in kaolin, used in most English china bodies

China Stone
Partly decomposed granite, rich in feldspar; vital ingredient of porcelain, known by the Chinese as "petuntse"

Chinese Export
Porcelain made in China for the Export Trade, in particular 18th-century wares shipped to Europe and America

Chinese Imari
Name given to Chinese copies of Japanese Imari patterns.

Chinoiserie
Decoration in Chinese style, but not copied directly from the Orient; a European adaptation of Chinese ornament.

Clobbering
Enamelling applied at a later date to add further decoration to plain white or blue-and-white porcelain, usually spoiling the original design

Cobalt
Basic ingredient of underglaze blue, used in its oxide form

Commedia dell'Arte
Characters from traditional Italian comedy, popular in Germany in 1700s

Crazing
Fine network of tiny cracks in the glaze of fired porcelain; used on purpose by the Chinese, but an unwelcome failing in much English bone china

Decals
Alternative name for lithographic transfers, from US term "decalcomania"

Deustche Blumen
Carefully painted flower decoration, developed at Meissen c.1740 and much copied in England

Dingyao
Ivory-tinted glazed porcelain made in China in the Song dynasty; decoration such as clouds often included

Doucai
Enamelled decoration, filling in outlines in underglaze blue; a refined form of decoration on Chinese porcelain from the 15th century

Empire Style
Development of the neo-classical style, originated in France and associated with taste of Napoleon – Roman, Greek, and Egyptian designs combined on a grand scale; in England Empire style closely associated with Regency

Enamelling
Process of decorating porcelain using colours mixed with a flux, which melt into the glaze at different temperatures

Famille Rose
Palette of colours, especially deep rose-pink, and style of decoration based on Chinese porcelain painting; introduced in Yongzheng period c.1730

Famille Verte
Similar palette of colours with prominent bright green, used on Chinese porcelain; introduced during Kangxi period at end of 17th century

Feldspar
Main component of china stone, used in most porcelain bodies

Firecracks
Cracks in surface caused by firing; manufacturing defect in early porcelain

Flatware
General term for plates, dishes, and saucers; as opposed to hollow ware, which is round vessels such as cups, jugs, and teapots

Foot-rim
Mostly hand-made turned base of cup, bowl, or vessel; may identify period

Gilding
Real gold applied to porcelain, usually as final embellishment, and burnished after firing to polish up; in 18th century it was mixed with honey but by 1790s this was replaced by mercury, for a smoother finish

Glaze
Layer, or skin, of melted glass put over most ceramics to keep them clean or to enable them to hold liquids.

Gothic Style
Ornament of medieval period, which enjoyed a revival in the 1830s and '40s; mostly influenced architecture, but had some effect on ceramics

Groundlay
Applying even background by dusting fine powdered colour on band of oil

Hausmaler
German term for enamelling done by decorators outside porcelain factory

Hard Paste
Term used to describe "true" porcelain, made from china clay and china stone, usually fused in a high glaze firing; Chinese and most European porcelains are hard paste, but very little was made in England

Hybrid Paste
The porcelain bodies used by many English factories from 1780s until c.1820; not hard paste in the "true" sense, but advanced forms of soft paste

Imari
Japanese decoration, late 17th century, with underglaze blue, overglaze red enamel, and gold; copied in China and used in England, especially Derby

Imperial Porcelain
Wares made for Chinese Emperor, or with his approval; best porcelain made at Jingdezhen for the Chinese market, not for export.

Indianische Blumen
Formal flower-painting style used at Meissen in 1720s; based on Chinese and Japanese painting, but style is much richer in colouring and design

Japan Patterns
Like Imari but with other colours, especially green; English adaptations, never direct copies of Japanese porcelain, popular during Regency period

Japanesque
Art movement inspired by wares and lifestyle of Japan, but something of an English obsession in the 1870s and '80s; Japanese styles were adapted to make them even more oriental in the eyes of English society

Jewelling
Decorating porcelain using tiny droplets of enamel to simulate jewels; popular in France in 19th century and in England at Coalport and others

Jiggering and Jollying
Processes of making flatware and hollow ware using rotating moulds

Kakiemon
Japanese porcelain from the late 17th century, much collected and copied in Europe, especially at Meissen and in England at Chelsea and Bow

Kaolin
Naturally occurring primary clay used in bone china; basis of true porcelain

Kraak Porcelain
Blue-and-white export ware from China in 17th century; name derives from Portuguese ships called "carracks"

Limoges Enamels
Decoration inspired by medieval French enamelling, involving building up a design in layers of white enamel on a dark glazed ground

Lithographic Printing
Photographic litho-printing using tiny dots of colour to produce an image transferred to surface; developed in late 19th century, used extensively today

Mark and Period
Chinese porcelain with reign mark of emperor, excludes later copies

Monochrome
Decoration in a single colour; name also associated with Chinese porcelain decorated with individual glaze effect

Moons
Tiny air bubbles trapped within the paste of Chelsea, and some other, porcelain, which produce light spots when held to a strong light

Neo-classical Style
Revival of interest in formal classical styles as reaction against frivolity of rococo; popular in England from 1770s, developed into excesses of Regency or Empire styles in early 19th century

Overglaze
Decoration in enamels or gold, fired on top of surface of glazed porcelain

Parian
White porcelain containing up to 70 per cent feldspar and 30 per cent china clay, mixed with a little crushed glass; also known as statuary porcelain, used to make copies of marble statues. It does not need a glaze but can be used to make creamy glazed porcelain

Pâte-sur-pâte
Building up a design by hand-painting with a white slip on a dark-coloured ground; a speciality of the Minton factory

Phosphatic
Type of soft paste porcelain containing calcined bone (or bone ash).

Picturesque Style
Style of painting used by English watercolourists – landscape altered to create a more attractive composition; popular at the end of 18th century

Press-moulding
A rolled-out slab of clay is pressed into a hollow mould to cast a vessel

Rococo
Art style using scrolls, rock, and shell forms, and asymmetry; developed in 1740s as reaction against more formal baroque, superseded by neo-classicism in 1770s but revived more strongly in 1830s and 1890s

Rose Medallion
American term for Canton porcelain in 19th century, featuring panelled decoration in famille rose enamels

Saggar
Box made of fireproof clay in which porcelain vessels are placed to protect them during firing

Scale Blue
Underglaze blue background formed by painting fine scale pattern, popular at Worcester in 18th century

Slip
Clay suspended in water, used for casting and decorating methods

Soft Paste
Term used to describe "artificial" porcelain bodies made from clay and forms of glass, fused in the biscuit-kiln and subsequently given a lower glaze firing; most 18th-century English porcelain is soft paste

Spur Marks
Small scars left on rim of plate or saucer by pegs on which piece rested during glaze firing; method used at several factories, notably Lowestoft

Steatatic
Type of soft paste porcelain containing soaprock, a type of steatite; used at Worcester and elsewhere in 18th century

Stilt Marks
Triangular arrangement of small scars, found on base of plates or saucers supported on clay stilts during glaze firing; usually on Chelsea porcelain

Throwing
Basic method of making any ceramic vessel, with clay, on revolving potter's wheel; many plainer early English pieces are hand-thrown, not moulded

Topographical
Painted decoration with accurate depiction of landscapes and scenic views

Transfer-printing
Design in ceramic colour is transferred from engraved copper plate to surface by means of a tissue-paper "pull"; developed in the 1750s, the process is virtually unchanged today

Translucency
Appearance of porcelain when held up to a strong light; colour varies between different bodies and makers

Underglaze Blue
Cobalt oxide is applied directly to biscuit surface and during glaze firing reacts to seal the blue colour permanently below the glaze; blue was only colour that could be used satisfactorily in this way

Vitrification
Point at which the particles forming porcelain melt and fuse together

Wreathing
Faint spiral grooves in surface of hard paste porcelain caused by vessel twisting in kiln; can be seen on most Plymouth and Bristol hollow ware

Wucai
Palette of enamels used overglaze on Chinese porcelain from the Ming dynasty

Further Reading

Marks

Chaffers, William
Marks and Monograms on Pottery and Porcelain (15th revised edition) (Reeves, 1974)

Cushion, John
Handbook of Pottery and Porcelain Marks (Faber and Faber, 1980, revised edition 1996)

Danckert, Ludwig
Directory of European Porcelain (NAG Press, 1981)

Godden, Geoffrey A.
Encyclopaedia of British Pottery and Porcelain Marks (Barrie & Jenkins, several editions)

General Books (World)

Battie, David (Ed.)
Sotheby's Concise Encyclopaedia of Porcelain (Conran Octopus, 1990)

Charleston, Robert (Ed.)
World Ceramics (Chartwell Books Inc., 1982)

Faye-Halle, A. and Mundt, B.
Nineteenth Century European Porcelain (Trefoil Books, 1983)

Lang, Gordon
Miller's Antiques Checklist – Porcelain (Miller's Publications, Octopus Publishing Group, 2000)

Litchfield, Frederick
Pottery and Porcelain, A Guide to Collectors, (5th edition) (M. Barrows & Co. Inc., 1951)

Morley-Fletcher, Hugo (Ed.)
Techniques of the World's Great Masters – Pottery and Ceramics (Quarto, 1984)

Sandon, John
Starting to Collect Antique Porcelain (Antique Collectors' Club, 1996)

Savage, George
Porcelain Through the Ages (Pelican, 1954)

Savage, G., Newman, H., and Cushion, J. *Illustrated Dictionary of Ceramics* (Thames and Hudson, 1992, reprinted 2000)

Oriental Porcelain

Ayres John, Impey, Oliver and Mallet, John
Porcelain For Palaces, the Fashion for Japan in Europe (Oriental Ceramic Society exhibition catalogue, 1990)

Donnelly, P. J.
Blanc de Chine (Faber & Faber, 1969)

Garner, Harry
Oriental Blue and White (Faber & Faber, 1970)

Godden, Geoffrey A.
Oriental Export Market Porcelain (Granada, 1979)

Howard, David
Chinese Armorial Porcelain (Faber & Faber, 1974)

A Tale of Three Cities, Canton, Shanghai & Hong Kong (Sotheby's, 1997)

Howard, David and Ayres, John
China for the West (Sotheby Parke Bernet, 1978)

Jenyns, Soames
Japanese Porcelain (1985)

Ming Pottery and Porcelain (1953)

Kwan, S.
Imperial Porcelain of the Late Qing (1983)

Macintosh, Duncan
Chinese Blue and White Porcelain (Antique Collectors' Club, 1986, reprinted 1994)

Medley, Margaret
The Chinese Potter (Phaidon, 1976)

Oriental Ceramic Society
Porcelain for Palaces (British Museum Press, 1990)

Sheaf, Colin and Kilburn, R.
The Hatcher Porcelain Cargoes (Phaidon, 1988)

Continental Porcelain

Fay-Halle, Antoinette and Mundt, Barbara *19th Century European Porcelain* (Trefoil, 1983)

Godden, Geoffrey A.
Godden's Guide to European Porcelain (Barrie & Jenkins, 1993)

Honey, William
French Porcelain (Faber & Faber, 1950)

German Porcelain (Faber & Faber, 1947)

Lane, Arthur
Italian Porcelain (Faber & Faber, 1964)

Langham, Marion
Belleek Irish Porcelain (Quiller Press Ltd., 1993)

Morley-Fletcher, Hugo
Meissen (Barrie & Jenkins, 1971)

Pauls-Eisenbeiss, E.
German Porcelain of the Eighteenth Century (Barrie & Jenkins, 1972)

de Plinval de Guillebon, Regine
Paris Porcelain 1770–1850 (Walker & Co., 1972)

Röntgen, Robert
The Book of Meissen
(Schiffer, 1996)

Ruckert, Rainer
Meissener Porzellan
(Hirmer Verlag, 1966)

Savage, George
18th Century German Porcelain
(Spring Books, 1958)

*17th and 18th Century French
Porcelain* (Barrie & Rockliff, 1960)

Savill, Rosalind
*The Wallace Collection, Catalogue
of Sèvres Porcelain (3 volumes)*
(Trustees of the Wallace
Collection, 1988)

Stazzi, Francesco
Italian Porcelain
(Weidenfeld & Nicolson, 1967)

Walcha, Otto
Meissen Porcelain
(Studio Vista/Christie's, 1981)

English Porcelain

Adams, Elizabeth
Chelsea Porcelain (British Museum
Press Ltd., 2001)

**Adams, Elizabeth and
Redstone, David**
Bow Porcelain
(Faber & Faber, 1981)

Bailey, Betty and Twitchett, John
Royal Crown Derby
(Antique Collectors' Club, 1976)

Berthoud, Michael
A Compendium of British Cups
(Micawber, 1990)

Bradshaw, Peter
Bow Porcelain Figures
(Barrie & Jenkins, 1992)

Derby Porcelain Figures
(Faber & Faber, 1990)

*Eighteenth Century English
Porcelain Figures* (Antique
Collectors' Club, 1981)

**Branyan, Lawrence, French, Neal
and Sandon, John**
Worcester Blue and White Porcelain
(revised edition)
(David & Charles, 1989)

Cox, Alwyn and Angela
Rockingham Pottery & Porcelain
(Faber & Faber, 1983)

Godden, Geoffrey A.
*British Porcelain, an Illustrated
Guide* (Barrie & Jenkins,
1990 reprint)

Caughley and Worcester Porcelains
(revised edition) (Jenkins, 1981)

Chamberlains-Worcester Porcelain
(David & Charles, 1989)

*Encyclopaedia of British Porcelain
Manufacturers*
(Barrie & Jenkins, 1988)

Lowestoft Porcelains (revised
edition) (Jenkins, 1985)

Staffordshire Porcelain
(Granada, 1983)

**Godden, Geoffrey A. and
Lockett, Terence**
*Davenport Earthenware,
Porcelain & Glass*

Holgate, David
New Hall and Its Imitators
(Faber & Faber, 1987)

Honey, William (Ed. Barrett, F.)
Old English Porcelain
(Faber & Faber, 1977)

Jones, A. E. and Joseph, Sir Leslie
*Swansea Porcelain, Shapes
and Decoration*
(D. Brown & Sons, 1989)

Jones, Joan
*Minton, the First 200 Years
of Design and Production*
(Antique Collectors' Club, 1993)

Messenger, Michael
Coalport (Antique Collectors'
Club, 1996)

**Miller, Philip and
Berthoud, Michael**
An Anthology of British Teapots
(Micawber, 1985)

Sandon, Henry
British Pottery and Porcelain
(John Gifford, 1980)

Royal Worcester Porcelain
(David & Charles, 1989)

Sandon, John
*The Dictionary of Worcester
Porcelain* (Antique Collectors'
Club, 1993)

*The Phillips Guide to English
Porcelain* (Merehurst/Murdoch
Books, 1989)

Sandon, John and Spero, Simon
*Worcester Porcelain, The Zorensky
Collection* (Antique Collectors'
Club, 1997)

Twitchett, John
Derby Porcelain
(Barrie & Jenkins, 1980)

Watney, Bernard
English Blue and White Porcelain
(Faber & Faber, 1973)

*Liverpool Porcelain of the 18th
Century* (Richard Dennis
Publications, 1997)

Whiter, Leonard
Spode (revised edition)
(Barrie & Jenkins, 1978)

American Porcelain

Atlee Barber, Edwin
*The Pottery and Porcelain
of the United States*
(Feingold & Lewis, 1979)

Cooney Frelinghuysen, Alice
American Porcelain
(Abrams, 1989)

Index

Acknowledgments

Author's Acknowledgments: I would like to thank my colleagues in the ceramics department at Bonhams, especially the department's administrator, Caroline Hilborne-Clarke. Also, other senior specialists at Bonhams: Mark Oliver, head of Late 19th- and 20th-century Design; Colin Sheaf, head of Asian Art; Chris Halton, head of Photography. In addition, Stuart Slavid of Skinner Auctioneers in Boston for help with the section on American porcelain, and the staff at Bronté Porcelain, Malvern, especially Bob Price for help with the chapter on the making of porcelain. I would also like to thank my father, Henry Sandon, for additional photographs and inspiration and finally, my wife, Kristin, for all kinds of help with research and for editing my manuscript.

The publisher would like to thank all those who contributed images and items for photography.

KEY:
b bottom **r** right **l** left **c** centre **t** top
BAL Bridgeman Art Library; BON Bonhams; BPC Bronté Porcelain Company Ltd. of Malvern; CH Chris Halton; CI Christie's Images; DB David Battie; JS John Sandon; OPG Octopus Publishing Group; SPL Sotheby's Picture Library; ST Steve Tanner; V&A Victoria & Albert Museum

Front cover c, cr, bl & br CI; **tl & tr** BON; **cl** SPL; **cr** CI
Back cover cl OPG/BON; **c & cr** CI; **b** OPG/CH/BON
Spine CI

1 CI; **3** BON; **6t** BAL/British Museum, London; **7tl** BAL/V&A, **tr** BON, **b** Stockspring Antiques/Robert McPherson; **8t** CI, **b** V&A; **9t & b** BON; **10t** BON, **b** CI; **11t** BON, **b** V&A; **12t** BON, **b** CI; **13l** CI, **r** BON; **14tl** BON, **tr & b** OPG/CH/BON; **15tl & tr** OPG/CH/BON, **b** BON; **16t** BPC; **17** BPC; **18** BPC; **19b** JS; **20** JS; **21t** JS/BON, **b** OPG/CH/BON; **22t** OPG/CH/B; **23** Roderick Jellicoe, 3a Campden Street, London W8 7EP; **24** The International Ceramics Fair and Seminar at the Park Lane Hotel, London; **25** JS; **26** BON; **27t & b** BON; **28** BON; **29l, r & t** BON; **30l** BON, **r** OPG/ST/JS; **31r & b** BON, **t** CI; **32l** CI, **r & t** OPG/ST/JS; **33l** OPG/Glade Antiques, **r** CI; **34l** CI, **r** OPG/CH/BON; **34b** BON; **35l** CI, **tr & br** BON; **36l** BON, **r** OPG/CH/BON; **37l** BON, **r** CI, **b** OPG/ST/JS; **38l** BON; **39l** BON, **r** OPG/CH/BON, **c** JS, **40l** BON, **r** CI, **c** OPG/CH/BON; **41l & r** BON, **42l** OPG/CH/BON, **r** CI; **43l & c** BON, **r** CI; **44l & r** CI; **45l** BAL/Hermitage, St Petersburg, Russia, **r** BON, **c** JS; **46l** OPG/CH/BON, **r** BON; **47l & c** JS, **r** The Wedgwood Museum Trust Ltd, Barlaston, Staffordshire; **48t & br** OPG/ST/JS; **49l** OPG/CH/BON, **r & b** BON; **50l & b** BON, **tr** JS; **51l** BON, **r** OPG/ST/JS; **52l & t** BON, **r** BAL/Private Collection; **53l & tr** JS, **b** BON; **54l** BON, **r** CI; **55tl, tr & br** BON, **bl** JS; **56tl & b** BON, **tr** OPG/ST/JS; **57l** S, **r** BON; **58l** CI, **r** OPG/ST/JS, **c** CI; **59l** BON, **r** OPG/ST/JS, **t** JS; **60l & r** BON, **c** CI; **61l** OPG/ST/Private Collection, **t** OPG/CH/BON, **br** OPG/ST/JS; **62l, r & c** BON; **63l** BON, **r** OPG/ST/Lynda Pine, **b** CI; **64t & b** BON; **65l, tc, tr & cb** OPG/CH/BON, **t & br** OPG/ST/JS; **66l** BAL/Joseph & Earle Vanderkar, London, UK, **r** OPG/ST/JS; **67l** CI, **r & c** OPG/CH/BON; **68l & r** BON, **69l & c** OPG/CH/BON, **r** OPG/ST/JS; **70l, r & t** BON; **71l** BON, **r & c** OPG/CH/BON; **72l, r & t** BON, **73l** BON, **r** CI; **74tl** BON, **tr** OPG/ST/JS, **b** JS; **75l** OPG/Butterfield & Butterfield, **r** BON; **76l** BON, **r & t** OPG/ST/JS; **77l & b** BON, **r** OPG/ST; **78l, r & t** BON, **79l & r** BON; **80l** OPG/CH/BON, **r** OPG/ST/JS; **81l** Dreweatt Neate Auctioneers, **r** BON, **t** JS; **82l** BON, **r** V&A, **t & bl** CI; **83r & tl** OPG/ST/JS; **84l** JS **84 r** V&A; **85l** BON, **r** CI, **c** JS; **86l, r & b** Esto Photographics/Lee Schecter; **87l** Skinner, Auctioneers and Appraisers of Antiques and Fine Art, Boston, MA, **r** CI; **88l** BAL/Metropolitan Museum of Art, New York; **r** JS/BON; **89r & bl** OPG/ST/JS, **tl** Esto Photographics; **90** BON; **91l & c** BON, **r** OPG/ST/JS; **92tl & bl** BON, **tr & br** OPG/CH/BON; **93l** BON, **r** JS; **94l** BON, **r** OPG/CH/BON, **c** JS; **95l & c** BON, **r** OPG/CH/BON; **96l & c** BON, **r** OPG/CH/BON; **97l** CI, **r & c** OPG/ST/JS; **98l** OPG/ST/JS, **r** OPG/CH/BON, **c** BON; **99l & t** OPG/CH/BON, **r** BON; **100l** OPG/ST/JS, **r** OPG/CH/BON; **b** BON; **101l** OPG/CH/BON, **r** OPG/ST/JS, **t** BON; **102l** OPG/CH/BON, **t** JS, **b** Royal Copenhagen; **103tl & bl** OPG/CH/BON, **tr** BON, **b** OPG/ST/JS; **104l** JS, **r** OPG/ST/JS; **105l & r** BON, **b** OPG/CH/BON; **106l** BON, **r** V&A; **107l & b** BON, **r** V&A; **108l** JS, **r** OPG/CH/BON, **b** BON; **109r** BON, **tl** JS, **bl** V&A; **110t** BON, **b** CI; **111t** OPG/Dragonlee Antiques, **b** BON; **112l, tr & br** OPG/CH/BON; **113l** CI, **r** BON; **114tl** OPG/ST/JS, **tr & b** OPG/CH/BON; **115l** V&A, **r** OPG/CH/BON; **116l** CI, **r & b** BON; **117l & t** CI; **r** OPG/CH/BON; **118l** CI, **t** BON; **119l & r** BON, **t** CI; **120l & r** BON; **121l** BON, OPG/ST/JS, **c** OPG/CH/BON; **122l** V&A, **r** SPL; **123l** CI, **r** V&A, **c** OPG/CH/BON; **124l & r** BON, **c** OPG/CH/BON; **125l & r** BON; **126l** BON, **r** CI, **t** SPL; **127l & t** OPG/ST/JS, **r** CI; **128l** V&A, **r** BON, **c** CI; **129l & c** BON, **r** OPG/CH/BON; **130l & r** BON, **t** CI; **131l** OPG/CH/BON, **r & t** BON; **132l & t** BON, **r** CI; **133l, r & c** BON; **134 l** JS, **r** BON, **c** OPG/CH/BON; **135l** CI, **r** JS, **t** BON; **136l** BON, **r** OPG/CH/BON; **t** BAL/Private Collection; **137r** OPG/CH/BON, **t** OPG/CH/BON, **b** OPG/ST/JS; **138l** OPG/CH/BON, **r** BON, **t** OPG/ST/JS; **139l** CI, **tr** JS, **br** OPG/CH/BON; **140l, tr & ct** OPG/CH/BON, **b** DB; **141l & t** BON, **r** DB; **142** BON; **143t** JS, **b** BON; **144** BON; **145** JS; **146t & b** BON, **147t** OPG/CH/BON, **b** JS; **148t** OPG/ST/JS, **bl & br** Q. W. Conservation; **149** JS; **150tl, tcl & tcr** BON, **tr, bl, bcl, bcr & br** OPG/CH/BON; **151** OPG/CH/BON except: Sèvres mark, 1846 V&A; impressed mark of He Chao Zong BON.